DOMESTIC VIOLENCE

DOMESTIC VIOLENCE

Facts and Fallacies

RICHARD L. DAVIS

Westport, Connecticut
London

Library of Congress Cataloging-in-Publication Data

Davis, Richard L., 1941–
    Domestic violence : facts and fallacies / Richard L. Davis.
      p.   cm.
    Includes bibliographical references and index.
    ISBN 0–275–96126–5 (alk. paper)
    1. Family violence—Government policy—United States. 2. Family
violence—United States—Prevention. I. Title.
HV6626.2.D39   1998
362.82′92′0973—dc21   97–27924

British Library Cataloguing in Publication Data is available.

Library of Congress Catalog Card Number: 97–27924
ISBN: 0–275–96126–5

First published in 1998

Praeger Publishers, 88 Post Road West, Westport, CT 06881
An imprint of Greenwood Publishing Group, Inc.

Printed in the United States of America

The paper used in this book complies with the
Permanent Paper Standard issued by the National
Information Standards Organization (Z39.48–1984).

10 9 8 7 6 5 4 3

To all the
children, women,
and men
who have endured

Police represent a closed society. They mistrust
outsiders. Cops know things you and I don't. It's
knowledge crafted out of years spent on the
street, sizing up and dealing with the volatile,
cunning, confused, comic, tragic, often goofy
behavior of human beings from every social,
economic and mental level. Police are privy to
special knowledge, most of which they share only
with other police and sometimes with their
families.
Fletcher, 1996, "What Cops Know"

Contents

Preface

Certainly not all readers will agree with my observations or the position set forth in this book. Certainly not all those I thank for their help have agreed with all the observations or positions set forth in this book.

In this book I seek to provide the reader with a series of serious questions regarding the status and relevance concerning the issue of contemporary domestic violence and its victims. It is not my intent to present inflexible propositions, but to make observations clear enough to be understood and thought about. It is not the purpose of this book to be critical but to be educationally provocative and to stimulate serious discussion. This book is intended for an extensive readership. For clarity and comprehension, I have sometimes stressed the same point more than once. In sum, what is at stake is whether our public policymakers are serious about the issue of domestic violence or whether they are just entangled in another political dance.

I thank Ruth Fishbach, Ph.D., Harvard University. She understood why, what, and where I had not explored. Without her encouragement, guidance, and most important her posing of the questions that had not yet been asked and answered, this book would not have been possible.

I thank Bonnie for her insight and prompting comments on the original work. I thank Fred for his assistance in defraying the cost of conveyance for the aforementioned work. I am grateful to Bridget, Lee, Beth, and Bill for their special assistance. I thank Donald and Sheila for their perspicacity concerning form.

To Ian and Dylan, special thanks for time stolen from your lives.

And to my wife Robin, at once my harshest critic and my biggest champion. I thank you for your long-suffering support and patience. And yes Robin, honest, the book is finished.

DOMESTIC VIOLENCE

1

Introduction

William Jennings Bryan: "I do not think about the things that I do not think about."

Clarence Darrow: "Do you ever think about the things that you do think about?"

Inherit the Wind

The predominant purpose of this book is to inject a rational and reasoned perspective into to the clamorous debate concerning domestic violence. For the purpose of this book, domestic violence is violence that occurs between couples who are living together or once did live together in a conjugal-styled relationship. I wish to bring to the attention of the American public in general, and to my colleagues in the domestic violence field in particular, my beliefs concerning the current extent and nature of domestic violence.

I examine the efficacy of our current, criminal justice driven domestic violence policies. I question the logic and wisdom of our public policymakers in placing so much emphasis on the overworked, frayed, and failing hands of the criminal justice system. I submit to feminists and victim advocates who want authentic domestic violence reform that they have not and will not receive true and verifiable domestic violence reform from their current public policymakers. They will not achieve their goal of ending or preventing domestic violence by placing their faith in the engagement of a floundering criminal justice system. In fact, the United States Department of Justice, Bureau of Justice Statistics *Sourcebook of Criminal Justice Statistics* does not include domestic violence as one of its 29 Part 1 and Part 2 criminal offenses. In fact, the 1994 edition does not include the term domestic violence anywhere in its 701 pages.

In 1963, Betty Friedan wrote *The Feminine Mystique.* "The problem lay buried," wrote Friedan, "unspoken for many years in the minds of American women." She spoke of this problem as "the problem without a name." What Friedan meant was the cultural, societal, and legal barriers that prevented equality for women in the workplace. This book is also about a problem that has been buried and unspoken of for many years. It is far more complex than the problem of gender equality in the workplace. It is the problem of domestic violence within the hearths of our homes and the hearts of our families. I believe that in every nuclear or extended family in America there is someone who has been abused or is an abuser.

This book endeavors to explain why the criminal justice system has failed to prevent the continued increase of domestic violence. There is a proper role for the criminal justice system in the intervention of domestic violence, and I will explain just what that proper role should be. I will also explain the manifold limitations of that participation. I explain what needs to be accomplished if we are to effectively combat the dilemma that haunts so many of us.

Although it is most often hidden from public view, violence in our homes is a problem that we all should be universally conscious of. Yet many of us, both men and women, often deny its existence. While most women are acutely aware of the problems created by domestic violence, many men remain in denial. This book is an attempt to help all of us become better communities of citizens who collectively must undertake the task of educating ourselves, one another, and, ideally, leaders of our schools, universities, business, and government. All are necessary to cast the light of awareness on this often silent and customarily hidden issue of domestic violence.

The truth is, that many men and some women, often display intolerance toward those who suffer this affliction. The question almost always asked is "Why don't they [the victims of domestic violence] just leave?" Society acknowledges that some people are afraid of high places and cannot climb to the top of a building or become terrified when crossing a high bridge. The mental state of many victims of domestic violence has often been psychologically altered or culturally conditioned and they cannot leave the abusive relationship without help. Victims of domestic violence often do not display rational or reasoned behavior because of a myriad of extraordinarily complicated circumstances. Their mental state has often been psychologically altered by an experience that often can leave them intellectually incapable of making rational decisions regarding that relationship. If society can accept and understand that some people suffer the fear of confined spaces or the fear of flying, then society should understand that some people experience the fear of leaving a relationship after being abused.

Too many times, as a police officer, I joined social workers who had to forcefully remove children from the home of their abusive parents. These children often would continue to profess nothing but love for their parents. They would most often not want to leave the home. Regardless of age, it is not unusual for strong emotions to flaw the rational decision-making process.

In Lowell, Massachusetts, four boys were beaten with a dog leash, a baseball bat, a chain, and paint mixers. They were forced to inhale cocaine, and smoke marijuana, and were injected with syringes by their father while they slept. They were also forced to engage in all kinds of sexual acts with both their mother and father. The parents were arrested and charged with rape, indecent assault, and assault and battery with a dangerous weapon, and the drugging of their four children. During testimony at the trial of their parents, the boys said they continued to care about their parents. "At times they spoke about their family life with aplomb."[1] Unconditional love is an enigmatic emotion to comprehend, but we must accept the fact that it exists. "People really believe that love will fix everything."[2] Unconditional love is not an emotion solely and exclusively sustained by children.

Many of us continue to refuse any display of empathy or compassion for the victim of domestic violence until that same calamity strikes one of our own family members or until a friend becomes an abuser or a victim. If we continue to wait for a personal family experience before we become believers, the visit of domestic violence to a family member or friend will be as inevitable as the visit of the Grim Reaper.

This book presents a synopsis of the subject for students, professionals, and the general public alike. It is the only book that I am aware of that provides analysis of domestic violence and recommendations for change from the viewpoint of a police officer. It is intended to be only a primer, for domestic violence is a very complex issue. I have tried to keep the exploration of the issue short, coherent, and, most important, comprehensible, for the typical reader.

My intent is to reshape understandings, misunderstandings, and misconceptions of domestic violence by both men and women. I provide uncomplicated and understandable direction that can lead to resolution. We have not yet found the solution to domestic violence because we rarely, as a society, address the inquiry correctly. The debate concerning domestic violence is too often dictated and directed by those with conflicting, emotionally held convictions.

Leading advocacy groups for victims of domestic violence claims that more than half of married women (about 27 million women) are beaten by men during their marriage and that more than one-third of married women (18 million women) are battered repeatedly. On the other end, a survey conducted by the National Institute of Mental Health found that about 3 to 4 percent of all families-1.8 million-have members who engage in "severe" violence that includes kicking, punching, or using a weapon.[3]

Domestic violence is most often presented on the one hand as an epidemic that views men as wild beasts, who are only loosely tethered by the constraints of civilization and who are aggressive, combative demonic primates who enjoy nothing better than battering, beating, and murdering women and children. On the other hand some do not view domestic violence as an issue at all. For them it is nothing more than a specious issue constructed and fabricated in the minds of feminists and is not a problem in America's enlightened modern society. The fact is that domestic violence is not as simple as men beating women. The nexus of the enigma is social, economic, and institutional power regardless of gender. Women have not been proven more moral then men, they simply remain less uncorrupted by institutional control and political power.

This book is an attempt to end the ambivalence of the majority of the American public, in particular American women, concerning domestic violence. Most of us as concerned citizens and occasionally even family violence professionals maintain ideas about convictions concerning domestic violence that are often inaccurate or fabricated "facts." Some authors present these "facts" simply to buttress their previously held convictions. Therefore, I have avoided skewing or distorting the facts so that the reader may make up his or her mind concerning the importance of the issue. I have come to believe that an even-handed review of the issue will demonstrate that domestic violence is an important topic that no reasonable and prudent person should continue to avoid. I have not anticipated, nor is it my intent, that everyone will reach that same conclusion.

My conclusion is twofold. One, regardless of the scope and size of the issue of domestic violence, it will not be resolved through the intervention of the criminal justice system. Two, the desired change that the majority of those concerned with the issue of domestic violence want, will not be effected until women control the majority of seats in the legislative bodies that create change.

Much of what I write is intended to challenge the conclusions reached by many domestic violence experts and to stimulate the debate. Most of the current literature concerning domestic violence is by academics and researchers who have produced works that frame the difference of conviction held by feminists or chauvinist writers. Often, however, the conviction of the academician or researcher is either absent or buried in obscure and unreadable technical language that most of us cannot interpret. I believe that this book provides an unbiased, uncomplicated, readable, and fair presentation of the issue.

Some of what I write is not measurable, or capable of being quantified by numbers or statistical fact. Some of what I write simply concerns human qualities by observation and a quantity of knowledge and expertise gained by my years of experience as a police officer. I have been able to observe at first hand that domestic violence is a problem that remains unseen in many American homes. Abuse by family members has never been a mystery to police officers, particularly those officers working in an urban setting. Regardless of the rhetoric, facts demonstrate that most of the abuse suffered by children and women occurs behind the closed doors of their homes and is committed by fellow family members.

Too many new police officers believe that their job will allow them to help solve many of our social ills. Police officers discover many hidden secrets in the private lives of American families. Their experience is an exceptional, exacting, and vivid journey into deviant behavior. Police officers today often deal with the maddest, baddest and saddest citizens our society has to offer. Police officers are trained to deny sentiment and emotion because their job is to be in control and to maintain control. This detachment is needed to avoid partiality and to preserve neutrality. Although the nature of police work encourages this emotional numbness, officers continue to be astonished and anguished by the harm family members do to those they profess to love.

I have included a number of appendices because they contain the laws, policies, and procedures that currently influence society's private and public perceptions of domestic violence. The appendices may not be as engaging and interesting as the preceding chapters, but for those who want a more complete understanding of the issue of domestic violence they are important. I have discovered many times that, although professionals may recognize the physical and emotional symptoms and needs of those involved in domestic violence circumstances, many of these professionals do not understand the complexities of the policies, procedures, and statute laws that direct the response of those in the criminal justice system. Just as important, the chapters that precede the appendixes will allow those in the criminal justice system who do comprehend the legal complexities to better understand the historical reasons and emotional rationalism of the victims of domestic violence.

The literature cited in this book is recent and offers fresh understanding or updated and conventional wisdom on the subject. In many instances, however, these sources present intense and specific political, polemic, and philosophical viewpoints. These works assuredly demonstrate that the only broad consensus in contemporary American society or the criminal justice system concerning the issue of domestic violence or our sex-role relationships will involve more than changing a few laws.[4]

Through this research I have reached a more complete understanding of this issue, I remain concerned because too many questions have yet to be answered. In the beginning, I had many of the same misconceptions of the issues as many average citizens, police officers, and professionals. I am not a feminist; I have been a registered Republican all my life and consider myself politically, a conservative. Over the last few years while remaining a political conservative, I have become, perhaps because of age, an empathetic humanist. It seemed to have worked for Teddy Roosevelt, and it seems to work for me.

I believe that it is time for many women who consider themselves to be liberal feminists to rid themselves of that identification in favor of being empathetic humanists. We must teach humanity the logic of correct behavior and not simply demand that their behavior change by means of legislation. I believe that it is time for the American dream of "all men are created equal" to be set aside for "all people must act as equals." Men and women are not equal psychically, biologically, or physiologically. We must replace the goal of equality of gender with one of equity of behavior towards each other. Equality of gender is an illusory goal that can not be achieved whereas equity can be rendered precisely. The difference between equality and equity is that we, men and women, are distinct in many ways and I believe that most of us elect to retain that distinction. We do not want nor can we expect that *everything* can be equal or the same for all of us. Equality and sameness are not synonymous. What we should endeavor towards is an equity of conduct that provides for fairness and impartiality of behavior towards each other. This is an educational process of learned behavior that must be taught in our schools and universities.

Men and women remain substantially divided on the issue of domestic violence. One can look at that division and be pessimistic. I persist in being optimistic but accept the fact that we have a long way to go. My familiarity with the problem of domestic violence draws from my ten years of street experience of responding to domestic violence calls as a cruiser officer, my eight years as a police detective and then sergeant, and my three years as a lieutenant training and lecturing on the subject.

Our society has come a long way in the last few decades, which are a mere blink in the eye of human history. Women continue to have expectations for continued and inevitable change, but many men and too many women continue to resist this change. Women, and particularly liberal feminists, must understand that we, as Americans, would not and could not have made this progress without the assistance of some men. I believe that it is time for the feminist movement to cease the chorus of lumping all men together in the theoretical dirty laundry basket. All men are not their antagonists. Many men, however, will continue to provide resistance because they view change as adversarial and potentially harmful to their traditional positions of economic and social control. Change in how we judge each other will be complete when some men and the majority of women decide that transformation must occur. Women who want change must use their newly won political capability and ability to implement that change.

Historically, over the last few thousand year's men have not conducted themselves as they should have. Unfortunately history has demonstrated that when one group of people can dominate another group and benefit from that domination, they have done so. Recently, however, many men have shown a better understanding of the fact that they cannot continue to live in what has traditionally been a man's world. Many men understand that society will be enriched by a sharing of power. I do believe however, that the majority of men will continue to resist change. The sharing of power is a political brass ring that will not be presented as a gift to women. It is now available to women who want it by means of our democratic process. Women should not just continue to lobby for help from their male public policymakers. *Authentic and certifiable progress in domestic violence will occur only when the majority of our public policymakers are women.*

NOTES

1. Paul Langer, "Boys Say They Care About Parents," *Boston Globe*, May 10, 1997, p. B5.

2. Jordana Hart, "Love Is Not Always the Answer," *Boston Globe,* May 14, 1997, p. A12.

3. Steven R. Donziger, ed. *The Real War on Crime: The Report of the National Criminal Justice Commission.* (New York: Harper Perennial, 1996) p. 156.

4. Peggy Reeves Sanday, *Female Power and Male Dominance: On the Origins of Sexual Inequality.* (New York: Cambridge University Press, 1981) p. 12.

2

Shift of Resolve

Irrationally held truths may be more harmful than reasoned errors.
T. H. Huxley (1825-1895)

Domestic violence is a perplexing and chronic paradox that has not been approached with circumspection. It has often not received the appropriate concern of many public policymakers. The majority of our contemporary public policymakers in America are men. They differ little historically from most other men who traditionally construct laws that will most benefit those who make the laws.[1] There may be more varied conceptions and convictions concerning how to create legitimate and coherent domestic violence public policies than any other contemporary political issue.[2]

The primary impediment to contemporary society's ability to reach consensus concerning domestic violence is that too much of what has been written about domestic violence, the studies, books, scholarly treatises, and numerous articles concerning domestic violence essentially support the particular author's previously held, particular point of view. The author's bias and ardent beliefs often distort much of what is written about domestic violence. This often presents the reading public with two fragmented and polarized conceptions of the problem. Women's advocates claim that domestic violence is a problem of epidemic proportions for women. Critics claim that this epidemic is only a "media epidemic" and that men are regularly being abused just as often as women are.

Many of these critics apparently consider our past history as virtually disassociated from affecting current circumstances. Virtually all historians understand that this is not so. There remains in all of us a biological and psychological connection between our past and our present behavior. Empirical knowledge and understanding of our past behavior between men and women is an important bond that continues to help us define our present conduct. Historically, change occurs only when decisions are made and choices are presented by an individual or group of individuals that change must occur. In our contemporary society neither change concerning domestic violence nor consensus on the issue will be reached *until women themselves decide that change must take place.*

There are exceptions to these biased presentations, and to date the most even-handed presentation of the problem of domestic violence is *Family Violence: Legal, Medical, and Social Perspectives* by Harvey Wallace. This book provides a comprehensive scholarly summary of family violence that includes the legal, medical, and social perspectives. It is a valued contribution to our understanding of family violence and should be requisite reading for anyone in the criminal justice field.

The primary concern of my book is to present an unbiased view of this complex issue. I have attempted to demonstrate my frankness and candor by using a rigorous technique of logic and empiricism. I may not have been thoroughly successful, and for any oversight I apologize in advance. Some of my own previously held beliefs in fact were altered during and as a result of this research.

Many of our current domestic violence public policy decisions have been made by those with good intentions. The problem is that many of these policies were formulated by men who have no real concept of the complexity of the topic, no authentic comprehension of this issue, and little to no understanding of the current limitations and past failures of the criminal justice system in guiding contemporary social issues or in altering individual behavior.

In 1984, the United States Attorney General's Task Force on Family Violence made recommendations in a final report released in September of that year. The report opens with advice that created many of our current domestic violence policy problems. "Progress against the problem of family violence must *begin* [emphasis added] with the criminal justice system."[3] That report played a major role in placing the emphasis for preventing domestic violence on the criminal justice system. This book will first and foremost attempt to demonstrate that the task force members offered very poor advice when they suggested that we *begin* ending a problem by *beginning* at the end. Indeed, perhaps we should begin at the beginning. "None of our current strategies have stemmed the single greatest threat to the safety of women: domestic violence. The federal Centers for Disease Control reports that more women seek treatment in hospitals for injuries from domestic violence than from all muggings, car accidents, and rapes *combined.*"[4]

Too often public policy decisions on domestic violence are based on information that has been received through passionate anecdotal reports supported by advocacy groups for battered women. More often than not public policymakers decisions are tempered by concern for votes in the upcoming election. Frequently data from recent National Institute of Justice empirical scientific studies, supported by qualitative research for foundation of fact, have not supported the position held by many of these victim advocacy groups and maintained by our public policymakers.[5]

We live in a society that has an obsession with "family values." Many in the media, most conservative politicians, and groups such as the Christian Coalition emphasize that the typical family unit represents the ideal and perfect living arrangement. Most of us like to believe that we live in a nation of families that personify "Ozzie and Harriet," "Father Knows Best," and "The Cosby Show." The truth is that many of our families are more comparable to "Roseanne," "Married With Children," and "The Simpsons."

There is an onerous side to family life that we as a society often shun. For many in this country, family life is a very private affair. Few families do not have a member who does not behave in a different manner at home than in social settings. Family members will rarely share this peculiar behavior even with friends in the social milieu. Some families can also teach children that combative, asocial, and violent behavior is acceptable in a family setting.[6] Often in the same family setting, many learn malevolence, hatred, and how and when to deceive each other.[7] Many studies demonstrate that animosity, prejudice, and violence are affected by genetic inheritance and learned behavior from family members.[8] Family violence is all too familiar to police officers. Approximately 50 million people each year are victimized by another member of the family.[9] Millions of men, women, and children flock to therapy groups to heal themselves from damage inflicted by their loved ones. A conservative estimate indicates that 10 percent of all women and 2 percent of all men have been molested as children. Strangers committed only approximately 8 to 10 percent of those molestations.[10] "But once the violence started, there was no end to it.... It demanded vengeance, or at least some answer, an endless series of biblical begats. A gun fired never stopped, it kept cutting through the lives of everyone around it, on and on. Like some unstoppable chain reaction."[11]

Today, the majority of Americans do not want to return to the "good old days of yore." Women, African Americans, the disabled, lesbians, gays, Asians, and Jews, among others in this country, have little desire for society to return to the values of the "fabulous fifties." It continues to astonish me that the majority of my peers often refuse to recognize or pretend not to understand why the fifties were not fabulous for more than 50 percent of Americans.

Women stayed at home cooking, sewing, and tending children while always enjoying those duties. My "fabulous fifties" high school history book rarely mentioned African Americans, and then most often in reference to Negroes on Southern plantations or during the Civil War. After the Civil War, with the exception of Booker T. Washington, Negroes conveniently disappeared. When they occasionally did surface in the general populace, they were okay as long as they appeared among us in small numbers or in sports. President Franklin D. Roosevelt did not live into the fabulous fifties but if he had we would still never have seen his wheelchair or crutches. The only gay people I knew of in the fifties were Caballeros. Jews were, of course, fiscally frugal, and Asians were small and shifty. Men, well of course, they were real men then. Ah, those fabulous fifties.

The status of the male-female relationship in the United States has been presented with the opportunity for more change in this century than in the entire history of humankind. In the nineteenth century, American women acquired the right to vote, which for the first time in the history of humankind gave women the right to share institutional power with men.[12] It was not until the nineteen century that the institution of governmental power was removed from the hands of the patriarchal political power brokers who controlled institutional government, which in turn has controlled social and economic power for the last five thousand years. The concept of women's emancipation has been finally delivered through the ballot box and is a late nineteenth-century idea that only recently has become accepted.[13] Some changes have already altered the relationships of wife to husband and of mother to child. It has also changed the relationship of women to other women. As Mary Catherine Bateson has written: "The biology that will continue to shape the destiny of human society is not sex, the relative differences in height and strength between men and women, the debatable difference in cognitive ability, nor even differences in endocrine systems and genitalia-but the human need for care, which both males and females can give."[14]

Neither in the family unit nor in the greater American society have we come to terms with this change. This complex relationship cannot be transformed by turning back the clock or by patchwork mending. It requires that both men and women adopt expectations of each other that are not constrained by gender stereotyping. Although the majority of abusers are men, all abusers are not men. Data on homicides in Chicago from 1966 to 1996 reveal that the female partner killed African-American men twice as often as African-American men killed their female partner.[15] The issue of domestic violence often transcends the issue of gender, and the disharmony often centers on whether we as humans can learn to share economic, social, and political power.

If the issue is merely gender, how do we explain the fact that many studies illustrate that same-sex domestic abuse in the lesbian and gay communities is often at the same level as that of heterosexual couples?[16] Curt Rogers, the executive director of the Gay Men's Domestic Violence Project in Boston conducted a 1997 study that found about one in four gay victims had suffered from domestic abuse. He believes that number is equal to the abuse suffered by heterosexual women, and that the issue is a power and control issue and not a gender issue.[17] In a survey of one hundred battered lesbians, sociologist Claire Renzetti discovered that four women reported that they could not go to the local women's shelter because their abusers worked there.[18] In the history of humankind those who have power, regardless of race, color, creed, national origin, or gender, seldom surrender their endowment of position and power without a struggle.

During the past decade, domestic violence has become an important, albeit misunderstood, political issue. Historically, society has been aware of domestic violence. Wife beating, child abuse, incest, and elder abuse, all occurring within the supposed ideal unit of the human family, are not new issues. In times of rapid social change, there are always Machiavellian machinations to prevent or slow societal transformation.[19] In current society, due to the tumultuous emotional change in the relationship between men and women, we often appear to be fretful, distrustful, and fearful of each other. Molly Chaudhuri, a lawyer and former prosecutor, observed: "It's when the most progress is being made that the violence is the most intense."[20]

The panacea for this human affliction will not be found by changing our criminal or civil court systems.[21] The shift of our resolve must begin in community intervention through a multi-strategy educational design. The use of civil restraining orders and mandatory arrest policies by police departments without proper criminal sanctions to cure the ills of domestic violence is a deception in which solid facts are scarce and it is difficult to tell fact from myth. Public social policy has been distorted by misinformation, incorrect analysis of studies, unjustified certainties, and the search for a quick fix by public policymakers. The lamentable truth is that many more blank spaces must be filled before we proceed any further.

An impartial look at the results of our current domestic violence policies is a sobering and disillusioning experience. Women's and victims' rights advocates, prosecutors, and legislators often line up like crows on a wire, disregarding National Institute of Justice studies that do not agree with policies they doggedly continue expound as gospel. Passion rather than reason and objectivity too often drive the advocates. Public policymakers strive to please everyone, and the only way to accomplish that is by using political smoke and mirrors to obscure facts contained in these studies.

In this book public policymakers guiding prevailing policy are urged to redirect their locus concerning domestic violence away from the criminal justice system and toward the educational system and preventive community based programs. Women must understand that if they want change, in democratic societies it is there for the taking. Naomi Wolf, a recent newspaper article notes, in her book *Fire With Fire*, wrote that political equality is within women's grasp if they choose to seize it. She believes that women are becoming more involved in politics but that they set their standards too low. "We are so acculturated to think of women with limits that we really don't get it yet."[22] In America over half the population is female yet in politics women remain the missing half. Who is preventing women from seeking elective office and from becoming the keepers of their own destiny? It is the responsibility of our society and, each of us as individuals within that society, to become more responsible.[23]

Society must blend empirical studies with emotionally held beliefs and become more committed to the logic of commonsense problem solving. Society must also become more reasonable and ask questions about who we are as a people and what the proper relationship between men and women should be.[24] We should come to understand that success is measured by what we put into life and not what we get out of it. These questions must include the logic of inquiry, explanation, and argument. Discussion must become much more frank and forthright. It must become the role of the community to define what our existing social arrangements should be in regard to gender and family. To reach accommodation, it is essential that we accept more alternatives than the criminal and civil justice system to produce this change.

Society must acknowledge the extent and limitations of the criminal justice system in adjusting the behavior of abusers.[25] The criminal justice system has not and cannot put an end to murders. The criminal justice system has not and cannot put an end to drug use. The criminal justice system has not and cannot be used as the guiding agency to end what has become an intolerable cycle of domestic violence. Columnist Ellen Goodman writes: "What is progress after all in the course of sexual politics? Is it marked by an increase in the number of men in jail? Or by a decrease in the number of assaults? I don't want to choose between law enforcement and 'crime prevention,' but I would chart the long run of progress by the change in men's behavior."[26]

Only the chronic portion of violent couples who will not curb their violent behavior can be overseen and disciplined with proper criminal sanctions through the courts. The beliefs held by the majority of men in America concerning equitable treatment of women will not be altered by the police departments and courts of this nation.

Society must expand the debate over the nature and content of the issue. Professionals in society must come to an agreement on terminology and research methodology. Many recent experiments concerning domestic violence have clouded the issue and have not cleared what the proper law enforcement role should be. Is the issue of domestic violence one of gender, or is it actually a struggle for economic, social, and political control? We must be able to get a better understanding of what make's domestic violence a problem in both the gay and lesbian and the heterosexual communities. We certainly must come to understand why so many women in contemporary society do not believe domestic violence is a problem. All women must come to understand that domestic violence, even for others, is *their* problem. There are few families in this nation that do not have a family member or a friend in need of understanding and support to break the cycle of violence that controls their life. Silence is acceptance and to accept is to condone.

We will not likely discover a solitary and distinct origin of all domestic violence, just as there is not a solitary and distinct remedy for cancer. It is time for public policymakers to understand that the solutions to domestic violence do not lie in the interventionist and reactive policies of the criminal justice system but rather in an effective change in the patterns of our social and cultural behavior.

Domestic violence is a quality of life issue for many women and men in this nation. To ensure that the quality of life will change for the better, more women must become part of the political process. We will not have policies in place that are designed to prevent the crime of domestic violence *before it occurs* until women in this nation understand that they must seek political office in numbers equal to men and create those policies themselves. It is difficult for many men to understand why they should challenge the historic and habitual conduct of men that has allowed them to become so entrenched in the social and institutional structures of power. There appears to be little reason for men to seek redistribution of resources and opportunities away from themselves and towards women. Many men continue to wonder how this social and economic change will make their lives any better and question what it will do for them or for their sons. I do not believe that many men believe that the concept of "What's in it for me?" is entirely a male concept.

Precipitating variables such as class and gender must be addressed in our schools and community with the goal of producing better citizens who must reach a better understanding concerning the complex issues of differing male and female values. We should better understand if these differing value systems are innate or learned behavior. Are men born to become more violent than women or is this difference a result of cultural patterns? *Long-term progress will begin only when we begin to treat the cause of domestic violence rather than continue our current policy of reacting to its symptoms.*

It is time that all men and women in our contemporary society begin to act more responsibly towards each other and undertake to answer the ancient question posited by Aristotle: "As a free people, how ought we order our lives together?"

NOTES

1. Richard Wrangham and Dale Peterson, *Demonic Males* (Boston: Houghton Mifflin Co., 1996), p. 242.

2. Richard J. Gelles and Donileen R. Loseke, eds., *Current Controversies on Family Violence* (Newbury Park, Calif.: Sage Publications, 1993), pp. 1-5.

3. *United States Attorney General's Task Force on Family Violence (1984) Final Report* (Washington, D.C.: U.S. Government Printing Office, 1984).

4. Steven R. Donziger. ed. *The Real War on Crime: The Report of the National Criminal Justice Commission* (New York: Harper Perennial, 1996), p. 146.

5. Jeffrey Fagan, *The Criminalization of Domestic Violence: Promises and Limits* (Washington, D.C.: National Institute of Justice, 1996), pp. 1-48.

6. Karen Wright and Devin Wright, *Family Life, Delinquency, and Crime: A Policymaker's Guide* (Washington, D.C.: Office of Juvenile Justice and Delinquency Prevention, August 1995) p. vii.

7. John B. Briggs and Devin F. Collins, *Evaluating the Quality of Learning* (New York: Academic Press, 1982), pp. 227-229.

8. Wrangham and Peterson, *Demonic Males*, p. 95.

9. James M. Henslin. *Social Problems*. (Upper Saddle River, N.J.: Prentice Hall, 1996), p. 402.

10. Harvey Wallace, *Family Violence: Legal, Medical, and Social Perspectives* (Boston: Allyn & Bacon, 1996), pp. 57-58.

11. Joseph Kanon, *Los Alamos*. (New York: Broadway Books, 1997), p. 27.

12. Wrangham and Peterson, *Demonic Males*, p. 245.

13. Robert C. Soloman, *Introducting Philosophy*, 5th ed. (New York: Harcourt Brace Jovanovich, 1993), p. 16.

14. Mary Catherine Bateson, "Holding Up the Sky Together," *Civilization* 2, no. 3 (1995): 29-31.

15. Wallace, *Family Violence*, p. 245.

16. Patricia Pearson, *When She Was Bad: Violent Women and the Myth of Innocence* (New York: Viking, 1997) p. 29.

17. Alexis Chia, "Abuse in Gay Partners Detailed," *Boston Globe*, September 3, 1997, p. B1.

18. Carl Sagan, *The Dragons of Eden* (New York: Ballatine Books, 1977) p. 190.

19. Patricia Pearson, *When She Was Bad: Violenct Women and the Myth of Innocence* (New York: Viking, 1997), p. 131.

20. Betty Grillo and Marleen Lee, "Domestic Violence Rate Still Reported to Be Alarmingly High," *Boston Globe*, October 29, 1995, p. 25.

21. Kathleen J. Ferraro and Lucille Pope, "Irreconcilable Differences: Battered Women, Police, and the Law," Ed. N. Zoe Hilton, *Legal Responses to Wife Assault* (Newbury Park, Calif.: Sage Publications, 1994) p.99.

22. Carolyn Barta, "Women to Be Major Force Entering the Next Century," *Charleston, SC Post and Courier*, March 30, 1997, p. 5G

23. Peter L. Berger, *Invitation to Sociology: A Humanistic Perspective* (New York: Doubleday, 1963) pp. 69-71.

24. Carl Sagan and Ann Druyan, *Shadows of Forgotten Ancestors: A Search for Who We Are* (New York: Random House, 1992), pp. 203-218.

25. Fagan, *The Criminalization of Domestic Violence*, p. 30.

26. Ellen Goodman, "I'd Have Let Him Walk," *Washington Post*, December 14, 1991, p. A27.

3

Roadmap

You can't get there unless you know where you're going.
Richard L. Davis (1941-)

Many of us, both men and women, remain confused by the issue of domestic violence. Those of us who have worked inside the criminal justice system and have received domestic violence training often have a better understanding of the problem than the general populace. Even so those within the system, because of their own childhood socialization, education, and the diversity and complexity of the subject, can find themselves inadequately prepared both personally and professionally to respond to and resolve many domestic violence incidents.

In the O.J. Simpson case, Mark Fuhrman, regardless of his flawed personality, was an alert and intelligent homicide detective. He received fifty-five official commendations during his twenty years with the Los Angeles Police Department. Many peers regardless of race, color, creed, or national origin respected him for his police work. Lead prosecutor in the Simpson case, Marcia Clark, following the first day of testimony, told him that "You're one of the best I've ever seen," and Johnnie Cochran, O.J. Simpson's lead defense attorney, described him as a "great witness direct from central casting."[1] Fuhrman, in his book, *Murder in Brentwood*, denies that the murder of Nicole Simpson and Ron Goldman was the result of domestic violence. "But how do you have domestic violence when the couple no longer lives together, no longer dates, and shares nothing but the custody of two children? What we do have is stalking, obsession, harassment, control, ego, and eventually murder."[2]

Fuhrman believes that Simpson was disturbed by his inability to control his relationship with his ex-wife. He writes that Simpson would often respond to this loss of control with threats, intimidation, and violence. Here Mark Fuhrman has described quite accurately what most of us would recognize as domestic violence. He became an eyewitness to this escalation of domestic violence between Simpson and his wife Nicole; years before he had responded to an intense and violent dispute between the couple. He responded again at the end of this cycle of violence to her murder. Yet, Fuhrman somehow remains unable or incapable of understanding that all of these emotions have created a jealousy so strong that it ends in rage and murder. The fact is that Mark Furman describes for us in his very own best selling book *precisely and in detail what domestic violence is* and then astonishingly and incredibly in this very same book and on those very same pages continues to deny that the murder of Nicole Simpson and Ron Goldman by Simpson was a result of this escalation of violence. He fails to understand that his own book provides the classic textbook example of the domestic violence cycle. I am sure that most of his readers will recognize what he describes as domestic violence, but why can't he? Where has he been for the last ten years?

Even more telling is his statement in the next to last paragraph of his book: "And when my son grows up, I hope he does not want to become a policeman."[3] Fuhrman also has a daughter but neglects to hope that she does not become a police officer. In this paragraph he unknowingly has demonstrated to us that he believes his son lives in one world and his daughter another. In Fuhrmans' world there is no equal opportunity of employment as a police officer for his daughter. I contend that Mark Furman is hardly alone in his beliefs, and too many men in America are still in denial of the issue of gender equity. The denial of equality can have menacing implications because not being equal means that women must be confined to being superior or inferior to men. Do you think men like Mark Fuhrman believe women to be superior or inferior? Dismayingly, Fuhrman does not even blink when he reduces his simple thoughts to the written page so that all of us can discover his naiveté.

Many professionals outside the criminal justice system believe that the prevalence and proliferation of domestic violence in society can best be altered and impeded through the intervention of the criminal justice system. Within the criminal justice system, the belief that domestic violence can or will be curbed through the use of our adversarial court system remains a topic of continued contention and dispute.[4] "Though the criminal justice system can arrest and punish perpetrators, we clearly must go outside the formal justice system to stop the cycle of violence that begins in the home."[5]

Some Americans believe domestic violence to be a central issue in our society, while others do not believe it to be an issue at all. This book is about domestic violence and attempts to present a unique challenge for both women and many men. It endeavors to provide a clear picture of domestic violence through a series of overviews of the problem as perceived by a police officer. It also seeks to present a more complete understanding of this formidable subject from the perspective of a police officer who has both worked the streets and who has researched the shelves of our libraries. It is from the point of view of a police officer, a student of history, a man, a father, and a husband who for twenty-one years often worked in the valley of despair that is domestic violence.

Domestic or family violence or intimate partner violence has roots deep in the history of humankind. Its nexus emanates from a social, economic, and political power and control struggle, most often between husband and wife or cohabiting partners. Civil rights battles in this country are not about "rights" or "equality". Rather, civil rights issues are grounded in matters of economics.[6] Domestic violence is not an issue of gender but rather is about how we make social and economic decisions in our homes or relationships. The person in the relationship that has control of the decision-making process will often use intimidation and/or violence to hold on to that control.

The obvious certainty is that for most of human history men have been in charge of making the family decisions. In our contemporary society each of the cohabiting partners, because of many twentieth-century social changes, wants to predominate in the decision-making process. Conflict and violence can result when there is no process in place that allows for a sharing of this responsibility. To be "in charge" is primarily a masculine concept. If a man loses his status as "authority figure" and his peers find out, he can lose his public reputation. "Honor was primarily a masculine concept, not always appreciated by wives who sometimes felt that a man's duty to his family was more important than pride in his reputation."[7] Who "wears the pants" in the family is often an essential component of this peculiar emotional masculine code of pride and reputation.

External power and control struggles between nations that cannot reach compromise often result in war. Quite often, the more powerful of the two warring factions wins. Family or interrelational power and control struggles are most often between men and women. Here as well the more powerful of the two will triumph. For the past five thousand years of recorded history, this contest has continued to be one sided. It is not a closely guarded secret that men have sustained their social and economic control over women through physical and institutional intimidation.

This is not to argue that a man *can not* be the victim of domestic violence or that women *can not* be the primary aggressors of a domestic violence incident. Men can be the victims of domestic violence and some women can be the primary aggressors. It is the more resolute or the more unyielding of the two, regardless of gender, whose will prevails. It should be apparent to any student of history, however, that men have dominated women through institutional mechanisms and the use of physical force. To deny that the dynamics of history have obliged women to play a submissive and subordinate role to men is to dispute historical fact. To deny, however, that many contemporary women in American society should not share the blame in the continuation of this submissive and subordinate role is to dispute historical fact. Contemporary women in America have no obligation to continue on the road most traveled. Why does male domination continue in America? Because men have been running things and women continue to let them do it by voting predominately for males to hold public office.[8]

Men remain our primary public policymakers. Many often behave as if they are disconcerted by the issue of domestic violence; they are not. A patrilinear legacy can be found among many of our wealthy and political privileged male family members that is akin to the arrogance of those in days of yore who held title by tradition and inheritance. Popular election to the Senate, after all, is only a twentieth-century idea. Many of us, principally women, who are not the majority of our public policymakers although they are the majority of our population, seem to understand the issue quite clearly.

Women are more often capable and competent in understanding domestic violence because of their proclivity for including compassion with reason and logic in the their decision-making process. Would we have been involved in as many wars over the millennia if women had been the leaders of nations? Women seem more apt than men to appreciate the complexity of domestic violence. I, of course, do not mean that all women exhibit this capacity and all men do not. Some women can be more violent than some men. This conclusion has been reached by examining the numbers of women involved in violent and nonviolent crimes as compared to men. I realize that I should avoid anecdotal evidence, but the behavior of my two boys as compared to their three sisters seemed to be, in a purely nonscientific manner, quite different. Proper and just change in public policy concerning domestic violence will come only when women who want that change are the agents who institute that change. Women should not continue asking their male public policymakers to create that change for them.

The lack of sympathetic understanding toward women by many men has its basis in the fact that, historically, men have displayed a pattern of systemic authoritative, aggressive and violent behavior. The reward for that type of behavior in the past has placed men in the position to retain social and economic dominance over women. Most men and indeed too many women in contemporary society continue to display little interest in dismantling these archaic societal foundations that have served men so well over the generations. I am not surprised by men's lack of interest for change, but I am often astonished by the continued disinterest of so many women.

Katherine Dunn, in the August 1, 1994 issue of *The New Republic*, writes that "An irritating by-product of the O.J. Simpson tragedy is the blizzard of balderdash about wife battering." In the same article "Truth Abuse" she seems to agree with some researchers that men and women batter each other at about the same rate. I would remind Dunn that there might be a reason why it is most often educated professional women, who are at or near the top of the socioeconomic ladder, who question the severity of the problems women face because of domestic violence. The reason, of course, as the Bureau of Justice Statistics has reported for the last twenty-five years, is that certain demographic groups have higher victimization rates than others. It is a fact that the violent crime rate decreases as income and education increases. I believe that few women at the lower end of the socioeconomic ladder will agree with her. While many professional women worry about the "glass ceiling," they seem to have forgotten that most working and minority women continue to worry about the "bottom line" of a food budget. The only glass these women worry about is the glass of milk they have to fill for themselves and their children.

The data in this book will indisputably demonstrate that in the field of criminal justice it is the men, principally young men, who perpetrate most of this nation's violent crimes. Their behavior is most menacing between the ages of approximately 13 and 30. The majority of domestic violence incidents also involve a male between the ages of 13 and 30. Data from the United States Department of Justice demonstrate a correlation between arrest rates with the age and gender of the defendant. "The same correlation holds true for victims. Women aged 19 to 29 are more likely than other women to be victimized by an intimate."[9]

No one in America, that I am aware of, has yet to provide empirical evidence that disputes that men of all ages are more likely than women to commit crime and in particularly violent crime. Men are much more likely than women to commit any type of domestic violence crime. An examination of any police department's records in America will reveal that the violent criminals who are arrested are overwhelmingly men and not women. Why is it then that many of us in today's society, including some family violence experts, continue to believe that this same type of violent and aggressive behavior by men in the public arena will not and does not continue in the sanctity of our homes behind closed doors.

A study conducted by Maria Roy, the founder and director of New York's Abused Women's Aid Crisis, reports that "ninety percent [of domestic violence abusers] do not have a criminal record, indicating the most offenders are not deviant outside of the family."[10] In fact on September 8, 1992, Massachusetts began the nation's first statewide, centrally computerized domestic violence recordkeeping system. In a sample of domestic violence restraining orders in 1992 and 1994, it was found that 70 percent of the abusers had a prior criminal history and 85 percent were male.[11]

As this book will illustrate some family violence experts have provided studies that contain statistics that they claim demonstrate women physically assault men as often as men physically assault women. Anyone who is familiar with crime statistics and most police officers who respond to domestic violence incidents realize that most domestic violence abusers are men who physically assault women. It is important to note in this section that data from studies in Massachusetts and elsewhere, as noted in this book, demonstrate that the majority of men who perpetrate domestic violence are predominately men with a history of criminal behavior. This does not, of course, preclude men without a history of criminal behavior from committing domestic violence. Data from Massachusetts studies and elsewhere, as noted in this book, indicate that approximately one in four males who are the subject of a restraining order do not have a criminal record.

If the reader is unwilling to accept criminal data that demonstrate male violence is commonplace, he or she may simply examine the history books. The history of humankind is a comprehensive record of women who have historically been considered as property by their husbands. It was often acceptable behavior for husbands to batter, torment, and otherwise mistreat their wives. In many nations today, that behavior continues. It is an undeniable recorded historical truth that male violent behavior has played a role in the historic male dominance over women.

Domestic violence, because of the unique complexity it presents to the victim, has become a challenge to the criminal justice system. Many public policymakers do not understand that there is little to no efficacy in our current criminal justice system.[12] My experience as a police officer has led me to believe that many of those who have an integral interest in criminal justice, that is those who make a living working for police departments, district attorneys, or the courts know there is little justice or compassion for the victim within the system. Few will admit it because of economic self- interest. It is important to note here that my contempt is not for those individuals working within the system, but for the *system itself.* Many individuals who work within the system continue to work long hours in a losing battle.

Many citizens who have been unlucky enough to become acquainted with the criminal justice system as victims have noticed the absence of any coherent, collective, coordinated system. The victim often discovers that the criminal justice system consists of multifaceted competing and independent agencies, each with diverse policies and strategies. Often victims are simply an afterthought for all three agencies.

These three agencies frequently have expertise in their own area but do not comprehend or appreciate the obstacles experienced by the other two. Worse still, these three agencies, the police department, district attorney's office, and the courts are often oblivious to the role the other is supposed to play in providing appropriate domestic violence services to those who have been abused.

This book hopes to help the reader reach a more complete understanding of the formidable subject of domestic violence. I have found only limited research concerning domestic violence from the perspective of the police. The police departments, after all, are the agencies that intervene in more domestic disputes than all other criminal or social agencies combined. "Living in our society is like living in a very tall building. The rich live on the top floors. The poor people live on the lowest floors. And only cops travel to all the floors. Only cops see it all."[13]

I find it interesting that as family violence experts search for solutions to domestic violence, they rarely give credence to the experience and knowledge of police officers who work the streets and enter the homes of so many family disputes. This lack of confidence and trust in the knowledge gained by these police officers is not unusual for those of us who are familiar with the criminal justice system. The Department of Justice and other federal criminal justice agencies in Washington, D.C., are layered with attorneys who rarely miss the opportunity to look down their litigious noses with revulsion at the mere thought that police officers may know as much or more about crime in this nation as they do.

Recently, a two-year effort was made by a group of thirty-four citizens who examined current criminal justice policy in the United States. The majority of the members on this commission were lawyers or members of academia. There were the required "token members" of this commission and so only two members had any real experience in policing.[14] How has it come to be, that lawyers and members of academia believe that they know more about the criminal justice system than police officers? Rather than recognizing how much assistance police officers could provide, lawyers and academics, when they are members of advisory boards or commissions concerned with domestic violence or any crime in fact, rarely miss the opportunity to discover corruption, lying, falsification of records, and excessive use of force by police officers.

In *The Real War on Crime* which is the report of the National Criminal Justice Commission, the editor, a lawyer, devotes eight pages to police abuse, police corruption, police lies about why they make arrests, and false police testimony in court. I looked everywhere in the book, and not to my surprise, I could not find a single paragraph, not a single sentence anywhere, in which the commission contended that any lawyers in the criminal justice system, anywhere, at any time, would do any of the above.

In an otherwise interesting book, *The Tough On Crime Myth: Real Solutions to Cut Crime*, author and lawyer Peter T. Elikann includes the following statement for no apparent reason other than it is difficult for most lawyers to pass on the opportunity to take a shot at cops: "The notorious testimony of police officer Mark Fuhrman at the O.J. Simpson trail was the most celebrated example of alleged perjury by a law enforcement official, a situation that many citizens believe is commonplace and pervasive."[15]

I would ask the lawyers on the above-mentioned crime commission report, Peter Elikann and all lawyers involved with the criminal justice system, to review pages 150-151 of the 1994 *Bureau of Justice Statistics Sourcebook*. In response to questions on lawyers honesty and ethical standards, 46 percent of Americans polled rated lawyers as low or very low. Only about 12 percent felt the same way about police officers. A 1993 Hart Research Associates survey found that only a fifth of those surveyed were comfortable describing lawyers as "honest and ethical."[16]

As for members of academia, I do not believe they would fare well in a poll asking the question; "What percentage of the members of academia live in the real world?" It is time for those of us within the criminal justice system to stop blaming each other when it is not individuals but an entire system that is creating these problems. Just as important, it would be helpful if our criminal justice experts in academia would recognize that police officers do know something about crime and could be helpful in providing information about how to control crime and domestic violence in particular.

Domestic Violence Report is published six times a year and is devoted exclusively to information concerning innovative programs, legal developments, and research concerning domestic violence law. It has twenty-two members on its advisory board, only two of whom appear to have any background as a police officer. One is a chief of police and the other a former chief. I am sure that both men are intelligent and capable. I am also sure that neither has had any field experience concerning domestic violence during the last decade. This may be an unusual concept, but I would think that some members of this advisory board should be from law enforcement who have actually worked in the field since many of the recent and dramatic changes in domestic violence intervention by law enforcement.

Violence Against Women is described by its publisher, Sage Periodicals Press as "The only scholarly journal dedicated to the problem of gender-based violence." It has an international editorial board of thirty-five members including physicians, psychiatrists, psychologists, family counselors, educators, social workers, attorneys, judges, but not nary a single, token police officer. The journal declares the following: "A primary goal of this journal, therefore, is to foster dialogue among those working in various fields and disciplines, as well as in agencies and other settings, and among those from diverse backgrounds in terms of ethnocultural and racial identity, sexual orientation, and experiences of victimization/survivorship."[17]

This book attempts to question why many of these family violence experts rarely understand or express little desire to recognize that many police officers want to help. Police officers are sincerely concerned about domestic violence and earnestly want to be included in this dialogue. I cannot understand why so many experts involved with the issue of domestic violence do not want input from police officers who, after all, respond to these domestic violence calls. And how is it that periodicals, such as the ones mentioned just above, continue to effortlessly dismiss the importance of the police officer, who respond to these troubled families and enter the homes of the abusers and victims by the hundreds of thousands when these officers have useful information for these experts? The fact that police officers are often viewed by these experts as having little real understanding of the issue of domestic violence is inexcusable as well as inexplicable.

I have seen few legitimate reasons written by experts who attempt to explain why police officers do not like to respond to domestic violence calls. While many of these experts are correct in their position that most police officers do not relish responding to domestic violence calls, these experts do not provide the right reasons for that reluctance. The reasons they give in various research papers and books are often far from the truth. It often seems as if these researchers have presented a series of Joe Friday-*Dragnet* like "Just the facts lady," television, movie, and detective novel explanations of police behavior, conduct, and function rather than reality.

While for many of these experts the study of family violence is still in its infancy, police officers have been aware of the problem of domestic violence for years. I can remember, to this very day, one of the first domestic violence calls that I responded to. I remember the names of those involved and can still recall how helpless I felt because there was so little I could do to change their behavior. I once brought them to court, this was before domestic violence laws were passed that allowed for arrest for domestic assault and battery. When the judge learned that they had informed me and my partner that one would not testify against the other, he chided us for wasting both his and the court's time. My partner and I finally told this same couple that if they did not stop their behavior the next time we responded to a family disturbance call we would arrest them for cohabiting, which was illegal and a felony in Massachusetts in 1976. The next time we were dispatched to that address the couple showed us that they were now man and wife. Twenty years later when I retired, police officers were still responding to domestic violence calls from that very same couple. These same police officers were also responding to the home of their daughter who, as children often do, followed in her parents' footsteps. Police officers will continue to have little success reaching harmonious resolutions of these disputes because the answers do not lie in the criminal justice system.

In most of the comprehensive works I have read concerning domestic violence, the concerns of police officers are rarely considered relevant enough to be included. When police concerns and opinions are included, they are often ridiculed and disparaged. It is odd that the agency that is widely acknowledged as the one that plays a pivotal role in domestic violence is viewed by so many domestic violence experts as not having a single, clear, or cogent concept of what should be done to prevent further escalation of this dilemma. Nothing could be further from the truth, and this book is an endeavor to present solutions from a police officer's perspective.

I was a police officer in Brockton, Massachusetts, from 1975 until 1996. Brockton is a blue-collar city with a 1990 census population of 92,788. When I became a police officer in 1975, we were trained to avoid arrest in family violence venues. Officers were instead trained to apply conflict resolution, mediate on the scene, and respect the desire of the victim. Much of the early critical feminist analysis of law enforcement response to domestic violence was directed toward police departments and individual officer response. Police officers were enforcing, both legislative and court laws that were approved and directed by public policymakers. Officers reacted, for the most part, as they had been trained to react. Most of the training police officers received were not in-house law enforcement concepts but consisted of the clinical and theoretical suggestions and agenda of sociologists and psychologists who were the family violence experts of their day.

A mantra repeated by feminists and many domestic violence advocates is the allegation that police officers treat domestic assault and battery differently from stranger assault and battery. The feminists assert that they have the data to prove this claim. I agree that research data will indicate that police officers often react to domestic violence assault and battery differently than stranger assault and battery, because often they do. And often they should.

The victims of stranger assault and battery usually have called the police with the intent to press charges and want punishment for their assailant. In these stranger assault and battery incidents the victims do not inform police officers that they do not want to press charges and that if charges are brought forward against their wishes by the police they will not go to court and testify. When victims are forced to testify, they often insist they will swear in court that nothing happened and that they did not want the assailant punished or arrested. If the wishes of the majority of stranger assault and battery victims the police respond to were similar to many domestic violence victims, then the research data would be similar to domestic violence assault and battery.

Domestic violence assault and battery is not a crime that is similar to most other crimes. Most of the complex circumstances surrounding both the abuser and the victim of domestic violence assault and battery are not present in stranger assault and battery. They are not the same crime and can not and should not be treated as if they are one and the same. While most victim advocates continue to demand that police officers treat domestic violence just like other crimes I assert that police officers should not because facts demonstrate that the circumstances surrounding both the abuser and the victim require a different criminal justice response.

Gender equity is an issue still in search of resolution and it will ultimately signal the beginning of the end of domestic violence. Gender equity is the best method to be used to achieve that resolution. I believe that until the last decade most Americans did not understand the complex nature of domestic violence and the quandary it presents to its victims. The circumstances that ensnare the domestic violence victim, as well as aspiration of and resolution desired by the victim of domestic violence through use of the criminal justice system, is more often than not very different from crimes such as stranger assault and battery.

Many feminists and victim advocates too often believe that if they could just get these jack-booted, gun-carrying male cops, who of course hate all women, to make an arrest every time they respond to a domestic violence call, incidents of domestic violence would decrease. The arrest by police officers does absolutely nothing to provide remedy to the many underlying problems within the family or between victim and abuser. To the contrary, data in this book clearly demonstrate that while police policies have changed dramatically over the last decade calls for restraining orders continue to increase. Across the nation as property crime and homicides drop, police arrests for domestic violence have skyrocketed, and domestic violence calls have not abated.

The numbers continue to increase because many victims seek the help of the criminal justice system at the advice of those outside the criminal justice system who have little to no understanding of the past and current failure of the criminal justice systems inability to alter human behavior. Victim advocates, many who often have little comprehension of the lack of compassion and concern for victims demonstrated in criminal justice system, continue to convince many victims of domestic violence that the criminal justice system is the answer to their problems. The criminal justice system is assuredly not the answer to those victims many who are only seeking to change the behavior of their abusers who they continue to care for.

Despite the many recent changes in police policies and procedures, domestic violence calls from victims pour into police departments and the courts seeking to end this enigma. These calls will continue to rise at an alarming rate because many victim advocates outside the criminal justice system continue to insist that it is the victims, only and best hope. It is not. Solutions to the dilemma of domestic violence require a formula that provides genuine caring and common sense. Both are certainly lacking in the legal labyrinth of our current criminal justice system. Many advocates continue to insist on help from our contemporary criminal justice system simply because they believe that something is better than nothing and anything is better than a past where the problem was ignored.

It is now time we begin to question the wisdom of our current reactive-oriented, criminal justice driven, domestic violence policies that are failing at the same alarming rate as our criminal justice driven, drug abuse policies failed. It is time to initiate honest evaluations of our current policies and attempt to reflect on why many of them have failed to provide what they promised. It is time to provide real relief for those caught in this complex, tortuous, and tangled web of domestic violence.

NOTES

1. Mark Fuhrman, *Murder in Brentwood* (Washington, D.C.: Regnery Publishing, 1997), pp. 100-103.

2. Ibid., p. 188.

3. Ibid., p. 321.

4. Steve R. Donziger, ed. *The Real War on Crime: The Report of the National Criminal Justice Commission* (New York: Harper Perennial, 1996), p. 158.

5. Ibid., p. 158.

6. Liz Winfeld, "Domestic Partner Benefits Getting to Be Routine," *Boston Globe*, March 23, 1997, p. E3.

7. James M. McPherson, *For Cause & Comrades* (New York: Oxford University Press, 1997), 23.

8. Joseph P. Kahn, "The Professor of Carnal Knowledge," *Boston Globe*, March 26, 1997, p. D1.

9. Donziger, *The Real War on Crime*, p. 156.

10. R. Barri Flowers, "The Problem of Domestic Violence Is Widespread," in Karin L. Swisher, ed. *Domestic Violence* (San Diego: Greenhaven Press, 1996), p. 13.

11. Donald Cochran, *The Tragedies of Domestic Violence: A Qualitative Analysis of Civil Restraining Orders in Massachusetts* (Boston: Office of the Commissioner of Probation Massachusetts Trail Court, October 12, 1995), p. 6.

12. Ibid., p. 181.

13. Connie Fletcher, "What Cops Know," *On Patrol* (Summer 1996): 44.

14. Donziger, *The Real War on Crime*, p. xi.

15. Peter T. Elikann, *The Tough On Crime Myth: Real Solutions to Cut Crime* (New York: Insight Books, 1996), p. 22.

16. Bob Garfield, "Do Lawyers Deserve Their Bad Name?" *Civilization* 4. No. 2 (1997): 51.

17. *Violence Against Women* (Thousand Oaks, Calif.: Sage Periodicals Press), 2 No. 4 (December 1996).

4

Pieces of the Puzzle

We do not deal with justice here; we deal with the law.
Herman Melville, *Billy Budd*

Domestic violence is one of America's most complex social problems.[1] There continues to be an emotional, polemical, and intense debate about how to end domestic violence.[2] To make the issue more complicated, endless ancillary debates have been held concerning the sum and substance of domestic violence. Many commentators believe that domestic violence is not as grave as feminists allege and that many women's advocates intentionally exaggerate and manipulate data to satisfy their own agenda. Other critics contend that women's abuse of men has essentially been ignored. While they often agree that the criminal justice system is not doing what it should be doing, they often disagree on *just what it is* the criminal justice system should be doing. Commentators, critics, women's advocates, and many within the criminal justice system do agree that regardless of who perpetrates domestic violence it is improper behavior that must be addressed.[3] This chapter seeks to provide a proper framework for those in contemporary American society who are not well versed in the issue. More than any other contemporary social problem, family violence challenges the public conscience, and there are no easy solutions.[4] Too many families continue to live in the shadow of this dark world; too many children will replicate the behavior of abusive adults.[5] We must acknowledge that domestic violence is more common than all other forms of violence combined.[6] Yearly reports issued by the Bureau of Justice Statistics, the Federal Bureau of Investigation, the National Victims Resource Center, and many other organizations actively engaged in studies of violent crime demonstrate that for women and children, statistically speaking, the home is the most dangerous place to be.[7] Their abusers, who have the potential to be killers, are not strangers. Those who claim love, even as they abuse and murder, are boyfriends, girlfriends, lovers, husbands, wives, mothers, and fathers. It cannot be denied that some women assault men, but because of the greater physical, financial, and emotional injuries suffered by women, they are now and have been, even before recorded history, the predominant victims of domestic violence.[8] In the words of Donald Cochran, Commissioner of Probation in Massachusetts. "These tragic tales of beatings and abuse are not being witnessed in the streets or television; it is happening right in the child's own home between his/her parents."[9] One of the first lessons police officers learn is that the most exacting and perplexing calls that society expects them to resolve is the family dispute.[10] Because of changes in statute law and police policies, more arrests for domestic violence are being made now than ever before.[11]

The traditional police approach has been to avoid intervention or arrest on the dual arguments that offenders would not be punished by the courts even if they were arrested and that an arrest might provoke the abusers into committing more serious violence, sometimes to themselves. Both of these contentions continue to have some merit. One of the prime concerns and complaints of many feminists, family violence experts, and other critics of police behavior is that the police treat domestic assault and battery differently from stranger assault and battery. I concede that police officers do react to domestic violence incidents on a case-by-case basis and I believe that much of their behavior is justifiable.

The absence of a positive decrease or productive change concerning the abuse of women and a lack of proper court-ordered sanctions for abuse violations seems to indicate that many of our current policies may just be "feel good" forms of behavior for the advocates of these reforms.[12] Linden Gross, the author of *To Have or To Harm: True Stories of Stalkers and Their Victims*, wrote that restraining orders or orders of protection by the courts are law enforcement's "knee jerk response" to domestic violence.[13] I agree that they are a "knee jerk response" but the fact is that restraining orders and orders of protection are not a response initiated by law enforcement but rather a response initiated by our public policymakers at the behest of victim advocates. They are just two of our many current domestic violence policies that are two simple and ineffectual answers to a complex problem. The rationale that these policies can and will provide deterrence is often lost in the irrational acts of the abusers.

Domestic violence is often an irrational act of rage and passion that can produce murder-suicides. In Massachusetts, a judge ordered a 32-year-old man to stay with his mother and stepfather after his wife received a domestic violence restraining order against him. He had not physically harmed his wife but had changed the locks on their house, disconnected the phone, and threatened her, and he refused to allow her to leave the house for four days. He was arrested by police for kidnapping, assault with a dangerous weapon, assault, and threatening to commit murder. In the court hearing, his mother testified that he was not a violent person; the judge apparently agreed and ruled that the accused was not a danger to himself or others and so released him without bail. Three months later he tried to contact his wife by phone at her parents' home, which was a violation of the court order. His wife reported the violation to the police. Before the police arrived to arrest him for the violation of the restraining order, he shot his mother, his stepfather, and then himself.[14]

Any police officer who has responded to only a few domestic violence calls can testify to the fact that both offenders and victims often demonstrate little rational cognitive behavior.[15] Most domestic violence incidents are committed by those where rational thinking has long been a stranger. The abusers rarely stop to think about the long term consequences of their actions. The victims are people who are often desperate and disoriented and who often have confused the emotion of passion for compassion. It may be impossible for a layperson to comprehend how difficult it is, for police officers to resolve a domestic violence dispute where no visible injury is present. It is often impossible for the officers to bring reason to a predicament that is controlled by impulse, emotion, desperation, and anger.

Although arrests, both "mandatory" for the violation of the order and "preferred arrest," by policy which in practice is "de facto mandatory," concerning most other forms of domestic abuse, are on the rise. Disturbing results have been obtained from multi-year federal research studies (see Appendix I), which indicate that arrest may help some victims at the expense of others. Some of these studies have also shown that arrest may assist the victim in the short term but increase the chance of future violence.[16] During the last two decades of police work, I and other police officers have come to understand that there will be no easy answers or quick-fix cures for domestic violence.

Evidence presented in this book and information in the Appendices illustrate that, when it comes to domestic violence, no one in the criminal justice system has made more changes in their past policies and procedures than the police.

I will present evidence that the prosecution and sentencing policies in many courts have changed very little.[17] The defendants' only certitude of anything swift and certain in the criminal justice system often stops at the arrest process.[18] In fact, arrest is often the only punishment the offender will ever receive. For most chronic offenders, this immediate arrest is only a temporary inconvenience and will not alter their behavior.[19] This fact is supported both by the extremely high rates at which some prosecutors do not go forward with the case after the police have arrested the perpetrator of the crime and the leniency of the sentence by the courts when they do.[20]

Many involved with domestic violence programs remain skeptical that the cure lies within the criminal justice system.[21] Domestic violence has been proclaimed a rising epidemic by public policymakers in Massachusetts.[22] Public policy in Massachusetts and nationwide, however, remains a crazy quilt-work of continually changing legal decisions, many driven by the most current and popular public opinion polls.[23]

There is no question that domestic violence is a crime, and it must be recognized as a crime by the criminal justice system.[24] An ambiguous or confusing message is sent to both abuser and victim when we begin with a civil restraining order, often-times issued from a civil court, by a civil judge who has no authority to act on any of the criminal elements found in the majority of the affidavits. In a civil case, because the verdict is decided on the preponderance of evidence standard, which is less onerous than the criminal prosecution hurdle of guilt beyond a reasonable doubt, the defendant can only be forced to pay monetary damage and the word "crime" is never applied.

The Massachusetts Probation Service registry of civil restraining orders summary for September 1992 to September 1995 shows that civil courts issued 20,714 orders across the Commonwealth. The civil court provides the plaintiff with a piece of paper, the civil restraining order, which offers no reliable relief and, in and of itself, provides no protection from the defendant. The defendant is reinforced in the belief that this incident indeed is a family matter. In fact, the *civil* hearing takes place in *family* court. There *cannot* be any criminal sanctions by the civil court for the abusive behavior. These tragic tales of beatings and abuse are muffled cries for help that have not been and can not be realistically addressed by the civil courts.

Dr. Park Dietz, a forensic psychiatrist who is a leading expert on homicide, has his own doubts about the effectiveness of these orders. "A restraining order is a way of getting killed faster," warns Dietz. "Someone who is truly dangerous will see this as an extreme denial of what he's entitled to, his God-given right. That slip of paper, which documents his loss, may be interpreted by the man as a threat to his own life."[25]

After two decades as a police officer, I have found that the criminal justice system remains a quagmire of ambiguity. In the courts, the truth is only what is opined by the newest or latest court decision. The truth then awaits another revelation of the newest truth that will arise from the next decision. The truth in the courts is often far from candid and forthright. The criminal justice system has become a procedure where people debate not about right and wrong, but about whether something is done by the rules and is procedurally correct.[26]

In 1992, a 27-year-old man in Massachusetts raped, bruised, battered, and killed a 5-year-old girl. He was arrested and evidence implicated him as the murderer. He confessed to committing the crime. Today 6 years later he has yet to be tried. He is still being held in jail where he has twice tried to kill himself. It is anticipated that the legal clash between the prosecutors, defense attorneys, and judges will linger into late 1998. The Suffolk County district attorney wants to use this case as a test for a new type of DNA testing. The defense wants the charges dismissed or to have his client released on bail.[27] In this particular case, the families of the victim and the defendant have become pawns in the great chess game that is our judicial system.

In a Lawrence, Massachusetts case, the defendant left a barroom after an argument with several members of a motorcycle gang. Some of the gang members followed the defendant and hit his car with beer bottles. The defendant fired several shots from a .24-caliber handgun at the gang, and a female gang member was injured by the gunfire. The defendant then went to the home of a friend, where he and the friend grabbed a AK-47 automatic rifle and a Mossberg 12-gauge shotgun and headed back to the bar. They were stopped by the police and arrested with the car full of weapons. The defendant admitted firing at the motorcycle gang members but stated that he had never meant to shoot the female member. He agreed through his lawyer to a plea bargain. When the defendant vacillated in court the judge decided he must have a trial and decides to let the jurors write down questions they have. During the trial, however, the judge read only the questions he wanted to read. The defendant was found not guilty of the crime that he had confessed to, and the owner of the automatic weapons had his case continued without a finding.[28]

O.J. Simpson, in criminal court, was found not guilty of killing two people by a unanimous vote of the jury. Twelve jurors must believe they reached a just verdict. In civil court, however, Simpson is found responsible for killing these same two victims and for the battery of his wife. Again, we had twelve jurors who believed they had reached a just verdict. This verdict was also by a unanimous vote of the jury.

Earlier, a judge in an unattached civil trial concerning custody of the children, allowed no testimony relating to the fact that Simpson may have battered and then murdered his wife and deemed him fit to raise his children, awarding custody of their two children to Simpson.[29] The judge, Nancy Wieben Stock, even suggested that Simpson posed no physical or psychological threat to the children and implied that she thought the children would thrive in Simpson's care.[30]

Simpson was acquitted under one set of rules of justice, the criminal justice system. He was found responsible for the death of his wife under another set of rules of justice by the civil court system. We are presented with two distinct and separate versions of the truth. The father who under one set of rules of justice did not kill their mother will now raise the children. But under a different set of rules of justice, they will be raised by a father who slaughtered their mother by cutting her throat and left her in a pool of blood while they slept in a bedroom upstairs.

Does anyone expect these children not to be troubled by these decisions which under different sets of rules provide no truth, no justice, and no closure to such a tragic event? I do not know if I am more troubled by this inexplicable occurrence or by the *Alice in Wonderland* judicious reasoning of so many attorneys who seem to believe that *this is justice.* Is this really an example of American jurisprudence? Do any of us expect these children not to be troubled by a justice system that now seems to believe that this jabberwocky of an American court system is our contemporary rendering of "justice for all"?

Do not be fooled into believing that the O.J. Simpson case is unique. In the California Rodney King case, the police officers who were videotaped beating him were acquitted in a criminal trial and were later found guilty in a civil-rights trial. In New York City, a man was acquitted of murder after being found with a bloody knife in his pocket at the crime scene and after twice confessing to the crime. Seven years later he was found guilty in a civil-rights trail.[31] Both of these cases were retried by federal prosecutors. If once you don't succeed, trial, trial again.

This system clearly has no heart, no soul, no compassion, and certainly no conception of how to reach resolution through common sense, logic, or rationalism. "The administration of justice," Charles P. Curtis, a Boston lawyer and legal philosopher once wrote, "is no more designed to elicit the truth than the scientific approach is designed to extract justice from the atom."[32] This is a system that is supposed to provide resolution to the dilemma that is domestic violence?

Timothy McVeigh, was recently convicted in the Oklahoma City federal bombing case that killed 168 people and injured 500 more in 1996. Many of the victims were children in the building's day care center. McVeigh, never in court, denied bombing the building but still his attorneys entered a not guilty plea for him. In July 1995, when he was providing information to his defense team, he was asked if it would not have been better if the building had been bombed at night, when there were would have been fewer people killed. He replied, "That would not have gotten the point across to the government. We needed a body count to make our point." When this information was first reported, McVeigh's attorney denied any knowledge of such a report. When the existence of the report could no longer be denied, his attorney said that, yes, there was such a report but it was only made up by the defense team. This report, because the information was provided by the defendant to his defense team, was not given to prosecutors and was never introduced to the jury.[33]

Maybe Johnnie Cochran, who was O.J. Simpson's lead attorney and professed many times to a national television audience that he and the rest of the defense team were concerned with a "search for the truth," could explain to the American public how in our current adversarial criminal justice system the defendant's attorneys are even remotely involved in the "search for the truth." It is the duty of the defense attorney to use smoke and mirrors to hide anything that is detrimental to his or her client from the jury. The defense attorney only technically remains an "officer of the court" just as the prosecutors are.

Timothy McVeigh's attorneys have no regard for the pain and grief suffered by the 168 men, women, and children McVeigh killed or any members of their families. Under our current adversarial court system they are not expected to show any such regard. After the murder trial of an infant, Massachusetts Judge Hiller Zobel wrote recently in the *Boston Globe* that, "The Court may not, however take into account the feelings of those the death has affected; the judge must focus entirely on the events of the trial. Thus although as a father and grandfather I particularly recognize and acknowledge the indescribable pain Matthew Eappen's death has caused his parents and grandparents, as a judge I am duty-bound to ignore it."[34] Timothy McVeigh exhibited no compassion for the men, women, and children he killed. How then can we expect half of the "officers of the court," the defense attorneys, to care about one abused woman or her children who have suffered at the hands of a domestic violence abuser? The answer is that the majority of defense attorneys do not care about the truth; it's no longer their job. They have no compassion for the victim because they believe that "they have a job to do." Their job is to get the defendant off by hook or by crook. This factious "search for the truth" is not to be found in our adversarial court system. Henry Friendly, a federal judge, once observed, "Under our adversary system, the role of counsel is not to make sure the truth is ascertained but to advance his client's cause by any ethical means. Causing delay and sowing confusion not only are his rights but may be his duty."[35] I do not argue with that observation but only question why defense attorneys continue to refuse to admit what is obvious to the rest of us.

Do not expect that defense attorneys in the criminal justice system are the only attorneys who throw logic and common sense to the wind. In a Torrance, California, murder case, prosecutor Todd D. Rubenstein told one jury that the evidence presented to them proved that their defendant was guilty. The jury believed him and found their defendant guilty of murder. In a second trial, with a second and different defendant, before a different jury, the very same Todd D. Rubenstein told this second jury that the evidence he presented to them should prove that their defendant was guilty of murder. This second jury also believed Mr. Ribenstein and found their defendant guilty of murder. Since no one I know will condone murder we must suppose that justice had prevailed. The government in its "search for the truth" had won the day. Truth and justice had been reached in our American judicial system.

There is one minor problem with these two separate trials. These two separate trials with their two separate decisions were reached from a single murder victim who was killed by a single bullet. If the truth has prevailed, this victim must have been killed twice but by a single bullet, fired by two different people, at the same time. In the first trial Rubenstein argued that, "It's unrefuted that John Windelman is the actual killer." In the second trial Rubenstein told the second jury that the evidence was "quite clear that Davis was the killer."[36] I think most of us understand that when you have only one bullet that killed a single victim, it is difficult to understand how two different murderers fired that very same bullet. This logic, it appears from this case, does not compute with our barrister. Both of the defendants, who now face life imprisonment, have defense attorneys who after the verdict was reached, argued that they did not hear the prosecutor's argument. This is not your "Dream Team" or maybe that is just what they were doing while their clients were being convicted.

Legal experts believe that Rubenstein's "legal argument" is solid. Laurie Levenson, a Loyola Marymount University law professor--someone from academia and is an attorney, and a former federal prosecutor believes that, "From a legal point of view, you may be able to explain this. But from a common-sense point of view, it's not fair."[37] Stated another way, what Laurie Levenson has confirmed is that there is no requisite for logic or common sense in the American judicial system.

David Nyhan, a *Boston Globe* columnist wrote recently, "The legal system is already a laughingstock. America's 980,000-odd lawyers clog arteries of commerce, harass school teachers and public administrators, pillage our estates and routine real estate transactions to line their pockets at the expense of pauperized clients."[38] Criminal justice historian David J. Rothman wrote the in a article entitled "The Crime of Punishment" for *The New York Review of Books*. "The least controversial observation one can make about American criminal justice today is that it is remarkably ineffective, absurdly expensive, grossly inhumane, and riddled with discrimination."[39] Is this really where we expect to find resolution to the problem of domestic violence?

All beliefs, either empirical or philosophical, must contain contextual evidence. Evidence of the truth cannot be applied abstractly, and it must be universally held to be true.[40] Both empirically and philosophically held beliefs should be as free of emotional bias as possible but not to the exclusion of compassion and common sense. Emotions so strong that they exclude common sense can have the effect of deluding a person into thinking that he may have reached the correct decision, when compassionate yet empirical evidence declares otherwise. Public policy must be based on convictions reached by empirical evidence, common sense, and reason, and not on emotionally held opinion. Public policy determination reached through anecdotal documentation of events has caused our public policymakers to rush to judgment and to put into place domestic violence policies that have not yet proven to be effective.[41]

PUBLIC POLICY TRANSFORMATION

The history of modern law enforcement began with the London Metropolitan Police District in 1829. Sir Robert Peel (1788-1850) was named the first chief, and because of his first name British police have forever since been known as "Bobbies." Peel assigned his Bobbies to walk specific neighborhoods and held them responsible for crime deterrence and the arrest of criminals who commit crimes in the officers' assigned areas. Peel also instituted the paramilitary command structure for the police. He wanted overall control to remain in the hands of civilians but believed that he needed to retain military discipline in order to ensure that the "Bobbies" walked their beats and enforced the law.[42] Across the Atlantic in America policing was developed using similar procedures.

The rise of "professional" policing in America is generally associated with August Volmer, who was chief of police in Berkeley, California, from 1902 to 1932. He introduced the idea of placing officers on bicycles because of the large size of their neighborhood patrols. Soon he introduced the first completely mobile motor patrol and placed the majority of his officers in cruisers. The radio-equipped police car allowed officers to respond to calls for service by being dispatched from the police switchboard. It remained police policy to place officers in cruisers because of the belief that their mere presence in the community would continue to deter crime as the walking beats had.

To this day the English "Bobbie" and the majority of the citizens of England have a special relationship of respect for each other. In America this is not the case for most police departments and the citizens they serve. This indifference or aloofness is in part due to the fact that American policing did not genuinely adopt a proper military discipline. Sir Robert Peel suggested that the officers needed military discipline to provide for an "esprit de corps."

In America, this British concept of military discipline for their police officers led many police departments to become para-military organizations. South of Berkeley, California, in Los Angeles, a man named William H. Parker, who had joined its police department in the 1930s, became chief in 1950. Chief Parker remade that department in the image of the United States Marine Corps. This caused many in the department to view their role as protecting the community rather than serving the community. Many police departments in America believed that the Los Angeles Police Department was the nation's most proficient and competent department, and it became a prototype for many other departments. Officers were trained to be objective and not to become personal or emotional. "All we want are the facts." In America, police officers, once "keepers of the peace" now became "crime fighters." In England, the respect between citizen and police officer remained a covenant, while in America wrote sociologist Egon Bittner, "Of all the institutions of city government in late nineteenth-century America, none was as unanimously denounced as the urban police." [43]

There was no cumulative body of theoretical or empirical research data that could demonstrate that police officers riding through neighborhoods in police cruisers could deter crime. The belief that their simple presence served as a deterrent continued to be held by the majority of those involved in law enforcement. Without any proof that this policy reduced crime, it was to remain accepted police procedure until the Kansas City Patrol Experiment which lasted from October 1, 1972 until September 30, 1973.

In the Kansas City study, the police patrols were divided into three comparable areas. In one area, patrols were increased two or three times their previous number. In another area, patrols were eliminated entirely, although the officers would continue to respond to emergency calls. In the third area no changes were made. After a year, the police checked to see how the crime rates differed in each sector and found no changes. The crime rates stayed the same in all three areas, and the general public of all three sectors scarcely noticed the difference. Adding or reducing police patrols had little to no effect on the crime rate. As Kansas City study noted: "Police patrol strategies have always been based on two unproved but widely accepted hypotheses; first, that visible police presence prevents potential offenders; second that the public's fear of crime is diminished by such police presence."[44]

The interpretations and findings of the Kansas City experiment were highly controversial. The major result indicated that no statistically significant differences were found in regard to fluctuations in crime in areas that had police patrols versus those in areas that had none. Most important to public policymakers, these findings should have demonstrated that ideas and principles ought to be subject to experiment and study before becoming policies and procedures.

That police officers mandated to arrest an offender, regardless of any and all circumstances, will deter crime has never been demonstrated. I have spoken with enough defendants to know that they do not expect to be caught. Massachusetts as well as federal public policy continues to proclaim that mandatory arrest is the most appropriate police response to domestic violence.[45] Although only the violation of the restraining orders contains the mandatory arrest provision in Massachusetts, the statute suggestion of "preferred response of arrest" has, because of liability issues, become a "de facto" mandatory arrest policy of many police departments not only in Massachusetts but nationwide.[46]

Police officers are often the first and almost always the only officials who respond to the family disturbance call. Although little to no valid evidence exists that arrest alone will change the behavior of the majority of abusers, many women's advocacy groups, district attorneys, the attorney general, the legislature, and the federal government continue to concentrate their attention on what proper police arrest procedures and police arrest policies should be.[47]

Many women's advocates, the bureaucracy of the criminal justice field, and some victims of domestic violence are convinced, in spite of any valid evidence, that the prevention orders will suppress further criminal behavior and injury.[48] Barbara Hart, the staff counsel for the Pennsylvania Coalition Against Domestic Violence, and other advocates believe the exact opposite will occur. They contend that when a prevention order is issued or the victim leaves the abuser, violence will escalate.[49] There is no evidence that restraining orders will have any effect in reducing the risk or seriousness of further violence. There are nonexperimental and experimental studies suggesting that some of these types of orders may *increase* the risk of further violence.[50] This information has not prevented our public policymakers from implementing these types of civil protection orders nationwide.

Many advocates believe that the offender will face legal consequences, thus demonstrating to the community that domestic violence is criminal behavior that will result in an increased number of prosecutions with proper sanctions imposed by the courts. This book demonstrates that the main players, the police, the offenders, and the victims know that little of the above takes place after the arrest.

Analysis of data from September 1992 to July 1994 from the Massachusetts district courts found that, after arrest for violation of a court abuse order, in Berkshire County, the toughest county in Massachusetts for these types of violations, 75 percent of the violators did not see a day in jail. In Nantucket County, not a single person was jailed.[51] In fact, across the Commonwealth, the majority of those who violated the order never saw as much as one day in jail.[52] In a domestic violence study in Minneapolis, Minnesota, sponsored by the National Institute of Justice, only 3 of the 136 perpetrators who were arrested were ever fined or incarcerated. "This is not the type of statistic that promotes confidence in the ability of police to protect the victim from further injury."[53]

There is little evidence, either from experiment or study, that contemporary police officers or police departments have treated arrest for crimes in a domestic violence venue less seriously from arrest for stranger/nonintimate violence, given the circumstances of the individual incident and taking into consideration the appropriate need and desire of the victim. In the May/June 1993 issue of *American Behavioral Scientist,* Eve S. Buzawa and Thomas Austin write, "We believe that police should increase their responsiveness to the desires of victims. . . . victim preference has long been recognized and generally accepted as the primary factor in determining proper police action."[54] Occasionally, the experts and those working the streets do agree. Most police officers I know believe that victim preference is and should remain an important concern.

The only study that I know of that found that the police made fewer arrests for domestic assault than for stranger assault, when the preference of the victim was considered, was conducted in behalf of the plaintiffs in a lawsuit against a police department.[55] One researcher involved in the study was an attorney who was working on behalf of the plaintiffs. There is little contemporary evidence that will demonstrate, when the level of injury and other factors, such as the willingness of the victim to press charges coupled with the amount of empirical and testimonial evidence necessary for conviction is taken into account, that there is a difference in arrest rates between domestic and nondomestic/stranger assault and battery.[56]

Massachusetts and other state legislatures have provided for more severe and more certain punishment for car theft, a nonviolent crime, than for wife battering. This would be a good question for the readers to pose to their local public policymaker. They could ask him or her why they are willing to assign greater sanctions for car theft than for spousal battery. Drop the policymaker a note and ask for their answer in writing.

In Massachusetts, General Law Chapter 266 Section 28 provides for a 2 1/2- to 15-year penalty that allows for parole or probation for a car thief. A second and subsequent conviction provides that a mandatory one-year sentence must be served and does not allow for parole or probation. Wife beating provides at the most only a 2 1/2-year penalty, and there is no mandatory sentence when a second and subsequent beating takes place.

Massachusetts laws proclaim that spraying of graffiti on a building is a felony--a serious crime. Massachusetts General Law 266 section 126A is a three-year felony.

Whoever intentionally, willfully and maliciously or wantonly, paints, marks, scratches, etches or otherwise marks, mars, injures, defaces or destroys the real or personal property of another including but not limited to a wall, fence, building, sign, rock, monument, gravestone, or tablet, shall be punished by imprisonment in a state prison for a term of not more than three years or by imprisonment in a house of correction for not more than two years.

The violation of a restraining order is a misdemeanor--a minor crime. All subsequent violations of a restraining order, under Massachusetts law, law that is passed by a legislature that is often influenced by fellow public policymakers, are misdemeanors. Such a violation is an arrestable offense but remains, by law in Massachusetts and in most other states, a minor crime.

Technically in Massachusetts and in most other states, there is still no such crime as that of "domestic violence" other than the violation of the restraining order. The assault and battery charge brought forward for those committing domestic violence in our homes is the same as the assault and battery charge brought forward for strangers in the streets. Evidently, the legislature in Massachusetts and elsewhere believes that it is a more serious crime to steal a car or to mar and injure a fence or a wall than it is to mar and injure someone who "has been given the protection" of a restraining order by the local court.

Today police make more arrests for domestic violence than ever before.[57] There is evidence that when arrest rates escalate, the prosecutors and the courts increase the rate at which the charges are dismissed.[58] Because of these contradictions and the complexity of the issue, most police officers I have worked with believe that there should be an exploration of just who in the criminal justice system is adhering to current domestic violence policy and who is not.

The U.S. Attorney General's Task Force on Family Violence made recommendations in a final report released in September 1984. The report began as follows:

Progress against the problem of family violence must begin with the criminal justice system. Social service agencies, schools, churches, hospitals, businesses, and individual private citizens must do their part as well, but it is law enforcement that must respond to the calls for help, prosecutors who must bring the perpetrators before the courts, and judges who must impose penalties that balance the interest of the victims and the requirements of justice.

The members of the task force did not seem to comprehend that by the time the abuser abuses the victim, it is often too late for the victim and the victim's children. The damage has already been done. To remedy the affliction of domestic violence, remedy must begin long before the reactive intervention of the criminal justice system.

Many citizens have lost respect for the judicial system.[59] The arrest rate for domestic violence in Massachusetts has increased fivefold since 1990.[60] "Still, more arrests for domestic violence are being made now than ever before."[61] It is the prosecutors, the courts, and the judges who are not imposing penalties that balance the interest of the victim.[62]

Newspaper reports often reflect public anger at the courts with their failure to protect those who have become victims of domestic violence. "The judicial system stinks," said Walter Buckley, whose daughter was shot by her estranged husband.[63] "In Massachusetts everyone has the rhetoric down." said David Adams, head of Emerge, the country's first treatment program for perpetrators of domestic violence. "But when you're dealing with individual cases, that's when the consistency really breaks down."[64]

In a recent Gallup poll conducted for the *American Bar Association Journal,* 45 percent of respondents said they respected the justice system less now than they did before the Simpson trial. "At its core, the Simpson case was a horrific yet routine domestic violence homicide."[65] "If you're rich, you can hire a (expletive) lawyer who will lie for you and manipulate the facts for you and probably set you free. . . . That's what I've learned," said Bob Tellison, a 28-year-old auto mechanic.[66]

The O.J. Simpson trail, from the first day of jury selection lasted three hundred and seventy-two days to the verdict. It cost the prosecution an estimated $9 million and the defense an estimated $6 million. The prosecution presented

99 days of testimony by 72 witnesses. The defense presented 34 days of testimony by 54 witnesses. There were two witnesses who would spend 9 days each on the witness stand. There were 857 trial exhibits and over 50,000 pages of official court transcripts. After just four hours of jury deliberation, Simpson was acquitted.[67] How or why do many still profess that the system of justice in America is not for sale and that the richest surely get more justice than the poor? Will those at the lower end of the social and economic ladder get less just treatment when it comes to domestic violence issues than those at the top of the ladder? If you have to ponder this question for any length of time, you are either rich, a lawyer, or possibly both.

The criminal justice system is a system that most police officers, most victims of crimes, and an increasing number of judges agree is not working.[68] Many, if not most, lawyers continue to insist that, while the American criminal justice system is not perfect it is the best in the world. Many lawyers argue that the American criminal justice system is one of the best in the world for the defendant. I agree that is true if you are a wealthy defendant. There are many defendants in jail just because they could not afford a good lawyer who could get them off. In America there can no longer be any question that we have a sliding scale for justice. The more money you have, the better justice system you will receive. I do not know of any lawyers who will argue that the best lawyers do not cost the most money. As for pro bono work, in Massachusetts less than one-half of 1 percent work in legal aid. The other 99.5 percent cannot find the time to help ensure equal access for the poor to receive the same type of justice that the rich get.[69] This is the system that the less affluent domestic violence victims will enter.

In 1971, a conference of prominent American and English jurists on administrative law concluded that "[t]he main value from the English standpoint was to observe the horrible American examples . . . and to learn not to do likewise."[70] Nationwide, after accounting for the likelihood of those getting caught and convicted, the length of actual incarceration is only about two years for murder, six months for rape, seven days for a burglary, and two to three days for car theft. While arrest rates continue to increase, the penalty paid for committing a serious crime has dropped over the past 30 years.[71]

The criminal justice system cannot be and should not be the lead agency to find the social and behavioral answers needed to prevent domestic violence. This extensive focus by public policymakers on the arrest of the perpetrator, after the crime has occurred, continues to take precedence over the advocacy of battered women and their children. Just as important is the education of society to understand that there is a problem within our homes.[72] In Massachusetts, "one of the supposed leaders in domestic violence policies, " shelters turn away five women for every two they accept. These same shelter turn away four children for every one they take in.[73]

Public policymakers continue to assume that the best policy for preventing domestic violence is punishing criminals after people are hurt. They continue to ignore the fact that the victims of domestic violence are also sentenced to a life of shattered dreams and broken hearts because these policies as designed have created little change in the lives of those in our society at the lower end of the socioeconomic ladder. It is simply abuse of another kind to be suffered by these victims of domestic violence.

By the very nature of the business, the criminal justice system is reactive and not proactive. Police respond after the crime is committed. The job of the police department is analogous to that of an ambulance service. The ambulance service picks up the injured person and brings that person to the hospital. The ambulance service does not provide preventive medicine or the very important aftercare. No one expects the ambulance service to play the lead role in the medical field.

I do not intend to offer only faultfinding, and in the ensuing chapters I will detail some of the following recommendations for change:

- If our public policymakers believe that domestic violence is a serious crime, then they should make it a serious crime by statute law. Domestic violence assault or assault and battery is still not a crime in most states. The violation of a court abuse order is a crime, but the actual act of spousal assault or spousal assault and battery is still the same crime with the same sanctions as hitting a stranger. The assault and battery of a wife or loved one remains the same as a misdemeanor charge of assault and battery of a stranger.[74] The Commonwealth of Massachusetts has only recently made certain acts of child abuse a felony. The same must be done with domestic violence.

- The criminal justice system should intensify its efforts and focus on the chronic and violent offenders.[75] Restraining orders should be criminal in nature and issued only by criminal courts. As long as they remain in family courts, many in our community will continue to consider domestic violence a family matter. There must be, at the very least, some probable cause that a crime has been committed before an order is issued. The order and its accompanying specific crime should proceed through the courts together. If the defendant is guilty, there must be an intensive probationary period for the first-time defendant and probationary visitations to the victim's home. Probation is currently a fundamentally flawed, matter-of-course, inefficient bureaucratic process used to clear overcrowded court dockets. Properly applied, it can become a most important weapon in the fight against domestic violence.

- The second and subsequent violation of a restraining order should include a mandatory one-year prison sentence that mandates successful completion of a proven and effective batterer treatment program. After release, there must be an intensive parole period for the defendant. Sanctions for all chronic offenders must be sure and swift.

- Nonviolent domestic calls, where there has been no assault, no assault and battery, no property damage, and neither party appears to want police intervention, must involve a process that would have the police notify women's advocacy groups for followup visits.

- There must be a procedure that engages both parties in the search for resolution. A prominent imperfection is the fixation by many that only one person is always the source of this disturbing dilemma.[76] "Goodness and badness don't come from sex. . . . We need to focus on real victims, irrespective of gender."[77] Both men and women may be in need of educational components to properly understand the demon inside many of us that gives birth to domestic violence.[78]

Society must recognize that the answers do not lie in the criminal justice system. We must involve physicians, nurses, psychiatrists, psychologists, family counselors, educators, social workers, attorneys, judges, and law enforcement personnel. Together we must find a common-core consensus concerning a public policy of gender equity and economic opportunity.[79] There must be a greater sense of moral concern and a greater search for social gender equity. There must be a challenge to the pessimism of present gender relations. Women must come to the understanding that they must challenge male domination politically, economically and socially by taking public office.

The study of American history demonstrates that our society has been one of social and economic domination of men over women. I believe that much of men's violence against women stems from the perception of male superiority that has historically entitled men to use authority over women, family members, and other perceived subordinates by exerting control over them through any means, including physical force. I also believe that this domination continues because too many women in this country refuse to be more vocal on issues that are germane to their own well-being.

Five thousand years of male domination will end when women learn to flex their recently earned political power. The world of politics is a rough and tumble world that most women do not want to enter. The motivation for this control is not one of uncomplicated gender domination but rather undiminished economic control and the power of decision making, regardless of gender, between two people.

The battle over superiority of race and nationality is also a guise for the real battle over economic control and the power of decision making. Hence, none of these battles can be decided until society recognizes that gender, pigmentation of skin, race, and ethnic background are all just a ruse. You cannot win the battle unless you know who the enemy really is.

It is in politics and business that men hold power over women institutionally. Through elected office, women can find themselves in a much better position to alter public policy and the public culture of male supremacy. In cultures where women have comparable political power with men, studies have shown, rape is rare or absent.[80] Most experts agree that rape is not always a sexual act but rather it is often a violent act involving considerations of power and control. Similarly domestic violence is often violent behavior that is driven by power and control issues. Could we not expect similar results concerning the issue of domestic violence if women have comparable political power with men?

The purpose of the following chapters is to bring about a deliberation and a redirection of the current unproductive public policy. Donald Cochran, the commissioner of probation in Massachusetts, believes: "This [domestic violence] is a problem that is going to require a considerable amount of new thinking. As probation executives we need to think creatively, we need to think boldly, because many of our prior expectations, beliefs and experiences surrounding family and inter-personal relationships need to be reexamined."[81]

Exploration of an understanding of domestic violence is not going to be accomplished in the criminal justice system. The biased and confined point of convergence on policing as *the* deterrent to battering is faulty and has led to limited understanding, stopping, and prevention of domestic violence.[82]

The search cannot *begin* with the reactive response of the police and courts. Society must understand that the police have broken their tradition of nonintervention into domestic violence. Their change in policy has not prevented domestic violence and demonstrates that serving restraining orders and imposing mandatory arrest without proper sanctions are not the answers. Since the inception of the Registry of Civil Restraining Orders in September 1992, the data demonstrate that domestic violence in Massachusetts has not moderated, but rather increased.[83]

Change must commence with a proactive policy by virtue of a complete community engagement. It is time to develop a coherent and comprehensive framework for defining domestic violence. Domestic violence still remains different things to different people. Clearly, much of the problem is due to men acting irresponsibly and violently as they have historically. It should be equally clear that some women must be taught that they must act more responsibly and become more accountable for their own actions or inactions, particularly when they are the parent of a young child in the home.

The proliferation of policies and the acceptance of these policies by many to a single, often misunderstood and misinterpreted, experiment, e.g. for example, the Minneapolis domestic violence study, have not worked. "There's a strong human tendency to seize on the most recent analogy that happens to fit one's prejudice in advance and tends to support what one wants to do anyway."[84]

There have not been adequate checks on the efficacy of our current domestic violence policies.[85] These policies, as currently promulgated, are doomed to fail because they provide intervention by a criminal justice system that lacks compassion and common sense, in a reactionary manner, after the domestic violence victim becomes just another statistical number.

NOTES

1. Richard J. Gelles, "Abused Wives: Why Do They Stay?" *Journal of Marriage and Family* 38 (1976): 659-668.

2. Harvey Wallace, *Family Violence: Legal, Medical and Social Perspectives* (Boston: Allyn & Bacon, 1996), pp. ix-xi.

3. Karin L. Swisher, ed., *Domestic Violence* (San Diego: Greenhaven Press, 1996), pp. 7-9.

4. Michele Bograd, "Battering, Competing Clinical Models, and Paucity of Research: Notes to Those in the Trenches," *Counseling Psychologist* 22, no. 4 (1994): 593.

5. Cathy Spatz Widom, "The Cycle of Violence," *National Institute of Justice: Research in Brief,* October, 1992, p. 5.

6. Steven D. Dillingham, ed., *Criminal Victimization in the United States 1991* (Washington, DC: Bureau of Justice Statistics, 1991) p. 69.

7. Ibid.

8. Richard Wrangham and Dale Peterson, *Demonic Males* (Boston: Houghton Mifflin Co., 1996), p. 26.

9. Donald Cochran, *The Tragedies of Domestic Violence: A Qualitative Analysis of Civil Restraining Orders in Massachusetts* (Boston: Office of the Commissioner of Probation Massachusetts Trial Court, October 12, 1995), p. 19.

10. Lawrence W. Sherman, *Policing Domestic Violence: Experiments and Dilemmas* (New York: Free Press, 1992), p. 1.

11. Meredith Hofford, "Family Violence: Challenging Cases for Probation Officers," *Federal Probation* (Sepeptember1991): 14.

12. Cochran, *The Tragedies of Domestic Violence*, p. 19.

13. Gavin DeBecker, *The Gift of Fear* (Boston: Little, Brown and Company, 1997), p. 192.

14. Matthew Taylor and Shirley Leung, "Son Had Been Called Dangerous," *Boston Globe*, April 29, 1997, p. B1.

15. Jeffrey Fagan, *The Criminalization of Domestic Violence: Promises and Limits* (Washington, D.C.: National Institute of Justice, 1996), p. 30.

16. Janell D. Schmidt and Lawrence W. Sherman, "Does Arrest Deter Domestic Violence?" *American Behavioral Scientist* 36 (1993): 601.

17. Hofford, "Family Violence," p. 14.

18. Fagan , *The Criminalization of Domestic Violence*, p. 50.

19. David B. Mitchell, "Contemporary Police Practices in Domestic Violence Cases: Arresting the Abuser: Is it Enough?" *Journal of Criminal Law and Criminology* 83, no. 1 (1992): 241-249.

20. Alison Bass, "The War on Domestic Abuse," *Boston Globe*, September 25, 1994, p. 1.

21. Ann D. Carden, "Wife Abuse and the Wife Abuser: Review and Recommendations," *Counseling Psychologist* 22, no. 4 (1994): 539.

22. Donald Cochran, *Project History of the Massachusetts Statewide Automated Restraining Order Registry* (Boston: Office of the Commissioner of Probation Massachusetts Trial Court, 1994), pp. 4-5.

23. Fagan, The *Criminalization of Domestic Violence*, pp. 49-51.

24. Anne Powell, "Comparison of Restraining Order Violators and Other Risk/Need Offenders." *Executive Exchange*, National Association of Probation Executives (Fall 1994): 4-5.

25. Ann Blackman et al., "When Violence Hits Home," *Time* (July 4, 1994) p. 21.

26. Harold J. Rothwax, *Guilty: The Collapse of Criminal Justice* (New York: Warner Books, 1996), pp. 18-19.

27. John Ellement, "Fight on DNA Test Case Gives Murder Suspects a Long Wait," *Boston Globe,* November 26, 1996, p. A1.

28. Mike Barnicle, "Case Becomes Open-and-Shot," *Boston Globe,* February 6, 1997, p. B1.

29. Peter S. Canellos, "Two Trails, Two Verdicts, Many Theories," *Boston Globe,* February 6, 1997, p. A1.

30. Associated Press, "Custody Ruling May Help O.J.," *Charleston, SC, Post and Courier,* December 22, 1996, p. 6A.

31. Fred Kaplan, "Two Found Guilty in Crown Heights Rights Case," *Boston Globe,* February 11,1997, p. A13.

32. Hiller B. Zobel, "The Jury on Trial," *American Heritage* 46, no. 4 (1995): 50.

33. Pete Slover, "Report Has McVeigh Describing Blast," *Boston Globe,* March 1, 1997, p. A3.

34. Hiller Zobel, "Zobel Cites Rationale for Reducing Murder Charge," *Boston Globe*, November 11, 1997, p. B4.

35. Philip K. Howard, *The Death of Common Sense* (New York: Random House, 1994) p. 86.

36. Associated Press, "Prosecutor Splits a Bullet." *Boston Globe*, May 27, 1997, p. A11.

37. Ibid.

38. David Nyhan, "Media and Legal System Will Suffer for Their Romp With Paula Jones," *Boston Globe*, May 30, 1997, p. A23.

39. David Rothman, "The Crime of Punishment," *New York Review of Books* (February 17, 1994): 34.

40. David Hackett Fischer, *Historians' Fallacies* (New York: Harper & Row, 1970), pp. 62-63.

41. Fagan, *The Criminalization of Domestic Violence*, p. 5.

42. Jeffrey Patterson, "Community Policing," *FBI Law Enforcement Bulletin* (November 1995): 5-10.

43. Ibid., 6.

44. George E. Kelling et al., *The Kansas City Preventive Patrol Experiment* (Washington, D.C.: Police Foundation, 1974) p. 42.

45. Fagan, *The Criminalization of Domestic Violence*, p. 10.

46. Sherman, *Policing Domestic Violence*, p. 14.

47. Fagan, *The Criminalization of Domestic Violence*, p. 12.

48. Ibid., p. 24.

49. Barbara Hart, "Battered Women and the Criminal Justice System," *American Behavioral Scientist* 36, no. 5 (1993): 624-638

50. Janice Grau, Jeffrey Fagan, and Sandra Wexler, "Restraining Orders for Battered Women: Issues of Access and Efficacy," *Women and Politics* 4 (1984): 13-28.

51. Bass, "*The War on Domestic Abuse*," p. 1.

52. Cochran, *The Tragedies of Domestic Violence*, p. 17.

53. Wallace, *Family Violence*, p. 207.

54. Eve S. Buzawa and Thomas Austin, "Determining Police Repsonse to Domestic Violence Victims," *American Behavioral Scientist* 36 (May/June1993): 610-623.

55. Eve S. Buzawa, Thomas L. Austin, and Carl G. Buzawa, "The Role of Arrest in Domestic Versus Stranger Assault," in. Eve S. and Carl G. Buzawa, eds. *Do Arrests and Restraining Orders Work?* Thousand Oaks, Calif.: Sage Publishing, 1996. p. 160.

56. Douglas A. Smith and Jody Klein, "Police Control of Interpersonal Disputes," *Social Problems* 31 (1984): 475.

57. William M. Holmes et al., *Mandatory Arrest and Domestic Violence in Massachusetts* (Boston: Statistical Analysis Center, Massachusetts Committee on Criminal Justice, 1993) p. 26.

58. Bass, "*The War on Domestic Abuse*," p. 1.

59. *Bureau of Justice Statistics Sourcebook of Criminal Justice Statistics-1994*, eds. Kathleen Maguire and Ann L. Pastore (Washington, D.C.: U.S. Department of Justice, 1994).

60. Holmes et al., *Mandatory Arrest and Domestic Violence in Massachusetts*, p. 14.

61. Sherman, Policing Domestic Violence, p. 14.

62. Bass, "The War on Domestic Abuse," p. 1.

63. Associated Press, "Father blames system for daughter's death, "*Brockton Enterprise* September 5, 1994, p. 9.

64. Bass, "*The War on Domestic Abuse*," p. 1.

65. Jeffrey Toobin, *The Run of his Life: The People v. O.J. Simpson* (New York: Random House, 1996) p. 12.

66. Adam Pertman, "Reverberations: A Year of Simpson," *Boston Globe*, June 11, 1995, p. 30.

67. Associated Press, "The Simpson Trials, by the Numbers," *Boston Globe*, February 11, 1997. p. A10.

68. Rothwax, *Guilty*, p. 233.

69. *Boston Globe*, "Defenders for the Undefended," October 11, 1996, p. A18.

70. Howard, *The Death of Common Sense*, p. 89.

71. Ernst Van Der Hagg, "How to Cut Crime," *National Review* May 30, 1994, p. 30.

72. Carden, "Wife Abuse and the Wife Abuser," p. 565.

73. Steven R. Donziger, ed., *The Real War on Crime: The Report of the National Criminal Justice Commission* (New York: Harper Perennial, 1996) pp. 156-157.

74. Murray A. Straus, "Identifying Offenders in Criminal Justice Research on Domestic Assault," *American Behavioral Scientist* 36, no.5 (1993): 589.

75. Ibid. p. 595.

76. Carden, "Wife Abuse and the Wife Abuser," p. 567.

77. Tish Durkin, "Domestic Violence Harms Both Men and Women, in "*Domestic Violence*. Karen L. Swisher, ed., (San Diego: Greenhaven Press, 1996) p. 69.

78. Wrangham and Peterson, *Demonic Males*, p. 241

79. Wallace, *Family Violence*, p. ix.

80. Peggy Reeves Sanday, "The Socio-Cultural Context of Rape: A Cross-Cultural Study," *Journal of Social Issues* 37 (1976): 5-27.

81. Donald Cochran, "Domestic Violence: The Invisible Problem," *Executive Exchange*, National Association of Probation Executives (Fall 1994): 1.

82. Elizabeth Stanko, "Domestic Violence" in Gary W. Cordner and Donna C. Hales, eds., *What Works in Policing: Operations and Administration Examined* (Cincinnati: Anderson Publishing, 1992). p. 58.

83. Cochran, *The Tragedies of Domestic Violence*, p. 19.

84. Donald Kagan, "History's Largest Lessons," *American Heritage* 48, no. 1 (1997) pp. 59-67

85. Fagan, *The Criminalization of Domestic Violence*, pp. 5-6.

5

Opening Closed Doors

No body of information can be fed into a computer in the hope that sooner or later it will spit out a universal solution.

Vaclav Havel (1936)

Assault and battery on a spouse or family member has traditionally been unlawful in America.[1] American common law, as well as the American statute law of assault and assault and battery, has rarely made exceptions for family and household members regardless of gender. However, children fighting on a playground, parents spanking their children, and teachers inflicting corporal punishment on children in school are some examples of assault and battery that are technically illegal and are rarely enforced and prosecuted. Not only do we live in a society that condones assault and assault and battery, but also in many sporting events, many of us accept it as part of the game. Many hockey fans have come to believe that the players, pummeling each other are an integral part of the sport. If a hockey player is not willing to fight, on the ice during the game, he often will lose the respect of the fans and his fellow players. The question of when it is appropriate to pummel and when not to pummel plays a role in the historically high rate of domestic or family violence in this country.[2]

Successful intervention by the criminal justice system in domestic violence has been consistently inconsistent. Domestic violence or family violence is caused by various peculiarly complicated behaviors that are not altogether understood by psychiatrists, psychologists, or sociologists.[3] Domestic violence differs significantly from most other forms of violent crime.[4] Most victims of a violent crime expect that their antagonist, the criminal (and in the eyes of most victims there is no question that their *antagonist is a criminal)*, if caught will be punished.[5] Most victims of violent crimes want their antagonist to suffer or experience the same type of pain they did because the antagonist has caused them, the victims, physical or emotional distress. Society in general anticipates that the legal sanctions suffered by the antagonist will create a deterrent effect not only on the antagonist and prevent the antagonist from repeating the act, but that it will further deter others in society who might have a desire to commit the same type of criminal behavior.[6] It has been my experience that most victims of crimes consider the greatest single failing of the criminal justice system is the courts inability to surely and swiftly punish their antagonist.

Regardless of what many women's advocates want to accept as reality, extensive research and repeated domestic violence studies demonstrate that the majority of domestic violence victims *are not* entirely concerned with punishment and deterrence of their abuser.[7] The majority of domestic violence victims hope that the criminal justice system can somehow control the behavior and conduct of their abuser/antagonist by the mere threat of criminal sanctions. Many who have been abused and have called the police claim that they still love their abuser. They want their abuser/antagonist to change his or her behavior, and many victims hope this can be achieved through some kind of behavior modification or counseling.[8] In some instances of domestic violence this is not true, and the victim does want help in leaving the abuser and hopes and expects that the abuser will be punished. To continue to deny that there is difference of expectations by the victims, as many victim advocates continue to do, is to deny the difference of help each victim wants, needs, and deserves. To continue to assert that in all instances the abuser should be arrested regardless of circumstances is to continue to defy logic and common sense. Many factors have produced this differentiation of expectations between victims of stranger crimes and those who are victims of domestic violence.

There can be little disagreement that historically most societies have been and remain patriarchal.[9] There are indeed some anthropologists who maintain that the evolutionary path that led us to patriarchy began some 5 million years ago.[10] Regardless of the date of the origin of patriarchy, to deny that we as humans live in a patriarchal society is to deny human history. "Written history starts a little later, with scraps of pottery from modern-day Iraq bearing witness to the Sumerian invention of writing in about 3100 BC. By then, the written record informs us, wars and the patriarchal systems fighting them were in full glory."[11] Few will argue that the history of patriarchy began before we reduced words to be written on pottery.

One of the few recorded exceptions of a completely patriarchal society would be the early kingdom of Mesopotamia which was under Babylonian rule over two millennia before the birth of Christ. The Code of Hammurabi provided that women could own businesses and buy property, and if a man divorced a woman the woman was entitled to the return of her dowry and the man would be required to pay child support.[12] In this historical period, the worship of gods and goddesses coexisted with or surfaced within male deity worship. As time passed, most of the female gods became subordinate to the male gods.

An old Jewish morning prayer states "Blessed art thou, O Lord our God, who has not made me a woman."[13] The Bible, however, gives some indications that Christ honored and worked with women: "For as many of you as were baptized into Christ have put on Christ. There is neither Jew nor Greek, there is neither slave nor free, there is neither male nor female; for you are all one in Christ Jesus. And if you are Christ's, then you are Abraham's offspring, heirs according to promise." (Galatians 3:27-29)

But much of the liturgical, theological, and biblical agenda of the Christian church has not been as kind. "Let a woman learn in silence with all submissiveness. I permit no woman to teach or to have authority over men; she is to keep silent "(I Timothy 2:11-12). "For the man is not of the woman, but the woman of the man. Let the women keep silence in the church for it is not permitted unto them to speak; but they are commanded to be under obedience, so saith the law. And if they learn anything, let them ask their husbands at home; for it is a shame for women to speak in the church" (I Corinthians 11.3).

As the goddesses were suppressed, it seems that so was the spiritual participation of women. In patriarchal societies, women often became property and were expected to be obedient to the rule of men.[14] Political systems have been, and for the most part remain, thoroughly male, with women silent and subservient.[15]

In the Middle Ages, the Christian church, the single strongest political force in Europe, felt threatened and was concerned that its base of power and control over Europe's rulers was diminishing. The Inquisition, in reaction to change of any kind, found women to be an easy target. From the fourteenth to the seventeenth century, witchcraft was the sin predominately of women. There was a popular saying, "One wizard to 10,000 witches."[16] The Inquisition lasted three hundred years. In Great Britain, it was not until 1784 that the Calvinist Parliament of Scotland declared an end to witch burning. In England, during the 1600s, the Quakers were one of the first religions that rejected the notion that women were not witches and that advocated equality of the sexes.

The history of statute law prohibiting family violence and permitting legal intervention in family violence began even before the settlement of Jamestown or Plymouth. As early as 1599, Puritan ministers in England condemned wife beating as immoral. While the English were involved in a civil war and a period of Puritan rule (1640-1660), there was an easing of control over the Massachusetts Bay Colony. The American Puritans drew up their own criminal code that was in part declaration of many Puritan biblical morals.[17] One early law provided that, "Everie marryed woman shall be free from bodilie correction or stripes by her husband, unless it be in his own defense upon her assault."[18] Several years later another amendment prohibited husband beating. There was little enforcement of these laws and many of them were primarily symbolic.[19] Between 1633 and 1802 there were only twelve recorded cases of men being brought to court for beating their spouse.[20] For this offense, the law provided penalties of fines, whipping, or both. Church courts also "shamed" offenders and decided whether to expel them from the congregation.[21] English Common Law during this period, however, continued to endorse the right of a husband to discipline his wife provided that he used restraint.[22] The English Common Law "rule of thumb," by which English courts may have acquitted husbands of beating their wives with a stick no thicker than a thumb, was never invoked and was never an issue in American courts.[23] Many judges in America would commonly dismiss spouse abuse charges on the grounds that "a husband was legally permitted to chastise his wife without subjecting himself to vexatious prosecutions for assault and battery."[24]

Public concern for family violence seemed to decline in the eighteenth century, with reduced enforcement of morality in general and a growing distinction between public and private conduct. American cultural values may have returned to the belief that what happened in families should be kept private and that the man was the head of the household. As the frontier spread west, the isolation of many families in the wilderness caused many to resolve matters on their own. To many men the old epigram, "A man's home is his castle," still incorporated his rights and indeed his obligation to be the disciplinarian.

At the end of the eighteenth century in France and British America, the right of the rulers of these nations to continue as the helmsmen of national institutional political power from their castle was being disputed. Ballots, cast by men exclusively, were replacing bullets and battalions as a method of governmental control. A revolutionary change of rationale for getting and retaining institutional power was now possible: at least for now it was to remain for men only. This democratic political process that began to provide equality for all men, the right to democratically cast a vote, would before long be available to women.

In mid-nineteenth-century America, increasing urbanization and a concern over immigration and crime gave birth to increased machinery for formalized social control. Local law enforcement organizations, including professionally styled police forces, replaced soldiers from the central government. Family violence or family disputes were within the jurisdiction of these police departments. This revolutionary change would play a most important role in democratic nations.

Yet more revolutionary changes in America were created by the economic transformations as produced by the Industrial Revolution. One change would take men out of the home into factories as laborers. This separation of job from home would create a "sphere of influence" and a "cult of domesticity" for women in the home. As men spent more and more time away from home, women became more and more responsible for the education and socialization of their children.[25] Women were allotted some of the most important roles in the rule of the castle. They were not in charge, but at least they were now participating. Women sought more participation in how the family should be organized and for the first time in millennia, because they lived in a democratic society, they would get more.

In New England and elsewhere, women began to attend public schools. In 1837, Oberlin College would open its doors to women who until then had been denied higher education because it was believed they would inevitably lower the academic standards for men. The second revolutionary change that would open the door for women to exit the home and continue the progression towards equity was that by the 1850s in Massachusetts nearly three-quarters of its public school teachers were women.[26]

In 1848, about three hundred people attended the first women's rights convention in the United States. The leaders of the convention were Lucretia Mott, a Quaker minister, and Elizabeth Cady Stanton, a speaker and writer. Both women had been active in the abolitionist movement. The convention presented a "Declaration of Sentiments," which declared in part: "[t]he history of mankind is a history of repeated injuries and usurpations on the part of man toward women, having in direct object the establishment of an absolute tyranny over her." The Declaration also stated, "that all men and women are created equal" and deserve their "inalienable rights" including suffrage."[27]

Prior to the Civil War, many women who worked as nurses for the armies during times of war were not always medical professionals. These women nurses were often camp followers who, along with providing some medical care, served as cooks and laundresses. During the war, the occupation of nurse was to find an official role in the United States Sanitary Service, a private organization that worked with the Army Medical Bureau. The courage that many of these battlefield nurses displayed "chipped away at the weaker-sex image."[28]

In the mid-1800s, a single act of adultery by a wife was grounds for divorce in South Carolina, but persistent adultery of a husband was required to prove marital infidelity.[29] In the 1880s, many district attorneys continued to refuse to prosecute wife abuse on the premise that women would retract the charges to allow their husband to remain employed.[30] By 1850 women began to organize nationwide and to demand a change of their status within American society.

By the 1870s, women's rights activists had established an autonomous women's rights movement under female leadership. Women joined temperance movements to stamp out the use of alcohol, and growing numbers of women began to participate in the suffragette movement. In 1871 an Alabama court found for the first time that "a wife had the right to the same protection of the law that the husband can invoke for himself."[31]

One day in 1874 a visiting nurse in New York City stumbled upon a 9-year-old who had obviously been beaten, was undernourished, and was chained to a bedpost. Wanting to take legal action, the nurse discovered that there was neither legislation nor a public agency to help her. She then appealed to the Society for the Prevention of Cruelty to Animals on the basis that the child was a member of the animal kingdom. The society assisted in removing the child from the home. With this action came the realization that there was no agency to help *humans* who were being abused. The first Society for the Prevention of Cruelty to Children was organized in New York City in 1875.[32] While children were first, would the realization that women also suffered abuse in their home be far behind?

Individual states established a number of innovative policies for control of domestic violence. In Maryland, Delaware, and Oregon, for example, whipping posts for wife beaters were legislated. Between 1901 and 1942, Delaware authorities flogged twenty-one men "fore wife-beating."[33] In 1906,The U.S. Congress defeated a bill to impose federal whipping of wife beaters. A study in Pennsylvania in the 1880s identified 211 wife beaters who were jailed, for an average of three months each.[34] By the turn of the century, legal aid for battered wives who sought assistance was established. Some courts issued promissory notes to husbands for moneys to be extracted from them in the event they would again abuse their wives.[35] These programs were expanded around the country by the Women's Club movement.

Wife beating was no longer to be condoned and was condemned publicly. There is little evidence, however, that these laws were widely being enforced. When they were enforced, the men who beat women would be arrested by men, tried by men, sentenced by men, and in many ways the criminal justice system was using men's standards and men's values to set policy. There also remained an image that these wife beaters were from the lower class and for the most part were drunkards. It was seldom acknowledged that refined or educated men also beat their loved ones.

Some women's rights organizations may have questioned whether this conundrum of domestic violence was a sign of something insufferable in the relationship between men and women that could not change. They began to question why this behavior remained an accepted component of our culture. Most women's rights organizations had little or no voice in law enforcement strategies or capacity to influence the public policymakers. They knew that what they needed to ensure change was the elective franchise.

In October 1917, Alice Paul, a leader of the women's suffrage movement, was arrested for protesting outside the White House in Washington, D.C. The term *suffrage* is from the Latin *suffragium* for the word "vote." Alice Paul had borrowed the militant tactics used by the British women's suffrage movement. Some of the methods used were chaining themselves to buildings and hunger strikes. She was sentenced to seven months in jail. During imprisonment she was force fed food to prevent her from going on a hunger strike. Later she was to comment that, "Well to me it was shocking that a government of men could look with such extreme contempt on a movement that was asking nothing except such a simple little thing as the right to vote."[36] In 1920, with the women's suffrage movement leading the battle, women won the right to vote. Alice Paul had known that the severe reactions to her tactics by those in power would attract public sympathy for the suffragette cause.[37]

That simple little thing as the right to vote, many men certainly must have known, could and would act as the linchpin that would allow women to vie for the institutional political power that had been in the hands of men for the last five thousand years. Prior to 1920, women, like my own grandmother, lived in a world that had changed little over the millennia as far as women's rights were concerned. Thanks to that "little thing as the right to vote," women in America would have the opportunity, heretofore never enjoyed, to share institutional political power with men. In Scott Turows' *The Laws of Our Fathers* a lead character speaks for all women when she states "But it's important in the lives of other people," Lucy answers. "And you did that. As a woman I know what that means, how *hard it was*...But I'm very proud of all of you, the women I knew who did all those things that their grandmothers or even their moms couldn't even dare to consider."[38] The right to vote was not given to women, they fought and fought hard to win that right.

In 1920, through the women's suffrage movement, women won the right to vote nationwide. President Woodrow Wilson at first opposed the suffrage movement and his wife detested them.[39] Public pressure because of hunger strikes and the jailing of suffragists convinced Wilson to end his opposition. In one of those never-ending historical curiosities Wilson suffered a stroke in 1919 and his wife, without public knowledge, made many presidential-level decisions for her husband.[40]

Many suffragists believed that their right to vote would act as a catalyst for social change, "A way to tap woman's greater capacity for human empathy, their status as the mother of the race."[41] The power to alter public policy *was* now in *their* hands. Men could not prevent them from going to the voting booth. Women now had the ability and authority to determine just what their role in society would be. The status of women in our society was now and remains in the hands of women. Many women believed that all they had to do to take that power was to mark the X or pull the handle at the voting booth to ensure their place in the political establishment. This democratic process never before available to women could guarantee their search for equity in society. Less than a decade later, women seemed to lose the momentum of their greatest victory. Many in the suffrage movement wanted to keep fighting but could not agree on what they now should fight for. The majority of women believed that they did not benefit from this newfound political power. For working class and minority women in some parts of the nation, it seemed that this hard fought struggle to win the right to vote created very little change in their lives. For most, black and Hispanic women, there was no change at all.[42]

By the early twentieth century, the telephone and the typewriter had provided a whole new category of jobs for women. Women were coming off the farms and out of the kitchen in large numbers to become important members of the labor force. Jobs involving typing and operating the telephone were considered "woman's work." During World War II, Rosie the Riveter, a brawny, yet feminine looking woman, dressed in overalls and had a rivet gun in her hand. She was this nation's homage to working women and exemplified the millions of home front heroines who served America's industrial machine, doing what up until then had been considered "man's work." Many women felt that they had now *earned the right of equality* in the workplace controlled by men. Their thank you from the millions of men, when they came home from the war, was that most of the women were sent home and the men went back to doing what after all remained the "man's work."

In 1960 President John F. Kennedy formed The Commission on the Status of Women, and in 1963, he signed into law the Equal Pay Act requiring employers to pay men and women the same wage for the same job. Could this become just another politically easy answer by our public policymakers to a difficult problem? Was this just going to be a lot of political smoke and mirrors?

In 1995, a full thirty-five years after passage of this law, women managers still earn 32 percent less than men; female college professors earn 22 percent less than men; female secretaries, typists, and stenographers earn 10 percent less than men; female elementary school teachers earn 12 percent less than men.[43]

These laws, nevertheless ignored by the very same federal officials who passed the laws with such a flourish, would when effectively combined with the 1964 Civil Rights Act mark the first major step in the federal governments ever hesitant recognition of gender inequality in the United States. Both these events would help the then stalled women's rights movement.

The 1960s and 1970s marked a revival of feminism and the creation of strong female support networks.[44] In 1963, *The Feminine Mystique* addressed an issue which its author, Betty Friedan, referred to as "the problem without a name." The problem was of course a system in America that led so many men to believe that it was their role to keep women "pregnant in the summer and barefoot in the winter."

In 1964 Howard W. Smith, a congressman from Virginia, looking for additional votes to kill the 1964 Civil Rights Act, added "sex" to the list of "race, color, religion or national origin." He assumed, of course, that he had added another reason for his fellow male federal legislators to vote against the act. To his astonishment and consternation not only did the bill pass but also he had unwittingly provided us with yet another historical curiosity. He had bestowed to women a legal process that would bring a litany of appeals in behalf of women's rights to the Equal Employment Opportunities Commission and the United States Supreme Court.[45] Another important role of the 1964 Civil Rights Act was that it would become a litigation mechanism that women would need to capture the attention of the criminal justice system.

Feminists and women victim advocates began to raise the issue of violence against women as a social problem. In 1966 the National Organization of Women was founded. Our public policymakers, our elected officials, fifty years after women gained the right to vote, were still largely male. With their newfound political power, certainly women have the opportunity to change the "old boy network" themselves. Research shows that women, when they run for elected office, win as often as men do.[46]

Today, nearly 52 percent of the electorate are women. In the 1996 presidential election, both the Republicans and Democrats made an effort to capture the woman's vote. There are 435 seats in the House of Representatives and women fill only 50 of those seats. In the 100-seat Senate, women fill only nine seats. If women expect true political, legislative and social change, they must understand that they have to get involved in the political process by running for office. There are more women than men in this nation, but few women hold political office simply because so few seem willing to run.

Men who have retained political and social control for the past five thousand years know that their continued control of political power in America allows them to retain their institutional and social control over women. Men have been offered no reason to change and are not about to alter that balance of power. The instrumentality of access to modify what goes on behind closed doors at home and the mechanism to change what goes on behind the closed mahogany doors of Capitol Hill are one and the same for women.

THE VICTIM

In Marvin Wolfgang's landmark study of violent deaths in Philadelphia for the period 1948 through 1952, only 12.2 percent of the 550 homicides with known suspects were committed against "strangers." Only 1.1 percent were committed against "innocent bystanders." The largest categories, 28.2 percent of victims, were "close friends." The next largest, 24.7 percent, were members of the family.[47] These studies confirm that murder is often familial. This data provided the first scientific data demonstrating that killers are most often men. For twenty-five years the United States Department of Justice has published a sourcebook of criminal justice statistics. For those same twenty-five years the data demonstrate that the violent criminals in America are overwhelmingly male.

Historically, males have always been more interested in dominance, aggression, and territory. Historical records demonstrate that males are more aggressive than females.[48] Men, especially young men, have always been at the heart of American violence.[49] Why is it so difficult for so many in societies today to understand that the male violence and male dominance over women are historical facts?

The 1994 Bureau of Justice Statistics Sourcebook (p. 468) reports that men committed 94 percent of this nations murders that year. Men also committed 79.9 percent of all the manslaughter, 93.5 percent of the kidnappings, 98.7 percent of the sexual abuse, 91.5 percent of all the assaults, 95.7 percent of the robberies, 95.7 percent of the arsons, 88.9 percent of all drug trafficking, 95.7 percent of all firearms violations, 97.6 percent of all burglary and breaking and entering, 96.3 percent of all auto theft, and 96.3 percent of all larcenies.

Interestingly, there are still some family violence experts who deny that the historic and universal pattern of violence by men will not and does not continue in our homes. They want us to believe that once the doors of the home are closed, women become just as abusive as men are in general society and that men in the home become just as quiescent as women.

John Leo, an editorialist for *U.S. News & World Report*, writes, "In fact, men and women abuse their partners at equal rates."[50] I agree with Mr. Leo that the media does report a lot of information that as he writes "seems so seeped in myths, bad stats and general misinformation."[51] In his article, he rails against reporting misinformation. I also agree with him that domestic violence in the United States should not be portrayed in the media, as being perpetrated by a nation of brutish men who, merely wander around and beat the tar out of innocent females. Nevertheless, for Leo to believe that we are a nation that has for the first time in the history of humankind, has become one where women are just as abusive as men behind closed doors in their homes and that patriarchy does not continue to play a role in the relationship of abuse of women by men, leads me to believe that Leo needs to read a few history books and some criminological literature. If he truly believes that men and women assault their partners at equal rates, I wonder if he also believes that men and women rape their partners at equal rates?

My background as a history major in college and my twenty-one years as a police officer have led me to believe that generally most of us do understand that men have historically exhibited more violent and abusive behavior than women. As previously noted, each year the United States Department of Justice prints mountains of documentation demonstrating that it is men in our society who commit the majority crimes and the vast majority of the violent crimes. To deny that the pervasive human pattern of aggressive male violence will cease once the male and female partners live with each other defies logic and common sense, and more importantly mocks all scientific evidence to the contrary. It is just as illogical to believe and is inconsistent with human history to assert that once a female finds a partner she becomes just as aggressive, abusive, and violent as her male partner.

Logic, common sense, and past historic empirical data to the contrary, sociologists Murray A. Straus and Richard J. Gelles, report that when women are married or cohabiting, they become primary aggressors just as often as men and are equally as abusive as men. "Previously published findings have shown that, in both surveys, the rate of wife-to-husband assault was about the same (*actually slightly higher*) [emphasis added] than the husband-to-wife assault rate.[52] Do Straus and Gelles believe that there is something about marriage or cohabitation that turns men from a history of combative and violent behavior into innocent victims, who are now being physically attacked by aggressive and violent women once they are married or cohabit? A recent Department of Justice study reports that among victims of abuse by spouses or ex-spouses women victims outnumbered men nine to one. In the boyfriend or girlfriend category women were almost eight times more likely than men to be the victim.[53]

I am not convinced that Straus and Gelles can explain just what causes this change of behavior between married or cohabiting men and women. Is it possible that they believe that marriage produces a castrational effect on men and a surrogate testosterone effect on women? Are their research and their evaluation design simply flawed? In another study, Straus reports that "Two recent gender-specific *estimates* [emphasis added] of rates for partner homicide indicate that wives murder male partners at a rate that is 56 percent (Straus, 1986) and 62 percent (Browne & Williams, 1989) as great as the rate of partner homicides by husbands."[54]

Straus and Gelles should question why these data differ from historic fact and again defy logic and common sense. One simple factor is that many men simply refuse and are ashamed to admit that they hit women. The 1994 Bureau of Justice Statistics Sourcebook reports (p. 334-335) that in 1993, 591 husbands and boyfriends died at the hands of their wives or girlfriends. The same sourcebook reports that 1,531 wives and girlfriends died at the hands of their husbands or boyfriends. That is close to the three to one ratio that has been constant for years. The annual FBI crime report released for 1995 announced that among female murder victims, 26 percent were killed by a husband or boyfriend. Wives or girlfriends killed 3 percent of male victims.[55] These are some examples demonstrating that data compiled by some family violence experts produced from surveys or research they conduct can produce imperfect findings. It may also be another example of how numerical facts can become twisted through statistical analysis.

THE CRIMINALIZATION PROCESS

Contemporary domestic violence programs for police departments first appeared in New York City. In 1965, the New York Police Department and the City University of New York received a grant from the U.S. Department of Justice. This was the result of the feminist organizations' placing of political pressure on public policymakers and engaging the civil rights movement that was sweeping the nation. Federal public policymakers decided that the Department of Justice should play that lead role.[56]

The Federal government's prodding caused many police departments to address the problem of domestic violence not simply as in the family dispute category but instead as criminal behavior. For the first time, a police department would be expected to train its officers not just to respond to these types of calls and resolve them as quickly as possible but to provide some type of help for the victim. The New York police were provided with training in crisis intervention by a psychology professor from the City University. They were trained to realize why domestic violence needs the attention of the criminal justice system. All calls for domestic violence were channeled to officers of the Family Crisis Intervention Unit. Officers were encouraged to negotiate the dispute at the scene, taking as much time as they needed. They were to refer the disputants to social service agencies, who would in turn refer both the abuser and the victim to agencies best suited to bring the problem to resolution. This mediation process, though it seemed neutral enough, often served the abuser's interest by decriminalizing the behavior of the abuser and rarely provided any sanctions for illegal abusive behavior.

The International Chiefs of Police national training manual specified that arrest was to be avoided whenever possible in responding to domestic disputes.[57] The concept was to build greater expertise for the responding officer through more concentrated experience with the problem.[58] In a society where men most often do the beating and women get beaten, it seems to me that this mediation process was a change from past procedure, but it was found to be an acceptable change by only half the population.

There was no empirical scientific evidence that established that the New York City Family Crisis Intervention Unit approach reduced domestic violence. In 1977, a survey of police agencies with over one hundred employees found that 71 percent of the departments reported a family crisis unit or at least a family crisis intervention-training program.[59] The adoption of this training, I believe, would help establish the police bias in favor of mediation and against arrest. This bias continued the police practice of believing that there was little, if anything, police departments could do that would prevent domestic violence.

The next study concerning domestic violence and the criminal justice system was the Kansas City, Missouri, homicide study. Data demonstrated that 40 percent of homicides arose from domestic violence disputes. In about half of these homicides, the police had been called five or more times in the two years prior to the murder. In February 1973, under a grant from the Police Foundation, a project team found a relationship between domestic disturbances and the violent crimes of homicide and aggravated assault.[60] It was possible that police departments could determine problem relations and ask for help from other agencies to prevent domestic violence.

I was a police officer in 1977, and the majority of domestic violence calls I was dispatched to around this time were, by law, misdemeanors with no powers of arrest. In the majority of the calls to which they responded, officers could not arrest the abuser even with probable cause. Officers could, at best, write a report and then apply through the courts for an arrest warrant or a show cause hearing. The court would decide if and when a warrant would be issued.[61] It was not unusual for this process to take over a month.

There was little a police officer could do about domestic violence arrest due to the limitations of Massachusetts law. Most officers with whom I had contact with over twenty years of service believed then, as they do now, that if they made an arrest the courts would do little to correct the actions of the abuser. Furthermore they believed that other governmental agencies would do little to *correct the precipitating causes* of domestic violence, which often left the victim and their children in the cycle of abuse. I believe they were right.

In 1977, Pennsylvania passed the first contemporary domestic violence statute. This occurred almost one hundred years after the first Pennsylvania "wife-beating study." In 1978, Massachusetts passed a similar statute: the Abuse Prevention Act, General Law c.209A, which allowed warrantless arrests for misdemeanor crimes involving domestic violence that police officers did not witness. The law was originally intended to provide legal remedies for battered women and to demonstrate that domestic violence was a crime. But because of its ambiguity and the fact that the order itself was civil, it began to be issued to both men and women, adults and minors, parents and their children, and even people who simply lived in the same household without any type of spousal relationship.

After passage of the Act, women's advocacy groups and others continued to protest that police inaction demonstrated their indifference to domestic violence.[62] They also claimed that police departments gave a very low priority to domestic violence. The *crime* of assault and battery, whether committed by a stranger or a family member, *remains a misdemeanor and is given a low priority because it is a minor crime*. All misdemeanors are given a lower priority than felonies. The public policymakers who proclaimed domestic violence to be a major problem have constructed it as a misdemeanor or a minor crime.

It is particularly difficult for an officer to make an arrest when both the victim and abuser deny that anything of a criminal nature has occurred. When both abuser and victim claim that there is no problem, and, there are no visible injuries present, there is little probable cause for arrest. The Abuse Prevention Act in Massachusetts allowed for arrest in unwitnessed misdemeanors. The "preferred" arrest policy in the Act was not uniformly understood nor implemented by many members of the criminal justice system. The language of the criminal justice system regularly has been that the police officer "should arrest," meaning that the officer has some discretion. That an officer "shall/must" is rarely if ever used but it is clear and understandable. I do not know to this day if anyone in the criminal justice system truly understands just what "preferred arrest" means." To my knowledge it has never been before or since used in the law enforcement lexicon.

During the late 1970s and early 1980s, many laws nationwide were further amended or introduced that signified that police officers were now to treat domestic violence as a crime. Many of these changes were in direct response to the concerted efforts of women's advocacy groups. In 1983, the Massachusetts Abuse Prevention Act was further amended, with additional regulations of police functions. The law provided for a standard police procedure that required all officers to adhere to specific guidelines. The criminal charge of assault and battery of a wife or loved one, however, remained unchanged. It remained the same as the misdemeanor criminal charge of assault and battery of a stranger.

Less acknowledged but most important catalysts of these changes, both in Massachusetts and nationwide, were the civil suits brought against police departments. In 1984, a Connecticut woman, Tracy Thurman, won $2.3 million in a lawsuit against the City of Torrington. Ms. Thurman had repeatedly called the police to arrest her husband for domestic abuse. During one incident the police told her that the only officer who could arrest her husband was on vacation. After repeated inaction by the police department, she was attacked by her husband and suffered multiple stab wounds that resulted in paralysis below the neck and permanent disfigurement. Introduction of the Minneapolis experiment's results at her trial by an expert witness may have given that experiment an indirect influence on policy and legislation nationwide through this critical case.[63] The Torrington Police Department has now changed its policy and practice of no arrest in domestic violence cases.[64]

Following the results of this case and other successful litigation by women against police departments, police administrators and public policymakers in Massachusetts and elsewhere expeditiously embraced pro-arrest or preferred arrest policies.[65] The International Chiefs of Police, public policymakers, and women's advocacy groups eagerly acknowledged the findings of the experiment done in Minneapolis.[66] By 1980, forty-seven states had some form of domestic violence legislation in place.[67]

Using a grant from the National Institute of Justice, the Minneapolis Police Department and the Police Foundation of Washington, D.C., conducted an experiment from early 1981 until mid-1982 testing the deterrent effect of arrest in domestic violence incidents. It was the first classic controlled experiment in history to determine the deterrent effects of arrest for any offense. A classic controlled experiment is a research design that allows scientists to discover the effect of one factor on another by holding constant all possible causes of those effects.

The design method was applied only to misdemeanor domestic assaults, in which both the abuser and victim were present. The police officers were empowered to make unwitnessed misdemeanor arrests. The incident had to have taken place within four hours of the officers' arrival. The officers' action was predetermined by lottery, and information regarding the action taken was given to a research staff for follow-up. The three standard methods used were to arrest the abuser, attempt to counsel both parties, or send the abuser away for several hours.

The results of this experiment were first reported in 1983. The Minneapolis experiment determined that arrest and a night in jail for the suspect cut in half the risk of repeat violence against the same victim over a six-month follow-up period. Both official records and follow-up interviews of victims seemed to demonstrate that "arrest worked best." The report then concluded that police in all states *should be allowed* to make warrantless arrests in misdemeanor domestic violence cases.[68]

The experiment had a small sample number, only 314. Minneapolis is unusual in respect to many other large cities in that it has a large white population, a large Native-American population, a very low rate of violence, a low unemployment rate, and few large low-income housing projects. There should have been some awareness that the results may have been quite different given the different socioeconomic demographics of many other cities.

The results and implications of the experiment were published in the April 1984 issue of the *American Sociological Review.*[69] Women's and victims' rights advocates, public policymakers, and police administrators used the report as proof that arrests had a deterrent effect on men who beat their wives. Women's and victims' rights advocates were assured by this report that the criminal justice system could be used to help prevent the reoccurrence of domestic violence. Police chiefs, concerned by criticism of their officers and worried about the possible financial burden of legal suits, welcomed the experimental results.[70]

The Minneapolis Police Department changed its domestic violence policy, and other departments quickly followed. A Police Foundation survey in the spring of 1984 found that only 10 percent of police agencies in cities over 100,000 people had pro-arrest policies for misdemeanor domestic violence. Two years later, the same departments reported that 43 percent preferred arrest for misdemeanor domestic violence incidents.[71] By 1989, 90 percent of police agencies nationally either encouraged or required arrest in such situations.[72]

Although this dramatic shift toward mandatory and preferred arrest policy reflects the current political trends and the wishes of women's advocacy groups, it was not the preference of the architect of the study, Lawrence W. Sherman, or his colleagues. Given the limitations of the study, they recommended against enactment of laws mandating arrest. In 1992, Sherman wrote. "But if any state legislatures should repeal a mandatory arrest law, it is states like Wisconsin that have black poverty ghettoes in large cities. The same would probably apply to the District of Columbia, Massachusetts, Missouri, and New Jersey"(p. 149).[73]

Their opposition to mandatory arrest laws failed to stop legislatures in most states from enacting either both mandatory or preferred arrest laws within a few years of the experiment. Most astonishing to me is the fact that the majority of mandatory arrest advocates whom I have met over the years continue to cite

Sherman and Berk (1989) as being *supporters* of mandatory arrest. These same advocates continue to state that the Minneapolis experiment favored mandatory arrest. *It did not.* The Minneapolis Experiment recommended that police in all fifty states *be allowed* to make warrantless arrests in misdemeanor domestic violence cases. The study clearly pronounces that:

It may be premature to conclude that arrest is always the best way for police to handle domestic violence, or that all suspects in such situations should be arrested. A number of factors suggest a cautious interpretation of the findings . . . . Until subsequent research addresses that issue more thoroughly, it would be premature for state legislatures to pass laws requiring arrests in all misdemeanor domestic assaults.[74]

Over the next few years, the U.S. Department of Justice, spent in excess of $4 million on replication studies in an effort to confirm the results of the Minneapolis study. The results of the studies in Appendix I demonstrate that arrest without proper sanctions did not have a consistent deterrent effect on the majority of domestic violence offenders. In fact, some of the studies state that "mandatory arrests in domestic violence cases *may cause more violence* against women in the long run."[75]

As acts of domestic violence increasingly became recognized for what they were, serious crimes deserving a serious response by law enforcement, there remained a movement that would allow much of this behavior to remain in our civil courts. Although many police departments would now begin to treat domestic abuse as a crime, many women's advocacy groups and public policymakers discovered what many police officers and others in the criminal justice system had known for years. Many victims of domestic violence are unwilling to file criminal charges against their spouse, do not want their spouse arrested, and if arrested the victim will ask that the case be dropped and often will refuse to testify in court.[76]

Beginning around 1976, women's advocacy groups pushed for state legislators to enact new laws that would allow victims of domestic violence to obtain civil restraining orders against their abusers. While these orders varied greatly, most allow the court to, on an *ex parte* [that is without the abuser present] basis, order the abuser to refrain from further abuse, vacate the home, include a "no contact order," and rule on the custody of children. Every state now has a law that will allow the plaintiff to obtain a civil restraining order against an alleged abuser. Implementation of these types of laws has created a real challenge for the criminal justice system.[77]

In 1979, Massachusetts issued 3,400 such orders; in 1993, the number issued had increased to over 52,000; and by September 1995 the total had reached an extraordinary 145,263.[78] Many of the plaintiffs seeking these orders were swayed, most often by women advocates, to believe that this order could help them prevent specific behavior of their abusers such as harassment, threats, and future or further violence. The truth was that when these policies were put in place, there was no study that had scientifically evaluated the effectiveness of civil protection orders in establishing safe conditions for the plaintiff or in preventing or reducing domestic violence.[79] "However, few studies have examined the effectiveness of restraining orders in reducing the incidence of domestic violence, and those few studies have been nonexperimental or quasi-experimental with designs that weaken any conclusion about their effectiveness."[80]

The ever-escalating number of civil orders may indicate the desperate longing of many victims that these orders will be the answer to their dilemma. This hope is fueled by public policymakers who continue to insist that these current policies can protect the victim. Worse still, the orders make that promise in writing and states in part "the court may enter such temporary relief orders without notice as it deems necessary to *protect* [emphasis added] the plaintiff from abuse." I believe that few criminal justice professionals believe that this piece of paper *provides protection*. I presume that many victims of domestic violence are so desperate for help that they do not or cannot, apply reason and logic to their circumstance and instead believe, simply because they *want to believe*, that this piece of paper is just what they need. Clearly, the ever-escalating number of restraining orders reflect that, with little to no demonstration or documentation of their efficiency, the courts have succumbed to the temptation of using these civil orders in lieu of criminal prosecution.

In 1987, the Massachusetts Abuse Prevention Act was amended again to further increase the powers and duties of police officers. The latest major revision took place in 1990. The Act would now *mandate* that a law enforcement officer *must* arrest anyone when he or she witnesses or has "probable cause to believe a person has violated a court order." Arrest is to be the "preferred response" for those instances where there is no court order, but where an officer witnessed or has probable cause to believe that a person has committed an act of abuse as defined under the guidelines of the Act. The majority of states have similar policies. Because of litigation concerns by police administrators, this 1990 change has created a "de facto" mandatory domestic violence arrest policy for most police departments.

Following this most recent change in the Act, a study with utilization of data from twenty-four Massachusetts police departments in 1992 showed that arrests increased dramatically. Overall, 37.8 percent of domestic violence incidents resulted in arrest, more than a five-fold increase in arrests. When a 209A protection order was in effect, offenders were arrested nearly half the time, 49.4 percent. Amazingly, many proponents of the law whom I know and met with at numerous domestic violence roundtables or conferences were dismayed and disappointed that the law that mandated arrest did not work all the time. They wondered why, as some data demonstrated, the police would make arrests only about half of the time the officers responded to these calls. I had to explain that it is eminently difficult for police officers responding to a domestic abuse call to arrest the abuser when the abuser has already fled the scene. The offender was arrested 80 percent of the time when the victim lived with the offender and, of course was present.[81] This falls short of the 100 percent arrest rate expected by some victims advocates under the mandatory arrest statute. Many offenders flee the scene before police arrive, accounting for many of the nonarrests.[82] During a three-year period, 1989-1991, domestic violence arrests in Massachusetts increased from 7.1 percent of all arrests in 1989 to 13.8 percent of all arrests in 1991.[83] More arrests for domestic violence are being made now than ever before.

This expectation of 100 percent arrest rate is just one demonstration of the discontinuity that remains between the ideological and actual use of policy as practiced by officers on the street. Public policymakers often provide theoretical answers for real problems, and hence results often do not meet their illusory expectations. Prohibition in the 1920s and forced school busing in the 1970s and 1980s are two other clear examples of their illusory contemplation of behavior transformation by edict of public policy that failed.

There is no well documented scientific evidence that arrest universally can reduce or ever has reduced crime or the likelihood of rearrest.[84]If there is no evidence that arrest can reduce crime why do so many domestic violence advocates and public policy makers continue to assure us that if an abuser is arrested, this act alone, will provide future protection for the victim? Most police officers I worked with believe, from their street experience, that arrest can and does play a role in deterring certain individuals in society. The shame and loss of integrity because of arrest may deter individuals who believe that their own self-interest is protected by a community commitment to the interest of others and who believe that it is their civic responsibility to uphold the law. Arrest may be a deterrence for people who are willing to balance their individual freedom with social responsibility. If there is no community commitment, no civic pride, no individual responsibility, no shame in being arrested, then the process of arrest provides no deterrence at all.

Studies demonstrate that arrest can deter some domestic violence in some cities but can *increase* it in others. Studies demonstrate that arrest can reduce domestic violence among employed people but often can *increase* it among unemployed people. Studies demonstrate that arrest can reduce domestic violence in the short run but can *increase* it in the long run.[85]Which of our domestic violence advocates and public policy makers want to take the credit, because of current domestic violence policies, for causing an *increase of violence* in the lives of these victims?

Prosecution and sentencing policies do not reflect sure, swift, and proper sanctions because of the increased numbers of arrests by police officers. Across Massachusetts the courts have not adapted in any systematic manner to the dramatic institutional changes concerning domestic violence by police departments. The increased numbers of arrests has often fostered extremely high rates at which either some prosecutors drop charges after the arrest or extremely high rates of dismissal by many courts. Some district courts, to the dismay (but not the surprise) of the arresting officers, dismiss between 60 and 75 percent of restraining order violations. In an analysis of data from the Commonwealth's district courts from September 1992 to July 1994, there were 5,060 violations of restraining orders in Plymouth County. Only 8 percent of the violators were sentenced to jail for these violations, and 66 percent of them were dismissed. During that same time period, the Brockton District court dismissed 77 percent of these violations.[86] It appears to me and to many of my peers that many judges want to remain steadfastly independent of the many constraints of domestic violence statute law. In some courts that I appeared in, it seemed to me, that many judges have had little to no training in the many recent changes concerning domestic violence. Even worse, some of the civil courts have had training independent of the criminal courts and they are headed in different directions. In some instances, however, and at certain times they seem to be on a collision course.

No comprehensive studies to date demonstrate that mandatory arrest policies and civil restraining orders without proper sanctions have prevented or even reduced the number of domestic violence incidents. In 1995 1,669 women and 2,209 children were given protection in Massachusetts shelters. Many others were told there was not enough room for them. Courts issued restraining orders 11,239 times, and hot-line phone services handled 92,255 emergency domestic violence calls.[87] These ever-escalating numbers *are all time highs*. Is it not time that our public policymakers come to some understanding that some of our current domestic violence policies may be harming some victims? Is it not time that we, at the very least, begin a dialogue that considers the notion that we may be doing something wrong? It is time to review our current policies and discover where we have gone wrong. It is time to admit that we may have made some mistakes in some of our domestic violence policies and it is not too late to correct those mistakes.

NOTES

1. Lawrence W. Sherman, *Policing Domestic Violence: Experiments and Dilemmas* (New York: Free Press, 1992) p. 45.

2. U.S. Commission of Civil Rights, *Battered Women: Issues of Public Policy* (Washington, D.C.: Government Printing Office, 1978).

3. Richard Wrangham and Dale Peterson, *Demonic Males* (Boston: Houghton Mifflin Co., 1996), pp. 242, 231-236

4. Jeffrey Fagan, *The Criminalization of Domestic Violence: Promises and Limits* (Washington, D.C.: National Institute of Justice, 1996), 28-31.

5. Kathleen J. Ferraro and Lucille Pope, "Irreconcilable Differences: Battered Women, Police, and the Law," in *Legal Response to Wife Assault,* N. Zoe Hilton, ed. (Newbury Park, Calif.: Sage Publication, 1993), 104.

6. Peter K. Manning, "The Preventive Conceit," *American Behavioral Scientist* 36, no. 5 (1993), p. 83.

7. Ferraro and Pope, "Irreconcilable Differences: Battered Women, Police, and the Law," p. 108.

8. Fagan, *The Criminalization of Domestic Violence*, p. 29.

9. Steven Foldberg, "The Inevitability of Patriarchy," in James P. Sterba, ed., *Morality in Practice* (Belmont, Calif.: Wadsworth Publishing Co., 1984), pp. 217-221.

10. Wrangham and Peterson, *Demonic Males*, p. 31.

11. Ibid., p. 172.

12. Charles Kenney, *Hammurabi's Code* (New York: Simon & Schuster, 1995), p. 289.

13. Diane Stein, *The Women's Spirituality Book* (St. Paul Minn.: Liewellyn Publications, 1993), p. 7.

14. Mary P. Fisher and Robert Luyster, *Living Religions* (Englewood Cliffs, N.J.: Prentice Hall, 1991), p. 27-28.

15. Wrangham and Peterson, *Demonic Males*, p. 242.

16. Matilda Josylin Gage, *Women, Church, and State* (Watertown, Mass.: Persephone Press reprint, 1980; original edition, 1893), p. 97,

17. Fagan, The *Criminalization of Domestic Violence*, p. 6.

18. Elizabeth Pleck, "Criminal Approaches to Family Violence, 1640-1980," *Family Violence*. Vol. 2 *Crime and Justice: A Review of Research*, eds. Lloyd Ohlin and Michael Tonry (Chicago: University of Chicago Press, 1987), p. 22.

19. Eve S. Buzawa and Carl G. Buzawa, *Do Arrests and Restraining Orders Work?* (Thousand Oaks, Calif.: Sage Publishing, 1996), p. 24.

20. Fagan, *The Criminalization of Domestic Violence*, p. 7.

21. Pleck, "Criminal Approaches to Family Violence," pp. 19-57.

22. Buzawa and Buzawa, *Do Arrest and Restraining Orders Work?*, p. 23.

23. Pleck, "Criminal Approaches to Family Violence," p. 22.

24. Buzawa and Buzawa, *Do Arrest and Restraining Orders Work?*, p. 24.

25. James M. McPherson, *The Battle Cry of Freedom* (New York: Oxford University Press, 1988), p. 34.

26. Ibid., 36.

27. John A. Garraty, *1,001 Things Everyone Should Know About American History* (New York: Doubleday, 1989), p. 64.

28. McPherson, *The Battle Cry of Freedom*, pp. 483-484.

29. Maxwell Bloomfield, "Law," in Charles Regan Wilson and William Ferris, eds., *Encyclopedia of Southern Culture* (Chapel Hill: University of North Carolina Press, 1993). P. 807.

30. Pleck, "Criminal Approaches to Family Violence," p. 31.

31. *Fulgham v. State,* 46 Ala. 146-147.

32. Robert C. Trojanowicz and Merry Murash, *Juvenile Delinquency: Concepts and Control* (Englewood Cliffs, N.J.: Prentice Hall, 1992), p. 428.

33. Robert G. Caldwell, *Red Hannah: Delaware's Whipping Post* (Philadelphia: University of Pennsylvania Press, 1947), p. 131.

34. Elizabeth Pleck, *Domestic Tyranny: The Making of Social Policy Against Family Violence from Colonial Times to the Present* (Chicago: University of Chicago Press, 1987), pp. 108-121.

35. Ibid., p. 42.

36. Robert S. Gallagher, "The Fight for Women's Suffrage: An Interview with Alice Paul," in John A. Garraty, ed., *Historical Viewpoints: Notable Articles for American Heritage* (New York: Harper & Row, 1981), p. 180.

37. Kenneth C. Davis, *Don't Know Much About History* (New York: Avon, 1990), p. 261.

38. Scott Turow, *The Laws of Our Fathers* (New York: Farrar Straus Giroux, 1996), p. 441.

39. James W. Loewen, *Lies My Teacher Told Me* (New York: Touchstone, 1995), p. 23.

40. Davis, *Don't Know Much About History*, p. 261.

41. Jean Bethke Elshtain, "What Feminists Could Learn from Ms. Anthony," *Civilization* 2, no. 6 (1995): 51-55.

42. Dallas Morning News, "75 Years After Suffrage," *Boston Globe*, June 4, 1995, p. 12.

43. Mary Leonard, "Dollar Power," *Boston Globe,* April 6, 1997, pp. D1-D3.

44. Susan Ware, *Partner and I: Molly Dewson, Feminism and New Deal Politics* (New Haven, Conn.: Yale University Press, 1987), p. 146.

45. Davis, *Don't Know Much About History*, p. 362.

46. Beverly Droz, "Massachusetts Women Politicians," *Boston Globe*, December 18, 1996, p. A24.

47. Marvin E. Wolfgang, *Patterns in Criminal Homicide* (Philadelphia: University of Pennsylvania Press, 1958), p. 207.

48. Wrangham and Peterson, *Demonic Males*, p. 108.

49. David T. Courtwright, "Violence in America," *American Heritage* 47, no. 5 (1996): 38.

50. John Leo, "The Media Misreport Domestic Violence," in Karin L. Swisher, ed., *Domestic Violence* (San Diego: Greenhaven Press, 1996), p. 80.

51. Ibid., p. 80.

52. Richard J. Gelles and Donileen R. Loseke, eds. *Current Controversies On Family Violence* (Newbury Park, Calif.: Sage Publications, 1993), p. 69.

53. Associated Press, "Home Violence Underreported," *Boston Globe,* August 25, 1997, p. A5.

54. Murray A. Straus, "Domestic Violence Is a Problem for Men," in Karin L. Swisher, ed., *Domestic Violence* (San Diego: Greenhaven Press, 1996), p. 54.

55. Associated Press, "Violent Crime Dropped in '95 in Major U.S. Cities, FBI Says," *Boston Globe,* October 13, 1996, p. A18.

56. Fagan, *The Criminelization of Domestic Violence*, p. 7.

57. Ibid., p.8.

58. Sherman, *Policing Domestic Violence*, p. 48.

59. Morton Bard and Harriet Connolly, "The Police and Family Violence: Practice and Policy," *Battered Women: Issues of Public Policy* (Washington D.C.: U.S. Civil Rights Commission, 1978), pp. 309-326.

60. Del Martin, "The Historical Roots of Domestic Violence," in Daniel Jay Sonkin, ed., *Domestic Violence on Trial: Psychological and Legal Dimensions of Family Violence* (New York: Springer, 1987). P. 3.

61. Joan Zorza, "The Criminal Law of Misdemeanor Domestic Violence, 1970-1990," *Journal of Criminal Law and Criminology* 83, no. 1 (1992): 46-72.

62. Ibid., p. 47.

63. Sherman, *Policing Domestic Violence*, p. 14.

64. *Thurman v. City of Torrington*, 595 F.Supp. 1521 (D. Conn. 1984).

65. Buzawa and Buzawa, *Do Arrests and Restraining Orders Work?*, p. 75.

66. Richard J. Gelles and Murray A. Straus, *Intimate Violence: The Definitive Study of the Causes and Consequences of Abuse in the American Family* (New York: Simon & Schuster, 1988), pp. 166-167.

67. Fagan, *The Criminalization of Domestic Violence*, p. 9.

68. Sherman, *Policing Domestic Violence*, pp. 2-3.

69. Lawrence W. Sherman and Richard A. Berk, "The Specific Deterrent Effects of Arrest for Domestic Violence," *American Sociological Review* 49, no. 2 (1984): 261-272.

70. Elizabeth Stanko, "Domestic Violence," in Gary W. Cordner and Donna C. Hales, ed., *What Works in Policing: Operations and Administration Examined* (Cincinnati: Anderson Publishing, 1992), p. 53.

71. Lawrence W. Sherman and Ellen G. Cohn, "The Impact of Research on Legal Policy: The Minneapolis Domestic Violence Experiment," *Law and Society Review* 23, no. 1 (1989): 123.

72. Sherman, *Policing Domestic Violence*, p. 14.

73. Ibid., p. 149.

73. Sherman, *Policing Domestic Violence*, p. 279.

74. Lisa G. Lerman, "The Decontextualization of Domestic Violence," *Journal of Criminal Law and Criminology* 83, no. 1 (1992): 217.

75. Peter Finn and Maria O'Brian Hylton, *Using Civil Remedies for Criminal Behavior: Rationale, Case Studies, and Constitutional Issues* (Washington, D.C.: National Institute of Justice, 1994), p. 66.

76. Andrew R. Klein, *Spousal/Partner Assault: A Protocol for the Sentencing and Supervision of Offenders* (Swampscott, Mass.: Production Specialties, 1993), pp. 1-3.

77. Gregg Krupa, "Concern Voiced over Restraining Order Abuse," *Boston Globe,* March 5, 1994, p. 24.

78. Finn and Hylton, *Using Civil Remedies for Criminal Behavior,* p. 1.

79. Fagan, *The Criminalization of Domestic Violence,* p. 24.

80. William M. Holmes, *Mandatory Arrest and Domestic Violence in Massachusetts* (Boston: Statistical Analysis Center, Massachusetts Committee on Criminal Justice, 1993) pp. 14-16.

81. Ibid., pp. 14-16

82. Ibid., p. 17.

83. Peter K. Manning, "The Preventive Conceit," p. 641.

84. Janell D. Schmidt and Lawrence W. Sherman, "Does Arrest Deter Domestic Violence?", *American Behavioral Scientist,* 36 (1993): 606.

85. Alison Bass, "The War on Domestic Abuse," *Boston Globe,* September 25, 1994, 1.

86. *Boston Globe,* "Easing Battered Lives," October 12, 1996, p. A18.

6

From Those in the Valley

Every society gets the kind of criminal it deserves. What is equally true is that
every community gets the kind of law enforcement it insists on.

Robert Kennedy (1925-1968)

Many police officers agree that police intervention in domestic violence is a
necessary element in the quest to solve the problem of domestic violence. Their
role should be to rigorously enforce existing laws. It is most important to note
that policing violence in the home is an *emergency* process to *stop* the violence,
restore the peace, and if necessary *arrest* anyone who has violated a law. The
police should provide the victim with information regarding what other agencies
are available for further assistance. These agencies should include the district
attorney's office, the court system, mental health departments, battered women's
shelters, transitional safe housing programs, and private practitioners.[1] Further
support must be provided through an integrative form of assistance through one
or more of these agencies.

While Massachusetts is a highly industrialized state, most of its police
departments are relatively small, and few have enough personnel to establish the
kinds of specialized units that the general public has come to expect through
television and the print media.[2] In police departments reporting more than
twenty-five domestic violence arrests annually, the number of arrests for
domestic violence increased by more than 100 percent in the early 1990s.[3] Most
of these arrests are by individual cruiser patrol officers just doing their job and
not by specific domestic violence units.

Most, if not all, police departments require demanding and inflexible
background examinations of job applicants, including a check to discover if the
applicant has a history of domestic violence. Most, if not all, police departments
have multidisciplinary training on domestic violence that begins in the recruit
academy and continues through in-service training throughout their entire
career. They receive training in child and elder abuse in their academies, which

continues through in-service training throughout their entire careers. They also have specialized domestic violence officers or units. Most, if not all, police departments have standardized guidelines to ensure uniform police procedures in responding to domestic violence calls and in guiding the conduct of the officers, if they themselves become involved in domestic violence. Finally, most, if not all, police departments have assistance programs that include appropriate resources and referrals concerning domestic violence for their civilian clerical personnel. "Actually, police departments are doing more these days to crack down on domestic violence, including abuse perpetrated by their own officers, the advocates say."[4]

Only a handful of other vocations, public or private, have a uniform, integrated standard of practice and multidisciplinary educational process regarding domestic violence as do the police departments. Some exceptions are Polaroid Cooperation, Marshalls, and Liz Claiborne. The majority of major cooperations are only now becoming involved with the issue of domestic violence and then often because they are beginning to realize those domestic violence victims who are their employees can affect the companies' bottom line. Each year, according to the Bureau of National Affairs estimates, employers lose $3 billion to $5 billion in productivity, absenteeism, medical bills and employee turnover.[5] One of the few governmental exceptions is Massachusetts. In August of 1997 by executive order, state supervisors have the authority to discipline state employees who have been charged with crimes that are interrelated with domestic violence. The state unions who contend that the process is illegal are currently contesting this executive order.[6]

Readers should review the policies of the Brockton Police Department contained in the appendices of this book and compare these policies to domestic violence policies where the reader works, if indeed there are any such domestic violence policies. The majority of physicians, nurses, psychiatrists, psychologists, family counselors, educators, social workers, attorneys, judges, and law enforcement officials other than police officers *do not* have policies similar to the Brockton Police Department. Nor are most employers mandated to report incidents of domestic violence. Police departments and a few others have come a long way in the past decade but many domestic violence advocates remain fixated on changes within law enforcement. Where are the physicians, psychiatrists, psychologists, educators, attorneys, judges, and politicians who should not be able to avoid the issue of domestic violence any more than police officers should? These other agencies and individuals have done little to institute policies and procedures that they must follow concerning domestic violence.

In Massachusetts the Kennedys publicly have been supportive of women's issues and in return for that public support they have received the almost unwavering support of women in elections. Women in Massachusetts more than any other voting block in the state have made the Kennedys almost invincible in the state's politics. But the private lives of the Kennedy men reveal that they have not "manifested in their private lives the respect for women implicit in their public positions."[7] Joseph P. Kennedy, the patriarch of the family carried on numerous affairs and all but public affairs with movie stars. This vision of a woman as nothing more than a sexual object was evidently passed down to his children. It is now generally accepted that both President Kennedy and his brother Robert carried on affairs even while in the White House. The Kennedy presidency was labeled as the "Camelot presidency," and suitably so because just as in the original Camelot the Kennedys believed they belonged to a privileged class and were not bound to the morality they preached for others. I have difficulty understanding how women in Massachusetts and elsewhere in this nation continue to vote into office men who in their private behavior demonstrate so little respect for women. I believe that it is time for us to demand that our publicly elected officials abide by the same moral beliefs they preach when they run for office.

Lesley Stahl, a co-host of the television show "60 Minutes", believes that "the police, for the most part, are sympathetic, and encourage a woman who is battered to call them any time she's been hit or even threatened.[8] In that regard, things are getting better. Is it better where you work? Has anyone at your job ever talked about domestic violence? Do any of your employers have any policies or procedures concerning domestic violence? Has Lesley Stahl been given any information about what she should do if she should have a problem with domestic violence by the producers of "60 Minutes"? I suspect that "no" is the answer to most of these questions.

The *Boston Globe* relates in a September 25, 1994, article that "Across the State, the data reveals enormous discrepancies in the way individual courts and district attorneys respond to violations of restraining orders." Is it logical that a domestic violence victim in Middlesex County should receive different treatment than a domestic violence victim in Plymouth County? Is it logical that a domestic violence victim in Texas should receive different treatment than a domestic violence victim in Massachusetts? The same article continues in reference to the prosecution: "But many district courts, the State's figures show, dismiss most such violations--sometimes even those involving assaults with bats, knives and other dangerous weapons."[9] The courts are issuing restraining orders in record numbers, the police are arresting violators of those orders in record numbers, and as a result many courts are dismissing violations of those orders in record numbers.[10] These facts do little to alleviate the Police general pessimism with regard to the effectiveness of the criminal justice system and its ability to impact social behavior.

Most police officers doubt that police intervention and the criminal justice system will resolve the problem of domestic violence. Astonishingly many public policymakers continue to believe that punishing abusers after their families have been harmed is more important than providing policies for preventing domestic violence in the first place.

In 1978 Massachusetts passed the Abuse Prevention Act and created restraining orders in matters of domestic violence. Among recent legal developments in Massachusetts are the following:

- Accused abusers must immediately surrender guns, ammunition, and gun licenses in their possession, ownership, and control once restraining orders have been issued against them.

- Judges may consider a woman's history of abuse when deciding whether use of force is justifiable as self-defense against abuse that could lead to death, serious injury, or rape.
- Authorities may prosecute restraining order violations, which are misdemeanors, either where the orders were filed or where the offenses took place.
- Police must make an arrest when they witness violations of a restraining order or have probable cause to believe a violation has occurred, or when a defendant has failed to surrender guns or gun permits.
- Police may testify about their first conversation with the victim if the victim is unwilling or unable to appear in court.
- Restraining orders cover not only spouses and household members, but also substantial dating relationships.
- Judges may consider the dangerousness of those accused of abuse when determining bail and may detain them without bail for trial.
- Authorities may enforce out-of-state restraining orders.
- Married people are no longer prohibited from testifying about private conversations during the course of the marriage.
- Emergency restraining orders can be granted twenty-four hours a day with a phone call involving police, the victim, and a judge.
- In cases of severe hardship due to a physical condition, emergency abuse prevention orders may be granted by telephone and someone else may appear on the victim's behalf in court the next day to request a temporary ten-day restraining order.[11]

These are all *reactive policies after the fact* that someone has been abused. These policies are analogous to building more hospitals for drivers injured in traffic accidents at a dangerous intersection rather than having the public works department make that intersection safer and educating drivers on traffic safety. These reactive domestic violence policies have taken on increasing prominence in Massachusetts and elsewhere. While these policies look great on paper, they have accomplished little genuine societal change. Certainly they have done little to prevent the almost two decades long rise in reports of domestic abuse and the issuance of restraining orders.

Those who pay the penalty for these misguided policies are the families who have been sentenced to shattered lives and broken hearts because of intervention that comes after these families have endured abuse. Why have these reactive policies become more important to most public policymakers than prevention efforts? How is it possible that our public policymakers do not understand that these policies provide little effective relief?

Resolution of the domestic abuse crisis will be achieved not through reactive policies but through education, a change in cultural values, gender equity, revision of opportunity structures, reorganization of social class systems and elimination of economic imbalance.[12] And yes, as the argument goes, we must start somewhere, and common sense alone should demonstrate that the criminal justice system is the wrong somewhere. The narrow focus on policing to prevent battering has led to limited inroads in understanding and preventing violence in the home.[13]

Police intervention is often proffered as a "proactive" approach. A true proactive approach requires that the police officer correct the underlying symptoms that are the real causes of the problems and then to focus on long-term care and prevention.[14] Completing the above process is a logistical, fiscal, and intellectual improbability for police departments to accomplish, given that the underlying symptoms are accurately listed.

Police actions are "reactive" approaches that occur after an incident occurs. Many of the policies enacted by public policymakers in recent years have done little to prevent new cases of abuse or to reduce the number of domestic violence reports filed by the police.[15] Over the last two decades, Massachusetts has experienced an unprecedented increase in reported incidents and arrests for domestic violence.[16]

Police officers are trained to view problems as incidents in which people break laws or create disorder. In retrospect, it appears that the police have had great difficulty responding to domestic violence incidents and taking the appropriate action. It is a valid argument, however, that in the past the "appropriate action" of police officers was in keeping with social mores of the time, and not an inappropriate action or inaction by individual police officers.[17] There is a valid argument that the majority of contemporary society has not agreed on what the "appropriate action" should be.

Historically, societal input and demands have defined the role of the police. A police "crackdown on crime" in any particular neighborhood or for any particular crime is almost always at the request of neighborhood residents or city and town politicians. Historically, the ballot box has defined the political personality of this country. Individual political personalities define when, where, and what kind of police actions most departments take. People and politicians complain to police departments about specific problems in their neighborhoods and the police respond to their complaints. Therefore, complaints about speeding cars will get you a traffic patrol; complaints about drug trafficking will get you drug enforcement officers; and complaints about domestic violence will get you domestic violence units or at least domestic violence training for the officers. It is not complicated, it is not perfect, and it is not always right, but that is the way it has always worked.

From a police officer's perspective, an arrest is difficult, if not impossible, to justify if there is a relatively poor chance of conviction or in the event of a conviction the court imposes no appropriate sanctions. The majority of police officers still question the logic of an arrest if there is not a follow-through by the victim, the prosecution, and the courts to validate the purpose of the arrest. That validation should be proper sanctions for those found guilty of a crime. The victim in domestic violence incidents often will plead with the officer not to arrest the abuser.[18] Most victims of domestic violence are more interested in their partner's rehabilitation or providing help for the abuser rather than in arrest and punishment. Most victims want to stop the violence, but few believe that arrest is the best way to achieve that goal.[19] Officers realize that, without victim cooperation, any charge will either be dismissed by the prosecutor or result in an acquittal for lack of evidence.

To make an arrest without the expectation that the arrest will result in a guilty finding runs contrary to all of the officers' previous training. Most police officers continue to believe the simple theory that they arrest the bad guy, the bad guy gets punished, and the victim feels satisfied.

As Kathleen J. Ferraro and Lucille Pope write, "For example, the use of citizens arrest is an option officers can employ when they are unsure of the strength of evidence." [20]In Massachusetts and many other states, however, a citizen's arrest can be made only when a felony has been committed. It is not a common sense option to suggest that police officers begin to search for reasons to validate an arrest when they are unsure of the strength of evidence. Ferraro and Pope's suggestion displays the limited conception of police work that even many criminal justice experts have about domestic violence.

Some of the literature produced by domestic violence experts stereotypes police procedure, policy, and behavior. One common myth in this literature is that police officers earn promotions by making felony arrests. "Another is that the effectiveness of police officers - a key aspect concerning promotions - is determined, in part, by how many of their felony arrests lead to convictions."[21] The truth is that the vast majority of police departments do not keep track of the arrest/conviction rate of their officers. If the department does have that type of information available, most good police administrators recognize that felony arrests, other than for detectives, is simply the result of the luck of being in the right place at the right time. Indeed, many police officers view it as being in the wrong place at the wrong time. More than 90 percent of felony cases are settled in "let's make a deal" agreements, that is, plea-bargains by prosecutors and defense attorneys.[22] A cursory inspection of the courts in this country reveals that the vast preponderance of cases, felony or not, never go to trial.

Ferraro and Pope are not alone in reaching yet another false conclusion: "Similarly, police departments seek to prove their efficacy by emphasizing the number of felony arrests and the number of convictions." How the district attorney or the courts administratively clean up their overcrowded criminal dockets has little or no relevance to whether or not an arrest was good. Felony or otherwise, it is the absence of crime that demonstrates that a police department is doing a good job, not the number of arrests.

By the 1900s, most contemporary police departments had begun to reflect the social ambivalence concerning domestic violence among the general public. Much later in the early 1960s and 1970s, there was a shorter period when the mediation process was emphasized. Neither method evolved from the officer on the street. Rather, both were reactions of police administrators and public policymakers who relied on the literature of psychologists and social scientists to establish policy. Both psychologists and social scientists believed that arrest was inappropriate because it exacerbated the violence, broke up families, and caused economic havoc following the abuser's job loss.[23]

The current trend toward arrest upon the officer's determination of probable cause or mandatory arrest by legislation reflects a change in statutory guidance and political demand.[24] The old police adage of, "You Call-We Haul-That's All" has never been more true than in the venue of domestic violence. A recent study suggests that most victims, over 85 percent, are highly satisfied with the responses of the police departments. When the victims stated that they wanted the offender arrested, the arrest generally was carried out even if there was no visible injury.[25]

This change has occurred because police officers have now been trained and encouraged to arrest for domestic assaults. New statutory specific policies have been legislated, and restraining orders are being issued by the tens of thousands. These changes reflect the change in how society views domestic violence coupled with public policy and legislative mandates.[26] Are these changes truly curbing domestic violence, or are they just a response to advocacy groups by police administrators fearful of legal repercussions and to public policymakers who have provided knee-jerk reactions amid growing political pressures?

Few who support the social and legal changes concerning domestic violence dispute the influence of the women's movement and battered women advocates groups. Not until the 1970s and early 1980s were many laws changed to reflect the desire of these groups to criminalize battering. The intent of these changes should be to prevent or deter the perpetrator from assaulting the victim. We must continue to understand that the criminal intervention is reactive in nature and deals with the abuser and the abused after the assault has occurred. Reactive criminal justice programs have only limited impact on preventing domestic violence. "In some respects, this is like responding to an outbreak of cholera by building more hospitals and morgues rather than by vaccinating those at risk."[27]

Only by working together can all segments of the system effectively intervene to assist the victim. There needs to be a collaborative effort between advocates, police, prosecutors, and judges. If the police are asked to make arrests but the prosecutor dismisses most of the cases, police officers will see their actions as a pointless exercise.[28]

Mandating police officers to arrest suspects who violate the restraining order will provide deterrence or protection only when all constituents in the system effectively intervene to provide proper sanctions for the abuser and assistance for the victim.[29] Insisting that police officers continue to serve thousands upon thousands of civil restraining orders and finding that many such orders are being used by prosecutors and the courts to avoid criminal prosecution,[30] will only confirm what many police officers and women's advocates have already surmised: the system is not working.[31] According to John Grisham: "There's a frustrating logic to this assembly line justice. Not far away, sitting over there in orange jumpsuits and handcuffs, are rapists, murderers, and drug dealers. The system barely has enough time to run these thugs through and allocate some measure of justice. How can the system be expected to care for the rights of one beaten wife?"[32]

Other than arrests by the police departments the Massachusetts criminal justice system seems to be a paper tiger in the area of domestic violence. Is consistency shown in the state's handling of domestic violence intervention? Across the Commonwealth approximately 86 percent of everyone who violated restraining orders never saw the inside of a jail cell other than when they were arrested by the police.[33]

IN SEARCH OF CONTINUITY AND CLARITY

To be effective, laws must be clear and understandable. The Abuse Prevention Act; Chapter 209A, signed into law in July 1978, allowed police officers to make warrantless misdemeanor arrests for some crimes committed in a domestic violence venue. Prior to this act, police officers, by law, were forbidden to make this type arrest. So that there will be no confusion for police officers, the law specifically states:

When there are no vacate, restraining, or no-contact orders or judgments in effect, arrest shall be the preferred response whenever an officer witnesses or has probable cause to believe that a person: (a) has committed a felony; (b) has committed a misdemeanor involving abuse as defined in section one of the chapter; (c) has committed an assault and battery in violation of section thirteen A of Chapter two hundred and sixty-five.

Section one defines abuse as: "The occurrence of one or more of the following acts between family or household members: (a) attempting to cause or causing physical harm; (b) placing another in fear of imminent serious physical harm; (c) causing another to engage involuntarily in sexual relations by force, threats or duress."[34]

On January 4, 1995, the Supreme Judicial Court of Massachusetts in the case of *Commonwealth v. Jacobsen* declared that police officers *do not* have the power to arrest without a warrant individuals who threaten to commit crimes covered by the domestic abuse statute. The court held that "A warrantless arrest for 'abuse' may be made under G.L.c. 209A s. 6(7), only if the police officer has reason to believe that a defendant's conduct placed the person in fear of imminent serious physical harm by virtue of meeting the element of the common law definition of assault. The appropriate complaint in such a circumstance would be one for assault under G.L.c. 265 s 13A."

The court ruled that if only threats are made and there is no menacing gesture or attempted battery, an arrest is unlawful. The court considered the applicability of the domestic abuse statute with regard to an arrest on a complaint for threats to commit "domestic violence." The court ruled that, at common law, police officers, in the absence of statute law, may only arrest without a warrant for a misdemeanor that involves a breach of the peace, is committed in the presence of the officer, or is still continuing at the time of the arrest. In the *Jacobsen* case the police had no evidence that the defendant had committed a felony or an assault and battery, or even simple assault. The complaint was only for a threat to commit the crime of "domestic violence." The court went on to examine the definition of abuse and ruled that because the complaint only alleged threats to commit "domestic violence" without an overt act to cause physical harm, the arrest was invalid. Thus, it took the Supreme Judicial Court of Massachusetts *seventeen years* to define what the appropriate complaint should be for law enforcement officers under the abuse section of this law. Thousands of abusers have been arrested over these seventeen years, and it was not until January 4, 1995 that the Supreme Judicial Court made a ruling on the appropriate complaint to issue in such a circumstance. Without question, everyone in the criminal justice system believed that, when the Abuse Prevention Act was passed seventeen years ago, this misdemeanor arrest power for law enforcement officers was the very nexus of the change. Everyone except the Massachusetts Supreme Court understood the intent. None of the sitting justices of the Supreme Judicial Court of Massachusetts understood that this change was supposed to have occurred some seventeen years ago.

Sydney Hanlon, a judge in Dorchester, Massachusetts, stated that batterers should not be held in jail until after there is a trial. She also believes that the court system is not equipped to protect anyone once a restraining order is taken out. Judge Hanlon states: "The system is not equipped to do that, and--and shouldn't be, frankly."[35] If the criminal justice system is not so equipped, why is it then that Judge Hanlon and the courts continue to issue restraining orders in Massachusetts at a rate of one every two minutes?[36]

In 1972, the executor of Ruth Bunnell's estate in California filed a wrongful death suit against the San Jose Police Department. Bunnell had called the police many times before her death to complain that her husband had abused both her and her two daughters. In September 1972, she called the police for help, telling them that her husband was on his way home and had threatened to kill her. The police told her that, in compliance with California law, there was nothing they could do to prevent him from returning home. With the *Jacobsen* decision, this is just where the Massachusetts Supreme Judicial Court would have placed domestic violence cases of this nature. By the time police did respond to the home, Bunnell had been stabbed to death by her husband. The California Court of Appeals upheld the trial court's dismissal of the case, stating that the police had never "induced decedent's reliance on a promise, express or implied, that would provide her with protection."[37]

In May 1992 the Massachusetts legislature passed a law that was intended, to prevent the stalking of victims of domestic violence. No where does it mention anything about any relationship between victim and stalker or domestic violence. The law, found in Appendix VII, appears to be misnamed because an abuser may still "willfully, maliciously, and repeatedly follow or harass another person" as long as the abuser does not threaten that victim with the intent to place that victim in imminent fear of death or serious bodily injury. Regardless of the law's intent, the abuser may continue to stalk as long as the abuser keeps his proper distance and is quiet about it.

This same "stalking law" can allow tenants who are stalked and threatened by the landlord to use this law. The law makes no mention of a relationship. Even after a restraining order is issued, the abuser can continue to stalk his victim as long as no threats are made and the abuser does not violate other provisions of the restraining order. Any reader who reviews this law will agree that it has glaring legal holes.

Another court ruling that has led to some confusion among police officers in Massachusetts who respond to domestic violence calls was handed down in 1995. On April 25, 1995, two Boston police officers responded to a 911 call reporting that a man was threatening to stab his girlfriend with a knife. When the officers arrived, they heard shouting and arguing through the apartment door. At first, the occupants refused to open the door. After the officers explained why they were there, the door was opened, but, upon entry, one of the occupants pushed and shoved both officers. He was arrested for assaulting a police officer. On September 11, 1995, Boston Municipal Court judge Mark Summerville found the defendant not guilty. Judge Summerville refused to hear any evidence about the 911 call, saying it was hearsay and inadmissible. Did he conclude that the officers had nothing better to do that night and just decided to drop by that address? "This man [the defendant] was practicing self-defense," Summerville said. "He was expelling people [the police] from this apartment who had no right to be there in the first place . . . they [the police] might even have been shot. You can use deadly force [shoot] to expel a person [the police] who has entered your castle without justification. The judge then went on to warn the officers that their actions could be considered "criminal." "I say to the police officers . . . you can never, ever enter a person's apartment in this manner . . . [a 911 call]. It's criminal and I don't want to hear about it."[38]

Public Safety in Massachusetts: An Overview of Critical Issues Facing Law Enforcement, a report prepared for the Attorney General's Office in April 1994 authored by Albert P. Cardarelli of the J. W. McCormick Institute of Public Affairs, University of Massachusetts at Boston, and Jack McDevitt of the Center for Applied Social Research, Northeastern University, states that:

The Act now mandates that law enforcement officers arrest anyone when he or she witnesses or has ". . . probable cause to believe a person has violated a court order." Arrest is now the *required* (emphasis added) response for those instances where there are no court orders, but where an officer has witnessed or has probable cause to believe that a person has committed an act of abuse as defined under the guidelines of the act.

The law speaks of *mandatory arrest* for violation of a restraining order and of *preferred arrest* where the officer has witnessed or has probable cause to believe that a person has committed an act of abuse. Nowhere does it state that an officer is required to arrest where there are no court orders. The Act defines arrest in the circumstances where there is no order as being preferred and not required under the abuse section. Officers are required or mandated to arrest only for *violation of an order* and arrest is preferred when they have witnessed or have probable cause to believe that a person has committed an act of abuse as defined by the law. Only the violation of a restraining order is mandatory. This preferred arrest policy seems to be confusing even to those in the Massachusetts Attorney General's Office and some experts in academia.

The Reference Guide for New Abuse Prevention Forms M.G.L. Ch.209A, a manual provided by the Administrative Office of the Trial Court and the Judicial Institute as an instructional guide for the criminal justice system, presents a sample affidavit filled out by a plaintiff:

Last night (Aug. 8, 1995) my husband Donald came home late from work. He had been drinking a lot. When I told him we had eaten dinner without him he became very upset and angry. He started screaming at me and shoved me into the stove. He called me a bitch and knocked me to the floor. He kicked me in the ribs. All this happened in front of my three kids. This has happened many times in the past. A year ago in June I had to go to the hospital to get 5 stitches above my eye from where he hit me. Once when I was pregnant with Tisha he kicked me in the stomach and I almost miscarried.

In Massachusetts, if this woman wants a restraining order, the fact that she is married means that she will have to go to probate or civil court and file for a restraining order. That civil court will bring no criminal charges because, among many reasons, they have no authority to do so. As this book demonstrates our system may allow her to file no criminal charges. There is a one in three chance that our system will allow the victim to dismiss the civil order within fifteen days. How much longer can this system be allowed to continue to disregard the legitimate intervention that the three children of the defendant need? How much longer can we allow those being abused to decide how much abuse their children must suffer?

QUAGMIRE

Our current system allows 37 percent of restraining orders to be dropped within fifteen days of issue. More than one-third of all plaintiffs will get no help for themselves or, more importantly, for the children. This is generally the result of the plaintiff's refusal to go forward. Our current system allows victims and their children, with histories worse than that in the preceding example, to return to the scene of the crime where behind closed doors the abuse often will continue. Current domestic violence policy provides little to no intervention for the victim or their children. For the majority of these victims this is not the first instance of abuse. Thirty-seven percent of the defendants in domestic violence cases indicate that they have an alcohol abuse problem and 27 percent mention a drug abuse problem and for none of them do we provide help. We do nothing more than wait until the victims and their abusers again come to the attention of the criminal justice system. Almost 15 percent of them will be back in less than six months.[39] We simply wait until "the victims decide they are ready" or until they and their children are abused again, and this sad slow dance will start once again.

There is little or no cooperation between the players in the criminal justice system. The players seldom even talk to each other, and when they do talk they seldom listen to each other's problems. If they did listen to each other, the *Commonwealth v. Jacobsen* decision would never have been handed down. If public policymakers want to mandate policy, why not mandate educational programs concerning domestic violence in our schools? Why not mandate training in domestic violence for all the educators of our children? Who is listening to the voices of the children while we allow the adults to continue this type of abusive behavior? There remain widely divergent individual and institutional views of the many participants despite what should be the common goal of all involved. That goal should be for immediate intervention, if not for the adults then at least for the children.

The March 1994 issue of the *Governor's Commission on Domestic Violence,* states: "Currently Massachusetts does not have a coordinated, accountable, statewide system to provide the support and safety planning necessary for abuse victims receiving civil protective orders." This statement was made years after passing this law. The Commonwealth and the rest of the nation have been issuing restraining orders for seventeen years and continue to do so by the thousands. All the while no carefully researched study has been written confirming that these orders have any long term consequences for either the abusers or the abused.[40]

Rather than becoming simply cynical, most police officers do not believe that the criminal justice system, with all its legal "simplistic mumbo jumbo," should be viewed as a panacea for domestic violence that is endemic in American society.[41] Included in the instructions to the plaintiff section of the Massachusetts abuse protection form, and on similar forms in many other states, is the following; "Under chapter 209A of Massachusetts General Laws, Judges can make Orders to protect people from abuse by family or household members."

Many police officers remain skeptical because seventeen years after passing a domestic violence law, we have failed to frame a coherent, consistent, and understandable procedure to effectively combat domestic violence.[42] On the last day of each calendar year the Boston Globe lists those killed during a domestic violence dispute. No judge in Massachusetts or elsewhere has the ability to make orders that can effectively protect people from abuse by family or household members. In this absence of any major study that can provide empirical evidence that demonstrate these orders work why do our public policymakers continue to promise that their current domestic violence policies and these pieces of paper can and will provide protection.

The needs and expectations of domestic violence victims vary dramatically. My twenty-one years of experience as a police officer allows me to take an educated guess that Massachusetts judges are not the only judges in this nation who, often reluctantly, sign restraining orders that make this false promise of protection. Arrest without proper sanctions and proper supervision of abusers and the issuance of restraining orders without valid programs in place to help the victims of abuse are surely doomed to continued failure.[43]

NOTES

1. Ann D.Carden, "Wife Abuse and the Wife Abuser: Review and Recommendations," *Counseling Psychologist* 22, no. 4 (October 1994): 567.

2. Albert P. Cardarelli and Jack McDevitt, *Public Safety in Massachusetts: An Overview of Critical Issues Facing Law Enforcement,* April 1994, p. 3.

3. Ibid., p. 6.

4. Marilyn Hancock, ""Dangers from Without and Within," *Brockton Enterprise,* October 1, 1995, p. 1.

5. Diane E. Lewis, "On the Job," *Boston Globe,* March 18, 1997, p. C16.

6. Doris Sue Wong, "Unions Question Domestic-Violence Order,"*Boston Globe* August 2, 1997, p. B2

7. Scott Leigh "The Decadence of Privilege," *Boston Globe,* May 4, 1997, p. E1.

8. *Battered*. Narr. Lesley Stahl, prod. Kathleen Sciere, *60 Minutes*, CBS, WBZ. Boston, April 30, 1995.

9. Alison Bass, "The War on Domestic Abuse," *Boston Globe*, September 25, 1994, p. 1.

10. Ibid., p. 1.

11. Kathleen J. Ferraro, "Scales Tip Against Dangerous Defendants," *Boston Globe*, December 2, 1996, p. B8

12. Lisa A. Frisch, "Research That Succeeds, Policies That Fail," *Journal of Criminal Law and Criminology* 83, no. 1 (1992): 212.

13. Elizabeth Stanko, "Domestic Violence," *What Works in Policing: Operations and Administration Examined*, eds. Gary W. Corner and Donna C. Hales (Cincinnati: Anderson Publishing, 1992), p. 58.

14. Robert Trojanowicz and Bonnie Bucqueroux, *Community Policing: A Contemporary Perspective* (Cincinnati: Anderson Publishing, 1990), p. 182.

15. William D. Baker, "A New Approach to Domestic Violence," *FBI Law Enforcement Bulletin* 64, no. 9 (September 1995): 18.

16. Cardarelli and McDevitt, *Public Safety in Massachusetts*, p. 17-18.

17. Stanko, "Domestic Violence," p. 49.

18. Eve S. Buzawa and Carl G. Buzawa, "The Impact of Arrest on Domestic Violence," *American Behavioral Scientist* 36 (1993): 558-573.

19. Peter G. Jaffe et al., "The Impact of Police Laying Charges," in *Legal Responses to Wife Assault*, ed. N. Zoe Hilton (Newbury Park, Calif.: Sage Publications, 1993) , p. 68-69.

20. Kathleen J. Ferraro and Lucille Pope, "Irreconcilable Differences: Battered Women, Police, and the Law," in *Legal Responses to Wife Assault*, N. Zoe Hilton, ed. (Newbury Park, Calif.: Sage Publications, 1993), p. 112.

21. Buzawa and Buzawa, "The Impact of Arrest on Domestic Violence," p. 154.

22. Steven R. Dozinger, ed. *The Real War on Crime: The Report of the National Criminal Justice Commission* (New York: Harper Perennial, 1996), p. 183.

23. U.S. Attorney General's Task Force on Family Violence, *U.S. Department of Justice Final Report*, 1984, p. 22.

24. William M. Holmes et al., *Mandatory Arrest and Domestic Violence in Massachusetts* (Boston: Statistical Analysis Center, Massachusetts Committee on Criminal Justice, 1993), pp. 14-16.

25. Eve S. Buzawa and Thomas Austin, "Determining Police Response to Domestic Violence Victims: The Role of Victim Preference," *American Behavioral Scientist* 36 (1993): 618.

26. Jeffrey Fagan, *The Criminalization of Domestic Violence: Promises and Limits*, U.S. Department of Justice National Institute of Justice (January 1996), p. 9.

27. Ronald Roesch, Stephen D. Hart, and Laurene J. Wilson, "Future Prospects for Intervention and Evaluation," ed. N. Zoe Hilton, *Legal Responses to Wife Assault* (Newbury Park, Calif.: Sage Publications, 1993), p. 299.

28. Bass, "The War on Domestic Abuse," p. 1.

29. David B. Mitchell, "Contemporary Police Practices in Domestic Violence Cases: Arresting the Abuser: Is it Enough?" *Journal of Criminal Law and Criminology* 83, no. 1 (1992): 243.

30. Fagan, *The Criminalization of Domestic Violence*, p. 24.

31. Marilee Kenney Hunt, "A Call for Court Advocates." *Governor's Commission on Domestic Violence*, May 1994, p. 1-2.

32. John Grisham, *The Rainmaker* (New York: Doubleday, 1995), p. 173.

33. Bass, "The War on Domestic Abuse," p. 1.

34. *Commonwealth v. Andres W. Jacobsen,* 419 Mass. 269 (Barnstable, Mass., 1995).

35. *Battered.* Narr. Lesley Stahl. Prod. Kathleen Sciere. CBS *60 Minutes.* WBZ, Boston. 30 Apr 1995.

36. Donald Cochran, *The Tragedies of Domestic Violence: A Qualitative Analysis of Civil Restraining Orders in Massachusetts* (Boston: Office of the Commissioner of Probation Massachusetts Trail Court), October 12, 1995. Executive Summary.

37. *Hartzler v. City of San Jose,* 46 Cal. App. 3d 6, 120, Cal. Rptr. 5(1975).

38. John Ellement, "Police Union: Judge's Ruling Morally Wrong," *Boston Globe,* October 20, 1995, p. 29.

39. Cochran, *The Tragedies of Domestic Violence,* p. 15.

40. Peter Finn, "Civil Protection Orders: A Flawed Opportunity for Intervention," in Michael Steinman ed., *Women Battering: Policy Responses* (Cincinnati: Anderson Publishing, 1991), p. 1.

41. David J. Hirschel and Ira Hutchinson, "Police-Preferred Arrest Policies," *Woman Battering: Policy Responses* (Cincinnati: Anderson Publishing, 1991), p. 68.

42. Hunt, "A Call for Court Advocates," pp. 1-2.

43. Niel Jacobson and John Gottman, *When Men Batter Women* (New York: Simon & Schuster, 1998), 278.

7

Mandatory Arrest and Restraining Orders

To become properly acquainted with a truth we must first have disbelieved it, and disputed against it.

Otto von Bismarck (1815-1898)

It is said that for every complex problem there is a simple and elegant solution that is wrong. I believe that our public policymakers love easy solutions. "Indians on good land? Move 'em out. You want Texas? Start a war with Mexico. Crime problem? Bring back the death penalty. Prayer in schools will solve the moral lapse of the nation. Busing schoolchildren will end racial segregation."[1] Problems with domestic violence in our homes? Make a law that will forbid it. Those who have been abused and are afraid of the abuser? Make a law that states we will arrest the abuser and then promise the victim that we will protect her. Have you got any other problems you want us to solve?

Mandatory arrest and the use of civil restraining orders without proper criminal sanctions are assuredly flawed solutions for preventing the complex enigma of domestic violence. Americans have historically objected to the government's attempt to legislate what they consider their private morality or family problems. Prohibition was a colossal failure, and the government's policies concerning abortion appease almost no one. Only when arrest policies are coordinated with valid intensive probation, judicial sanctions for chronic abusers, and substantial and intensive community supervision by community domestic violence services coupled with early intervention educational programs in our schools will we begin to have progress.

The use of civil domestic violence abuse prevention orders, mandatory arrest of violators of those orders by police policy, and de facto mandatory arrest by preferred arrest policies for domestic violence often are most often not followed with proper criminal sanction by the courts.[2] In most of the states that have preferred arrest policies, because of the fear of lawsuits by police departments and the inability of nearly anyone to understand just what is meant by "preferred arrest," police departments often require their officers to arrest someone in almost all domestic violence incidents.

The Abuse Prevention Order, commonly referred to as a restraining order, attempts to prohibit an abuser from further abusing the victim of domestic violence by issuing a civil protection order that demands the abuser vacate the home, stay away from both the home and the plaintiff, and have no contact of any kind with the plaintiff or the plaintiff's children. Under current Massachusetts law, similar to many other laws nationwide, a police officer who has probable cause to believe that a criminal provision of a domestic abuse restraining order has been violated is *mandated* to arrest the abuser even though the act is a misdemeanor. The criminally enforceable provisions of restraining orders are only those sections to vacate, stay away, and too have no contact with the plaintiff or the plaintiff's children.

This mandated arrest provision is unique in that a police officer is provided with no discretion to determine whether or not to make an arrest. This impugns the tradition of victim preference and officer discretion to respond to the desire and concerns of the victim that has long been recognized and generally accepted as an important role in determining proper police action.[3] Mandatory arrest, and hence disregard of the victim's desire may also reinforce the belief of many women that the patriarchal institution of state government is still "Big Brother" and not "Big Sister." The law implies that women, at least some women, are incapable of making rational decisions on their own.

The only empirical scientific study to date that examines the complex but important relationship of mandatory arrest and domestic violence in Massachusetts concludes that, while arrest rates increased, the injury rates of victims and the number of domestic violence calls to police did not decrease. That same report proclaims: "The findings of Sherman and Berk in Minneapolis (1984) encouraged arrest in cases of domestic violence."[4] What the report does not announce is that the Minneapolis study *does not* encourage the arrest of all suspects of domestic violence incidents. The experiment contained cases in which police were *empowered* to make arrests. In the second paragraph, of the first page, Sherman and Berk determine that "It may be premature to conclude that arrest is always the best way for police to handle domestic violence, or that all suspects in such situations should be arrested. A number of factors suggest a cautious interpretation of the finding."

The Massachusetts study omits that Sherman and Berk do not prefer mandatory arrest laws. In fact, Professor Sherman has written that Massachusetts, by passing "mandatory arrest" laws for misdemeanor domestic violence violations, has not helped but rather has compounded the problem. Sherman's report is resolute in its finding that mandatory arrest laws are unwise and should be repealed.[5] Professor Berk is not as certain, yet he concludes, "A better policy than simple mandatory arrest for all offenders, regardless of risk category, would be to couple an arrest for high risk offenders with additional measure to protect victims."[6]

No study nationwide has produced any empirical scientific evidence that mandatory arrest laws have been effective in reducing the number of assaults and abuse calls.[7] Such calls to police departments, both in Massachusetts and nationwide, continue to increase. The Massachusetts Trial Court operates a Judicial Response System, a statewide emergency program designed, to assist law enforcement in resolving emergency legal situations by providing the services of a judge by phone when court is closed. In fiscal year 1985, 324 calls were placed; in fiscal year 1994, 14,878 calls were placed. Requests for restraining orders accounted for 13,374 of the total.[8]

After the Minneapolis study and with support from the National Institute of Justice, further studies were conducted in Omaha, Nebraska; Charlotte, North Carolina; Milwaukee, Wisconsin; Metro-Dade (Miami), Florida; and Colorado Springs, Colorado. A study in Atlanta, Georgia, was funded, but to date no results have been published. Interestingly, I placed many calls to the National Institute of Justice and could not locate anyone who knew anything about the Georgia project. When the findings of these studies (included in summary form in Appendix 1) were released, the results were mixed. In general, the studies showed that arrest by itself may not be the primary factor in modifying future violent behavior.[9] Those involved in the studies were not invited to appear on a series of television shows, as was Professor Sherman after the original Minneapolis study. *In fact, these studies seem to have been universally ignored by public policymakers, women, and victims' right advocates.* In an even more bewildering development, the results from most of these followup studies, which for the most part did not substantiate the outcome of the Minneapolis study, were vilified and criticized by the *very people* who enthusiastically supported the conclusions reached by the Minneapolis study.[10]

Some of these latest studies contain results that are complex but challenge the central premise that arrest works best in all domestic violence circumstances. Some of these most recent studies produced evidence that in some cases arrest would *increase* the frequency of future domestic violence.[11] In Milwaukee, Omaha, and Colorado Springs, results from the studies demonstrated that those who were unmarried or unemployed and were arrested because of domestic violence, became even more violent after the arrest. Among married and employed suspects, arrest did have a deterrent effect.[12] Arrest results vary from city to city and from individual to individual. A summary of these studies to date indicates the following,

- Arrest reduced domestic violence in some studies but increased it in others. Milwaukee, Charlotte, and Omaha produced evidence that arrest *increased violence* in some cases. Colorado Springs and Metro-Dade reported that the risk of further violence was reduced.
- Arrest reduces domestic violence among employed people but increases it among unemployed people who often believe they have nothing to lose.
- Arrest reduces domestic violence in the short run but escalates violence later in older and distressed urban cities.

- A small but chronic portion of all violent couples produces the majority of domestic violence incidents.
- Many offenders who flee before police arrive are substantially deterred from future violence by warrants for their arrest.
- Police, because of prior calls for service, can determine which couples are most likely to suffer future violence.

These results suggest that arrest alone is not consistently the correct course of action.[13] All intervention cannot and should not be by mandatory arrest policies or civil restraining order. In these studies, the majority of those arrested were released within a few hours, and only a small number were held overnight. The legal sanctions were limited to the arrest process.[14] For sanctions to be effective, some sure, equitable and swift discipline or punishment must come from the actions of prosecutors and judges whose job is supposed to mete out sanctions when and if the abuser is found guilty.

Results from a study released in January 1991 reveal that almost half of the female victims who reported they were victims of intimate violence said that violence was a private or personal matter and they did not report it to the police.[15] Schools, separate treatment programs for both perpetrator and victim, shelters, and other community intervention and education may better assist some of these perpetrators, particularly those who are not chronic criminal offenders, and many of the victims.[16]

I have found no studies or data to provide any credible reason for mandatory arrest policies, particularly without proper sanctions anywhere in the criminal justice system. Logic alone should lead us to conclude that, if mandatory arrest policies deterred criminal behavior, the same policies would be used in drunk driving, drug interdiction, and child abuse. Some of these crimes include mandatory sentencing policies but not mandatory arrest policies. "The logical and empirical links between knowledge of the law and sanctions, arrest, consequences of an arrest, and alteration of future behavior have never been adequately presented."[17]

Nowhere is there a carefully documented, well-organized, original, and convincing body of evidence that mandatory arrest has caused any change in criminal behavior.[18] "There is little conclusive evidence of either deterrent or protective effects of legal sanctions or treatment interventions for domestic violence.[19] The conclusion I have reached, along with many others I have worked with in the criminal justice system, is that these procedures are just highly visible, inexpensive attempts by public policymakers to persuade women's and victims' rights advocates and battered women's groups that they, the public policymakers, are doing *something/anything* to combat domestic violence.

The police and court logs that are printed in many of this nation's daily and weekly newspapers can provide a carefully documented, well-organized, original, and convincing body of evidence that much of our current domestic violence policy remains as follows: "have the police arrest the abuser, have the court system let them go." What we are left with is the familiar refrain of "arrest them, let them go, arrest them, let them go". That is the only real *something/anything* that public policymakers have given us to combat domestic violence.

Many public policymakers and some practitioners in the criminal justice system believe that women will be safer once they have been separated from their abuser. The truth is that, in Massachusetts, mandatory arrest policy or not, the abuser is most often legally separated from the victim for only a matter of hours when arrested by the police. Quite frequently, there is evidence[20] that the violence inflicted after separation of the couple can be substantial,[21] in fact, in certain circumstances violence may even escalate.[22] It is a fact that, "75 percent of spousal murders happen after the women leaves."[23]

Even though no major study has been done on the effectiveness of civil protection orders concerning their effect in reducing spousal domestic violence[24] and there is a complete absence of any scientific empirical data on the efficacy of these orders,[25] they are now available in fifty states. Both Peter Finn and Sarah Colson are aware of the lack of any credible or convincing evidence that demonstrated that restraining orders could effect violence recidivism[26] when they wrote that "Properly used and enforced, protection orders can help prevent specific behaviors such as harassment or threats which could lead to future violence. They also can help provide a safe location for the victim, if necessary, by barring or evicting an offender from the household, and establish safe conditions for any future interactions, for supervised child visitation (Finn and Colson, 1990, p. 10).

A restraining order may be effective to deter the rational, reasonable, and stable person who is not likely to and has no history of acting out in a violent manner. If a person is rational, reasonable, and stable there should be little real need of a restraining order. With this segment of the population and properly implemented, restraining orders may prove to be effective. This is not, however, the person that law enforcement frequently has as a client.

Other than the eviction process, which is almost always accomplished with the aid of the police, Finn and Colson readily concede that they know of no scholarly apparatus, scientific study, or empirical data showing any evidence of what they conclude will be or has been accomplished. This lack of scientific study or empirical evidence did not stop Finn and Colson from being confident about achieving the proper results. Am I missing something here?

If empirical data from the National Institute of Justice studies demonstrate that the issuance of these orders in Massachusetts and elsewhere can *encourage rather than deter acts of violence,* as some of the studies have demonstrated, who will take responsibility for precipitating the violent actions of the abuser because of the issuance of the order? Are we to continue believe that it is always better to do something rather than nothing? Am I wrong to question the wisdom of issuing a domestic violence protection order if there is data that under certain circumstances the issuance of a domestic violence protection order may actually be the catalyst of further violence?[27]

REEXAMINATION

Many advocates believe that Massachusetts does not have a coordinated, accountable statewide system that provides the support and safety planning necessary for abuse victims receiving civil protective orders.[28] Most advocates agree and data continues to demonstrate that enormous discrepancies exist in the way individual courts and district attorneys respond to violations of restraining orders.[29] No one can dispute that restraining orders are being issued in ever-increasing numbers in Massachusetts. The numbers speak for themselves. From September 1992 to September of 1995, the state commissioner of Probation Registry of Civil Restraining orders summary lists the issuance of 145,263 orders from both civil and criminal courts.

Data demonstrates that few abusers are convicted and imprisoned for any length of time.[30] In the Minneapolis, study only 37 of the 802 arrests had initial charges filed, and only 11 convictions resulted (1%), this despite the fact that victims went to meet with prosecutors in half the arrest cases.[31]

In 1994, the Brockton District Court made 327 dispositions for violation of restraining orders. The court dismissed 202 of the violators, 112 were found guilty, 9 not guilty, and 4 were transferred to other courts. Of the guilty dispositions, only 37 were placed in jail, 21 were placed on probation, 18 received suspended sentences, 13 were placed in programs, and 23 were continued without a finding.

In 1994, the Brockton District Court made 713 dispositions for the misdemeanor crime of simple assault and battery. The court dismissed 523 of the violators and found 172 were found guilty, 14 not guilty, and 4 were transferred to other courts. Of the guilty dispositions, only 58 were placed in jail, 22 were placed on probation, 28 received suspended sentences, 10 were placed in programs, and 54 were continued without a finding. These dispositions reflect the Brockton Police Department increased the number of domestic violence arrests because of mandatory arrest laws. The courts continue to treat the violations of the restraining order as a simple misdemeanor that is not much different from simple assault and battery. In deference to the courts, the crime of violating a restraining order *remains a simple misdemeanor* no different from that of the simple assault and battery in Massachusetts and most other states.

The Brockton Police Department made 897 arrests in 1994 for various criminal charges in a domestic violence venue. Some experts believe that most police officers now take the crime of domestic violence as a serious matter while the courts continue to treat these matters as simple misdemeanors. If there continues to be few serious dispositions for these arrests, some officers are likely to resist making arrests or at the very least to question the logic of such a policy.[32] The majority of professionals in the criminal justice system know that defendants must be swiftly and surely held accountable by proper sanctions for their criminal acts. The majority of professionals in the criminal justice system know that this rarely occurs.

Based on my twenty-one years of experience I do not believe that police officers will go it alone for very much longer. Most police officers I have worked with, contrary to popular belief, do care about domestic violence, particularly when they see its effect on children. The "lock them up and let them go" process, however, will do a lot to speed up the burnout many police officers experience in their careers. In Massachusetts, fewer abusers are being placed in counseling programs today than a few years ago. David Adams, director of EMERGE, the first counseling program in the state, continues to have fewer placements from the courts than he had a few years ago.[33]

A two-year study by Andrew Klein, chief probation officer of Quincy District Court, suggests that civil intervention, especially largely unenforced civil intervention, will not deter repeat criminal activity among men who display a pattern of chronic domestic abuse.[34] "Grau, Fagan, and Wexler (1984) found no significant differences in subsequent abuse between women receiving restraining orders and women receiving other interventions. Moreover, they reported that subsequent violence was more likely among men with histories of severe domestic violence or prior records of stranger crime."[35] In a study of stalking cases sponsored by the San Diego District Attorney's Office, almost half of the victims who received restraining orders reported that they, "felt their cases were worsened by them."[36]

Like the blind men holding on to different parts of the elephant, advocates of civil restraining orders often disagree on the purpose of the order. Few, if any, who are concerned with domestic violence will dispute the fact that restraining orders were originally created to protect women who were being battered by their husbands or boyfriends and wanted help from the criminal justice system. Few, if any, who are concerned with domestic violence can look you in the eye and tell you that these civil protection orders really do provide the protection they promise. Dr. Susan Cayouette, clinical director of the Emerge battering treatment program has said that "Getting a restraining order or a divorce can give a woman a false sense of security: if a man is determined to find her and hurt her, it's pretty hard to prevent that."[37]

The accounts below are from the log of the fifteen calls received by a Massachusetts judge during just one twelve-hour shift of the statewide emergency Judicial Response System. The Judicial Response System provides emergency judicial assistance 365 days a year, 24 hours a day, when court is not in session.

5:00AM Restraining order issued for a wife whose ex-husband broke into her apartment and raped her: victim required hospitalization.

12:45PM Restraining order issued for a woman whose estranged husband had stalked her and left messages on her answering machine threatening to cut her into little pieces.

1:45PM Restraining order issued for woman whose boyfriend was drunk and had assaulted her.

2:40PM Restraining order issued for mother of two children who was punched in the mouth with closed fist by boyfriend because she wouldn't give him money for more beer.

3:20PM Restraining order issued for young woman who was dragged out of her car by boyfriend and banged against the hood until she lost consciousness because he said he couldn't live without her.

3:45PM Restraining order issued for elderly woman who was verbally abused by alcoholic husband who had trashed their home.

4:30PM Restraining order issued for a young woman who had been hit in the head with a shovel by boyfriend and was being treated at the hospital.

5:10PM Restraining order issued for mother of three children whose estranged husband threatened to kill her if she was with another man.

6:00PM Restraining order issued for young woman whose ex-boyfriend broke into her apartment and choked her until she passed out.

8:00PM Restraining order issued for mother who was assaulted by her daughter, a drug abuser trying to obtain money for drugs.

8:15PM Restraining order issued for mentally disabled mother who was attacked by her daughter.

8:30PM Restraining order issued for man whose former girlfriend had broken windows in his truck and threatened him over the telephone.

9:35PM Restraining order issued for young woman who was hospitalized with a fractured skull after being kicked repeatedly in the head by a former boyfriend.

9:50PM Restraining order issued for mother of two children whose estranged husband broke into her house and repeatedly punched her in the face in front of the children.

9:55PM Restraining order issued for young woman whose ex-boyfriend had rammed his car into her car, dragged her out of her car, and kicked her in the stomach.

These desperate calls for help represent only one night and just a few of the 13,374 calls concerning domestic abuse in the period July 1992 to July 1993.[38] To those who believe that domestic violence is a fifty-fifty deal between men and women, I would suggest that they review these records and then tell me where I've gone wrong. These records are not surveys or statistics; they are the real deal.

In 1994, the Administrative Office of the Trial Court and the Office of the Commissioner of Probation conducted a study to determine how many of these orders are followed up in court during the next few days and what is the profile of the defendants in these cases. Within two court days 97 percent were followed up with further court action. The most disturbing result is that only 35 percent of these defendants would have a criminal charge filed against them. Almost two-thirds of the perpetrators of these crimes would never receive any criminal sanctions for their abusive behavior that was brought to the attention of the judicial system.[39] Read the fifteen log items again and try to determine which ten of these perpetrators deserve to be let off with no sanctions from the criminal justice system. Why is it that, once the criminal justice system is aware that someone has their skull fractured, or arm broken, or has been hit in the head with a shovel, or raped, the system is allowed to condone those actions by ignoring them? Ten of those perpetrators committed *crimes against women and children,* and the criminal justice system did nothing to bring the perpetrator to task. Carol Arnett, the executive director of the Los Angeles County Domestic Violence Council says, ". . .shelter workers have watched the criminal justice system fail to protect, and often even endanger women for so many years that we are very cautious about recommending restraining orders."[40]

It seems that the criminal justice system, because of the specificity and rigidity of inflexible rules, often has abandoned its moral and ethical responsibilities for the victims of domestic violence and their children. In Lawrence, Massachusetts, a couple was charged criminally for leaving their dog unattended in a parked car on a hot day. In that same car, also left unattended, were two children ages 4 and 5. The couple *was not* charged for leaving the children unattended. A spokesperson for the Essex County district attorney said, "Clearly this is a gap in the law, but as far as we know, child neglect is a civil matter that we don't get involved with."[41] This spokesperson knows that by following the letter of the law he or she can avoid any personal responsibility or accountability. The capability of "passing the buck" has become a rite of passage in the world of the criminal or civil justice system. An avalanche of institutionalized, procedural, and bureaucratic protocol has desensitized the reasonable and prudent person, once the bedrock of our judicial system.

The courts should and most often do know that in the majority of domestic violence instances the plaintiff of the restraining order has a history of being abused and that children are involved. The courts should know and most often do know that in the majority of instances the plaintiff of the restraining order is looking for help. In their affidavit, almost 50 percent of the victims describe being hit. One in every four plaintiffs describes the defendant's causing property damage. Over 50 percent of the victims in the affidavit report being threatened. From the profile of most of the defendants, they are generally no strangers to courtrooms. Over 70 percent have previous court arraignments for criminal activity, and almost half have a prior criminal history of a violent offense against a person.[42] Yet the civil and criminal justice system allows more than one-third of the orders issued during a routine court business day to be closed within fifteen days, with no further response from the criminal justice system other than a lot of paperwork by a lot of people with little sense of accomplishment. Lawrence W. Sherman suggests that restraining orders may be a cruel hoax on the victims. He also states that, "Until such rigorous testing is done, perhaps police should be required to advise victims that the orders may have quite limited practical value."[43] Police officers may not be criminologists or social scientists but they understand very early in their career that criminal laws can act as a deterrent on the general populace, but for those who have a history of arrest and criminal behavior most law have little to no affect in altering their behavior.

How long must behaviors similar to those listed above be allowed to continue before the public policymakers and women's rights advocates realize that their current strategies of preventing domestic violence are not working? A forceful police response to domestic violence will not work without a commitment to prosecution and without more sure and swift sentencing practices where warranted as well as laws with teeth in them. How about mandatory sentences for all second and subsequent offenses? These sanctions must be coupled with supportive and therapeutic services for both the perpetrator and the victim to deter reoccurrence.

Studies reveal that women in Massachusetts are in danger of abuse either if they stay with their abuser or if they leave them. They are in danger whether or not they take out a restraining order.[44] Civil restraining orders, most without sanctions, that are issued approximately every two minutes by courts in Massachusetts rain down upon the criminal justice system like confetti at a parade. More than one out of every three orders issued or more specifically, *37 percent* of those orders will be *canceled fifteen days later.*[45] The criminal justice system will take no action on more than one out of every three orders issued. Often, nothing is done in those instances where women have been beaten and children terrified. There will be no change in the behavior of the abuser if there are no sanctions associated with their aberrant behavior. Little of these current reactive policies shield or protect the 43,000 children who witness this violent behavior.[46] In homes where domestic violence occurs, children are abused at a rate 1,500 percent higher than the national average.[47]

I believe that criminal restraining orders with sure and swift sanctions, such as intensive probation or incarceration for chronic offenders, could provide some effective short-term protection that many victims need to restructure their lives. These criminal restraining orders should be issued for spousal abuse only when there is probable cause to believe that a crime has been committed. Although the original intent of restraining orders was to prevent women from being abused I believe that anyone who lives in a conjugal styled relationship should be included. A violation of this order should be a felony and a second or subsequent violations of the order should include a mandatory sanction.

The long-term effects of legal sanctions as a deterrent for domestic violence abusers are still not understood.[48] "We simply do not know what the effects of legal sanctions for domestic violence are. . . "[49] A study done by the U.S. Department of Justice reports, "given the prevalence of women with children who utilize restraining orders, their general ineffectiveness in curbing subsequent violence may leave a good number of children at risk of either witnessing violence or becoming victims themselves."[50] Why do we continue, full steam ahead when we know there are icebergs in the water?

Mandatory arrest without sure, equitable, and swift sanctions and the use of civil restraining orders with few if any criminal sanctions will continue to occasion ineffectual impact on the behavior of those involved.[51] Given the history of the incapacity of our criminal justice system to curb violence I can find no historical evidence that it can produce the demise or even a decline of domestic violence. While most crimes are declining, aggravated assaults involving domestic violence continue to rise unabated.[52] Violence within the family remains a crime that is culturally relative. If we begin behavioral modification role modeling by allowing mothers and fathers to spank their children "for their own good" where do we end?

There is simply no empirical evidence that either civil restraining orders or mandatory arrest policies with little sanctions by the courts have or can fulfill what public policymakers have promised.[53] "The case must be issued, tried, and the defendant convicted of a crime if the criminal justice system is to fulfill its short term responsibilities to the victim."[54] We must remove the relatively small number of chronic violent offenders from the homes and the streets. If these abusers do not want to change their behavior then it is up to society to provide change for them. Incapacitation for the small number of chronically violent offenders is the best short term solution.

If it is the purpose of deterrence to let potential offenders know that those who break the law will swiftly and surely be punished, there is no question that we have failed. I know of no one in our contemporary criminal justice system that genuinely believes that domestic violence offenders or any other offenders are swiftly, surely, and equitably punished. Solving the problem of domestic violence cannot be accomplished through makeshift measures. What we need is a thorough reform of the criminal justice system and we must create a single unifying philosophy of sanctions as well as educational programs. What is the purpose of the criminal justice system for domestic violence abusers; retribution, deterrence, rehabilitation, or incapacitation? Do we have an amicable and unified criminal justice *system* that can provide any of the above?

Appendix 1 provides a summary of the major studies funded by the National Institute of Justice. The majority of these studies *do not* provide any data that attests that restraining orders or mandatory arrest should be the preferred police response to domestic violence. Some of these studies demonstrate that the mandatory arrest policies sought by many domestic violence advocates may in the long run *increase* the abuse suffered by some victims. I believe that the body of research to date demonstrates that data is insufficient to determine proper policy choices for all agencies involved in domestic violence intervention. I beseech those who continue to be concerned with emphasizing police policies and intervention to read these studies. The majority of feminists and other advocates for victims of domestic violence that I have met over the last few years continue to claim, some in writing, that the first of National Institute of Justice studies, the Minneapolis study urged mandatory arrest of all abusers by police. The study *never urged arrest in all domestic disputes as a police policy* by rather urged officers be *empowered* to arrest. How so many people can remain so confused about such a consequential and significant fact continues to mystify me.

To date there are no National Institute of Justice studies the can demonstrate that the use of civil restraining orders has or can reduce domestic violence abuse. This is not to deny that under certain circumstances some victims of domestic abuse may find civil restraining orders or mandatory arrest helpful. This is also not to deny that under certain circumstances some victims of domestic abuse may find civil restraining orders or mandatory arrest harmful.

NOTES

1. Kenneth C. Davis, *Don't Know Much About History* (New York: Avon, 1990), p. 255.

2. Jeffrey Fagan, *The Criminalization of Domestic: Violence Promises and Limits.* U.S. Department of Justice, National Institute of Justice (January 1996), p. 15.

3. Eve S. Buzawa and Thomas Austin, "Determining Police Response to Domestic Violence Victims: The Role of Victim Preference," *American Behavioral Scientist* 36 (1993): 621.

4. William M. Holmes, *Mandatory Arrest and Domestic Violence in Massachusetts* (Boston: Statistical Analysis Center Massachusetts Committee on Criminal Justice, 1993), p. 1.

5. Lawrence W. Sherman, *Policing Domestic Violence: Experiments and Dilemmas* (New York: Free Press, 1992), p. 22.

6. Richard A. Berk et al., "A Bayesian Analysis of the Colorado Springs Spouse Abuse Experiment," *Journal of Criminal Law and Criminology* 83, no. 1 (Spring 1992): 199.

7. Peter K. Manning, "The Preventive Conceit," *American Behavioral Scientist* 36, no. 5 (1993): 641.

8. *Judicial Response System*, Commonwealth of Massachusetts Administrative Office of the Trial Court (October 1994), p. 3.

9. Eve S. Buzawa and Carl G. Buzawa, "The Impact of Arrest on Domestic Violence," *American Behavioral Scientist* 36, no. 5 (1993): 569.

10. Richard J. Gelles, "Constraints Against Family Violence," *American Behavioral Scientist* 36, no. 5 (1993): 575-586.

11. Berk et al., "A Bayesian Analysis of the Colorado Springs Spouse Abuse Experiment," p. 198.

12. Janell D. Schmidt and Lawrence W. Sherman, "Does Arrest Deter Domestic Violence?" *American Behavioral Scientist* 36 (1993): 601-609.

13. Ibid., p. 606.

14. Fagan, *The Criminalization of Domestic Violence*, p. 15.

15. Caroline W. Harlow, *The Female Victims of Violent Crime.* Washington, D.C.: Bureau of Justice Statistics (January 1991), p. 3.

16. Robert T. Sigler and David Lamb, "Community-Based Alternatives to Prison: How the Public and Court Personnel View Them," *Federal Probation,* June 1995: 3-9.

17. Manning, "The Preventive Conceit," p. 86.

18. Sigler and Lamb, "Community-Based Alternatives to Prison," p. 3.

19. Fagan, *The Criminalization of Domestic Violence*, p. 25.

20. Andrew R. Klein, *Spousal/Partner Assault: A Protocol for the Sentencing and Supervision of Offenders* (Swampscott, Mass.: Production Specialties, 1993), p. 9.

21. Sherman, *Policing Domestic Violence*, p. 169.

22. Barbara Hart, "Battered Women and the Criminal Justice System," *American Behavioral Scientist* 36, no. 5 (1993): 626.

23. Gavin DeBecker, *The Gift of Fear* (Boston: Little, Brown and Company, 1997), p. 184.

24. Fagan, *The Criminalization of Domestic Violence*, p. 24.

25. Buzawa and Buzawa, *Domestic Violence: The Criminal Justice Response* (Newbury Park, Calif.: Sage, 1990), p. 119.

26. Janice Grau, Jeffrey Fagan, and Sandra Wexler, "Restraining Orders for Battered Women: Issues of Access and Efficacy," *Women and Politics* 4 (1984): 13-18.

27. Sherman, *Policing Domestic Violence*, pp. 170-171.

28. Marilee Kenney Hunt, "A Call for Court Advocates," *Governor's Commission on Domestic Violence* 1, no. 2 (1994): 1-2.

29. Fagan, *The Criminalization of Domestic Violence*, pp. 15-18.

30. Donald Cochran, *The Tragedies of Domestic Violence: A Qualitative Analysis of Civil Restraining Orders in Massachusetts* (Boston: Office of the Commissioner of Probation Massachusetts Trail Court, October 12, 1995) p. 17.

31. Sherman, *Policing Domestic Violence*, p. 347.

32. David J. Hirschel and Ira Hutchinson, "Police-Preferred Arrest Policies," *Women Battering: Policy Responses* (Cincinnati: Anderson, 1991), p. 67.

33. Alison Bass, "The War on Domestic Abuse," *Boston Globe*, September 25, 1994, p. 1.

34. Andrew R. Klein, "Re-Abuse in a Population of Court-Restrained Male Batterers: Why Restraining Orders Don't Work," in Eve S. Buzawa and Carl G Buzawa eds., *Do Arrests and Restraining Orders Work?* (Thousand Oaks, Calif.: Sage Publications, 1996), p. 211.

35. Fagan, *The Criminalization of Domestic Violence*, p. 25.

36. DeBecker, *The Gift of Fear*, p. 187.

37. Alison Bass, "The War on Domestic Abuse," *Boston Globe*, September 25, 1994, p. 1.

38. Donald Cochran, *Project History of the Massachusetts Statewide Automated Restraining Order Registry,* Massachusetts Trial Court Office of the Commissioner of Probation, 1994, p. 22.

39. *Judicial Response System,* Commonwealth of Massachusetts Administrative Office of the Trial Court, October 1994, p. 6.

40. DeBecker, *The Gift of Fear*, p. 189.

41. Caroline Louise Cole, "After Pair's Arrest, DA Says Neglect Law Covers Pet, Not Kids," *Boston Globe,* May 24, 1995, p. 28.

42. Cochran, *The Tragedies of Domestic Violence,* Executive Summary.

43. Sherman, *Policing Domestic Violence*, pp. 242-243.

44. Klein, *Spousal/Partner Assault,* p. 9.

45. Cochran, *The Tragedies of Domestic Violence,* Executive Summary.

46. Ibid.

47. Otto Johnson, ed. *1996 Information Please Almanac* (Boston: Houghton Mifflin Co, 1996), p. 430.

48. Fagan, *The Criminalization of Domestic Violence*, p. 30.

49. Ibid., p. 40.

50. DeBecker, *The Gift of Fear*, p. 187.

51. Manning, "The Preventive Conceit," p. 648.

52. Massachusetts State Police Crime Reporting Unit, *Massachusetts Crime Index.-1960/1993* (December 1994), p. 7.

53. Sherman, *Policing Domestic Violence*, p. 238.

54. Harvey Wallace, *Family Violence: Legal, Medical, and Social Perspectives* (Boston: Allyn & Bacon, 1996), p. 212.

8

A Domestic Violence Prototype: Teaching, Enforcement, and Mediation

Skill to do comes of doing.
Ralph Waldo Emerson (1803-1882)

The National Institute of Justice experiments produced diverse results. The one reassuring conclusion for the criminal justice system is that all six experiments determined that *a small share of violent couples produces the majority of habitual domestic violence incidents.*[1] The criminal justice system cannot prevent domestic violence.[2] However, it can anticipate which couples are most likely to suffer future violence.[3] The most effective criminal justice policy is one that will identify repeat offenders and will address those locations that generate repeat domestic violence calls. The criminal justice system could then ensure that the perpetrator encounters sure and swift sanctions or proper program placements and that victims receive assistance by fast-tracking these cases.

This policy must be linked with a procedure that establishes a protocol for interagency cooperation. Special emphasis must be placed on a communitywide response through cooperation among law enforcement, prosecutors, the judiciary, battered women's shelters, outreach programs, and neighborhood watch groups.

The city of Boston has recently received national attention for its extraordinary success in reducing firearm violence among youth. By the beginning of 1997, Boston had achieved a violent crime rate level that had not been seen since the 1960s. No juvenile has been killed with a firearm in Boston since July 1995. The city of Boston has a comprehensive strategy of prevention, intervention, and enforcement. Through partnerships and alliances with all individuals and organizations who work collaboratively rather than competitively and executing a multistrategy approach crime is down to its lowest level in twenty-six years.[4]

In 1988, Massachusetts launched a program called *Saving Lives* in six communities. Involved in the pilot programs were schools, colleges, police, citizens, and local government executing a multistrategy approach. The program's goal was to reduce drunken driving and its related problems. The result was 42 percent fewer alcohol-related fatal crashes in Saving Lives cities than in the rest of the state.[5]

Education and prevention instruction concerning domestic violence must begin in the schools with K-12 training and be continued by colleges, police, citizens, and local government executing a multistrategy approach that addresses prevention, education, intervention, and corrections. It is important that these agencies consider such variables as gender differences, socioeconomic conditions, employment status, and racial and ethnic factors.

The city of Brockton, Massachusetts, with a Federal census of 92,788 residents in 1990, is a microcosm of many of this nation's older cities. The city has not escaped the national dilemma of domestic violence. The census demonstrates that Brockton's population experienced one of the greatest racial transformations of any city in Massachusetts. The city's overall population fell from 95,172 to 92,788. The white population decreased from 87,422 to 74,499, while the African-American and Hispanic populations more than doubled. The number of African-Americans increased from 4,929 to 12,028 and Hispanics from 2,142 to 5,860. There is also a population of legal and illegal immigrants, many from Haiti and Cape Verde. Community leaders of each of these groups claim to have a population of about 10,000. City officials estimate the population to be between 2,000 and 8,000 for each group. This multicultural, multiethnic population has created for the Brockton Police Department what criminologist Lawrence Sherman calls "The Different Folks Dilemma."[6] In summary, the dilemma is that "*the equal treatment of mandatory arrest does produce unequal results.*"[7] The approach must be "different strokes for different folks."

A HOLISTIC APPROACH

Early in 1997, the Brockton Police Department in concert with the Brockton Family and Community Resources Domestic Violence Action Program developed a task force approach to domestic violence. An explicitly trained, domestic violence team consisting of a Brockton police sergeant and a multilingual civilian domestic violence advocate will provide the linkage for this collaborative procedure. The Brockton Police Department does not intend to establish a program or to place responsibility for responding to domestic violence on a single individual or specific division. The individual responsibility process will develop an "It's not my job mentality" for those who are not expressly involved in the process. The danger of having a "Domestic Violence

Unit" is that members of the organization will believe that domestic violence is the sole responsibility of that specialized unit.

The Teaching, Education, and Mediation *(TEaM)* not only involves the *whole department* in this new organizational principle and philosophy, but also *integrates all other agencies* in the community that will build a greater sense of trust and acceptability between the community and the criminal justice system. The Brockton Police Department recognizes that as more social responsibilities are placed on its officers, this greater sense of accountability will often be accompanied by greater frustration, which is often the result of the officers' realization that they are not able to solve or interpret complex social problems. The *TEaM* must assure the officers that they are not alone and that others in the community do share accountability. A cohesive communitywide task force approach must ensure that community agencies and service providers will work together with the police and respond in an integrative manner. Officers repeatedly spend time interviewing adult witnesses, collecting evidence, filing incident reports, and making arrests only to find that, too often, that is the end of the process.

The *TEaM* must ensure opportunities for all agencies to spend time with police officers in police cruisers, in the police station, and, most importantly in the streets and homes of the community. The job of a police officer is hard to describe and even harder to comprehend. There is nothing more unrealistic than TV and movie versions of a cop's job. It is like the game of baseball. You cannot watch a baseball game to understand how to hit the ball; rather you have to play the game to appreciate the difficulty of the task. The officers must be afforded the time to be with other agency members in their environment. This will expand the ways in which both officers and other agency members view each other.

The *TEaM* will be housed at the Brockton police station and will review police reports detailing domestic violence calls. It will provide information, safety planning, options, and referrals to victims and participate in education and prevention forums throughout the city. Accomplishing these goals and objectives involves three major components:

1. To use a police sergeant and a multilingual civilian domestic violence advocate to coordinate a communitywide task force. The task force will consist of agencies, departments, and groups, including health professionals, school personnel, battered women's advocates, shelter personnel, the media, business, court personnel, mental health professionals, law enforcement, probation/parole, neighborhood watch members, members of the Brockton Community Policing Leadership Council, the District Attorney's Office, and representatives from the various cultural and linguistic minority groups. Jointly, they can assess the needs of the community and evaluate the efficacy of services that are already in place. The duty of the two-person *TEaM* is to insure that the communitywide task force will work closely with the police department to develop a systems approach that includes all aspects of the community.

2. To provide educational instruction in grades K-12. The *TEaM* will have the responsibility to "train the trainers" within the school department and address domestic violence issues in the classroom. This will be accomplished through a series of seminars and public speaking engagements aimed at education administrators, teachers, guidance counselors, and community groups. The teams will educate school personnel about the warning signs of dating violence and how they should respond to it. They will provide the teachers with the areas of resources for the victims and abusers. They will help the school develop a policy that will protect the safety of students or staff who disclose abusive situations. They will help incorporate preventive education into the school's health education program. They will train teachers in how to organize peer education and support programs. They will inform teachers about the warning signs and about community resources for abused or abusive students.

The *TEaM* will not use the prevalent educational format that emphasizes a teacher-directed process but will employ a collateral teaching-learning model. Training will be primarily learner and problem centered. Too many of these children will be familiar with violence within their homes. The focal point of training in grades K-6 will be conflict resolution and mediation. Grades 7-12 will emphasize preventing teen dating violence. All grades will be given the clear message that violence and harassment are antisocial behavior and will not be tolerated.

The *TEaM* will assist in developing a violence prevention plan that includes input from staff, parents, and students. Training will be presented in violence prevention skills, and information will be furnished on making safer choices both in school and at home. Each will emphasize equity of gender and respectful relationships as a partial resolution of the problem of domestic violence.

3. To provide training for police officers that is not classroom structured. Specific classroom and roll-call training for police officers relative to domestic violence is important and will continue. Emphasis will be placed on the first-line supervisors--sergeants--for their most important responsibility is the training of their subordinates. In any learning process, the learner should be motivated, and the first-line supervisors should be held accountable for motivating their subordinates. It is understandable that the *TEaM* will not always be able to change long-standing attitudes, and so it remains the responsibility of the first line supervisors to change long-standing behavior.

The *TEaM* will initiate field-training procedures as the paramount form of instruction. Indeed, field training may be the most crucial element in changing the culture within the police department. This "on-the-job" training tends to outweigh whatever officers learn in the academy and later during in-service training.[8] In the field training experience, the officers will be provided with individualized learning experience. This training will be used to establish acceptable police behavior and to ensure compliance with department procedures during a domestic violence call. When the training and learning experience is both visual and hands on, it can potentially increase the officers understanding and acceptance.

Training will be accommodated to develop skills in the individual officers that will provide expected and productive action. Too often classroom training anticipates the same results from all learners and in the same amount of time. Classroom training expects that the individual officer will learn in the same way and does not allow for the differences of officers' abilities and learning skills. Learning is improved when officers are allowed to understand the results of their efforts and when they receive accurate feedback about the progress that has been achieved because of their efforts. The officers must be allowed to use their experience, expertise, and particular ability to add to the learning procedure. Adults learn best when they feel the need to learn and when they have a sense of responsibility for what, why, and how they learn.[9] This teaching/learning effort can be used to motivate each officer to participate actively in the training. The officers will be more receptive to learning if they are included in the procedure, and gratification is often achieved from the learning process when the officers have been provided with every opportunity possible to participate.[10]

It will be the responsibility of the *TEaM* to influence the officers' desire to learn by demonstrating to the officers that this training is germane to their personal and professional needs and goals. Police officers learn best through an informal setting in their normal work environment and when the training provides them with a skill or knowledge that is relevant and allows them to perform their job more efficiently and provides results more effectively.

The *TEaM* will provide monitoring on the streets during work hours as the officers respond to calls for service. This monitoring process is most important, for it will provide the *TEaM* with the ability to adjust the methods of instruction and materials to meet the needs of the officers. The officers should be assured that the *TEaM* is there not to supervise but to be a helpful resource. The *TEaM* may lead the officers towards the proper solution, but the purpose of this training is to allow the officer to learn how to solve the problem. The monitoring will include:

- The early detection and correction of performance problems, as well as the detection of opportunities for performance improvement, including investigation, report writing, and victim safety at the scene.
- The mobilization of widespread commitment to continuous improvement in performance.
- More efficient uses of other community support resources.
- It is expected that the goals, objectives, and outcome of this learning/monitoring process will be both measurable and observable and should include the following:
- The victims of domestic violence will be assisted with developing personal safety plans and will receive support services and options for continued recovery and safety from the appropriate agency of the communitywide task force.
- Every police officer of the Brockton Police Department will be available to respond to a domestic violence call with the aptitude to gather specific pertinent information to assist with the prosecution of perpetrators.
- Arrest of domestic violence perpetrators should result in swift and sure sanctions: incarceration, probation, or treatment programs monitored by the court.
- Education of children in K-12 should result in the decrease of domestic violence in the home and the individual safety of children during domestic disputes.

- The community will take responsibility by responding effectively to end domestic violence. Neighborhood Watch members will be trained in current laws and will be provided with appropriate material to disseminate to neighbors. This information will demonstrate that there are ways to help victims of domestic violence. This will send a message that neighbors do care and will provide help when needed.
- While most police departments acknowledge the importance of outreach, when it is time for implementation of new programs, too often they ignore opportunities to include the entire community in the planning activity. Not only is the community's input constructive, but this inclusion will provide a means of access to forging new and more open alliances between the citizens and community agencies. All voices must be heard and their input incorporated.

This demonstration of action will be accomplished through the collaboration of schools, media, health organizations, business, police, courts, the fire department, battered women's programs, mental health agencies, and neighborhood watch programs. The community is the fabric, and the *TEaM* will act as the tool to weave everyone together and ensure that tasks are completed on schedule.

Rigorously evaluating implementation efforts, identifying reasons for implementation successes and shortfalls, and then using the results of the analysis to refine action plans and communication strategies will provide a framework for continuous improvement that will support effective efforts on a yearly basis.

Victims of domestic violence will be given an anonymous questionnaire to complete and return by preaddressed, stamped envelopes. Answers to these questions will provide important information about the effect of this procedure. The results of these questionnaires can be analyzed, with strengths and weaknesses addressed by the Domestic Violence Task Force. This process will ensure progress and provide a means of detecting weakness in the process or timetable.

A PROACTIVE POLICY

The primary reason why innovative policing initiatives do not achieve their potential is that communities and police departments view these programs as something to be done by police departments in addition to the department's other operations. These innovations must be both the principle and philosophy that underlie all its day-to-day functions not just of the police department but of the entire community.

Establishing a community-based program and unit is relatively easy. Actually implementing these programs and ensuring community participation is a daunting task, however. It must be the paramount responsibility of the *TEaM* to create an interdisciplinary system of training for all the agencies. All of these agencies have expertise in their own area of specialization. The *TEaM* must ensure that all agencies come to understand and appreciate the difficulties experienced by each individual agency.

All agencies must understand that while boys are responsible for the majority of these violent episodes, girls are also involved. Girls can and do participate in bullying, hair pulling, fistfighting, name-calling, and ganging up on other students. Thus, domestic violence is not just gender based, and it can be found in gay and lesbian as well as heterosexual relationships.

The narrow focus on the criminal justice system as *the* deterrent to battering is misguided and has led to only limited results in preventing domestic violence.[11] The current approach is one of intervention and not prevention. The very premise of *preventing* the *crime* of domestic violence with the assistance of a *civil* order *after* the crime has occurred defies logic, reason and common sense. Clearly, this is one topic that needs reexamination.

Both the entire community and the police department must be held accountable for their individual actions. Violence is learned behavior both within and outside of school. It is the responsibility of the community to establish community-based activities that promote nonviolent values and teach nonviolent alternatives to resolve conflict. This is the essential ingredient in the definition and success of community-based programs. Society must blend the National Institute of Justices empirical studies with their individual emotionally held beliefs and become more committed to the logic of commonsense problem solving.

The effectiveness of any intervention must begin with a distinct and harmonious communitywide understanding of the enigma of domestic violence. It is myopic to believe that the criminal justice system can provide the resolution of the puzzle that is domestic violence. We must begin again, with a collaborative and mutually determined response that makes more sense than reacting after the victim is beaten. We must hold more than just the criminal justice system responsible for this change.

NOTES

1. Lawrence W. Sherman, *Policing Domestic Violence: Experiments and Dilemmas* (New York: Free Press, 1992) p. 214.

2. Peter K. Manning, "The Preventive Conceit," *American Behavioral Scientist* 36, no. 5 (1993): 639-650.

3. Janell D. Schmit and Lawrence W. Sherman, "Does Arrest Deter Domestic Violence?" *American Behavioral Scientist* 36, no. 5 (1993): 601-609.

4. Paul F. Evans and Alan Fox, "Our Anticrime 'Miracle'," *Boston Globe,* February 18, 1997, p. A11.

5. *Boston Globe,* January 26, 1997, p. E6.

6. Sherman, *Policing Domestic Violence,* pp. 154-187.

7. Ibid., p. 185.

8. Ron Sloan, Robert Trojanowicz, and Bonnie Bucqueroux, *Basic Issues in Training: A Foundation for Community Policing,* Nov. 1992, National Center for Community Policing, Michigan State University, November 1992.

9. Barbara Duffy, "Using a Creative Teaching Process with Adult Patients," *Home Health Nurse* 15, no. 2 (1997): 102-108.

10. Keith F.Killacky, *Towards a New Model in Police In-Service Training* (Quantico, VA: FBI Academy, n.d.) pp. 7-8.

11. Donald Cochran, *The Tragedies of Domestic Violence: A Qualitative Analysis of Civil Restraining Orders in Massachusetts.* Boston: Office of the Commissioner of Probation Massachusetts Trial Court, October 12, 1995, p. 19.

9

The Winds of Change

Where there is no vision, the people perish.
Bible, Proverbs

Traditionally, the criminal justice system has employed sanctions, treatments, and rehabilitation to correct criminal behavior. This philosophic belief is empirically problematic, however.[1] I do not believe that many domestic violence abusers "weigh up the possibilities in advance and base their conduct on rational calculation."[2] I do not believe that just before striking a victim an abuser will stop and calculate the odds that he or she may be arrested and if arrested then try to calculate what sanctions he or she will face in our contemporary court system. I believe that once the chronic offender is arrested and determines that the sanctions are minimal, these lenient sanctions imposed by our courts are not effective in deterring future abuse by the chronic abuser with a criminal history. In Massachusetts, as we have noted, approximately three out of every four abusers have a criminal history. The majority of abuser are not deterred by our current policies.

This book demonstrates that a traditional criminal justice approach using mandatory arrest policies and civil restraining orders as currently promulgated has not been effective in *preventing* domestic violence. I also seriously question how effective these policies are in providing proper sanctions, either through intensive probation or incarceration, for the perpetrators of domestic violence. Federal policies that are championed by the Violence Against Women Office of the Justice Department have dramatically altered police policies and procedures but have had little to no effect on our courts in imposing proper sanctions or deterring the chronic criminal domestic violence abusers. Simple common sense should lead us to understand that proactive prevention efforts cannot come through the reactive process of the criminal justice system. A more logical concept is to understand that the courts will only take domestic violence seriously when domestic violence becomes a serious crime, that is, when it is made a felony.

An effective effort to remedy the domestic violence cycle must include unified communitywide prevention and intervention strategies for abusers/victims who believe they do not need or do not want the intervention of the criminal justice system as well as intervention for the chronic abusers/victims by the criminal justice system.

The city of Boston, Massachusetts, and a number of other communities nationwide have reduced juvenile crime in a sensible fashion, relying on coordinated and cooperative multistratagey programs. The tactics are quite simple. They target gangs, which is where many of the serious chronic juvenile offenders are found; they then ensure swift court appearances and stiff sanctions for those found guilty. Stiff sanctions must begin with intensive probation and incarceration only for chronic offenders. This process is coupled with increased educational and recreational opportunities for young people in high-crime areas. A particularly beneficial component of these programs is the constant followup by police and probation officers with joint visitations to the homes of the troubled families[3].

The chronic abusers and victims of domestic violence are often caught in a cycle of criminal behavior and codependency relationship that our arrest and rising per capita incarceration rate will not remedy.[4] Often, both abusers and victims are entrapped by the primal social power and economic dependency, coupled with an emotional relationship bond that is at the heart of human intimate behavior. Wanting relief, these codependent people will often engage in obsessive/compulsive processes to alleviate the pain, or they will deny that any problem exists. Much of this love and avoidance behavior by the abuser/victim is in response to a lifetime of societal attitudes or childhood familial trauma.[5] Use of the criminal justice system as an instrumentality of formal social control to change the behavior of these abusers and victims will have little to no effect.

The struggle to conquer this "enemy within our homes" has no unified national, state, county, district attorney, court, or police policy. The problem is that public policymakers who are driven by budgetary constraints and election cycles are directing the process. These same public policymakers often chose the same easy answer that they provide for many of our other social problems; they choose to engage the criminal justice system.

Most abusers do not stumble across this aberrant behavior when they reach adulthood and understand that there are laws against it. The Minneapolis study on domestic violence reported that 85 percent of the men arrested in this study had been victims of or had witnessed domestic violence as children. In Massachusetts, 56 percent of restraining orders mention the presence of a child during the incident of domestic violence.[6] A 1985 Massachusetts Division of Youth Services study found that children who witness violence at home are 24 times more likely to commit a sexual assault, 75 percent more likely to commit a crime against a person, and 50 percent more likely to abuse drugs or alcohol. It also found that 63 percent of the 12 to 20 year- old-males in jail for murder killed their mother's batterers.[7]

The social and community environment often plays a part in addictive personalities and antisocial or criminal behavior.[8] There is no reason to believe that it is not the same with chronic domestic violence abuse. A recent study by the Massachusetts Probation Department found that a defendant who has a criminal record is twice as likely to violate a restraining order than someone with no prior arrest record. More than three out of four abusers who have restraining orders issued against them have a prior criminal arraignment.[9]

Prevention efforts cannot *begin* with a reactive criminal justice system; rather they must begin before children attend school. Early intervention may even include prenatal drug exposure and hyperactivity. Health services and early infant care providers should note family characteristics. The home environment, family dynamics, and parental stability play a major role in shaping children's future adult behavior.[10] Good parents must act responsibly and teach their children proper behavior.

Head Start programs that combine the nurturing of children with home visits to their parents and other preschool programs along with elementary schools must provide children with anti-violence instruction and training. These programs and others like them should address the root causes of domestic violence by emphasizing the importance of violence prevention and gender equity to the parents as well as children.[11] It is at this very early age that boys begin to assimilate to a culture that depicts men as strong, competitive, violent, and unfeeling.

At this early age, boys and young men are not yet socialized to be aggressive and combative. They should not be socialized to hide their emotions or be taught that crying is a shameful act that men just do not do. They should not be desensitized to pain and taught to disconnect from expressions of emotions. "Get in there son and rip their heads off." "Suck it up, son," is the implicit, all-too-American message we teach boys.[12] Often these lessons are taught through violence in the media, sports, toys, and by the behavior of adult males in their family.[13] It is in these early ages that stereotyping often leads to an imbalance of control/power in male/female relationships. Boys learn to be tough, and many take pride in being disrespectful. Girls learn to be compassionate and gentle.[14] It is through this socialized learning process that some segments of our society often foster aggressive conduct and condone abusive behavior in young men.[15]

The *Washington Post* reviewed records of professional and college football players with incidents of violent behavior toward women. Of those that were reported to the police, just one of 141 cases was a player disciplined for his violent behavior by a team or the league. While the National Collegiate Athletic Association has policies concerning players who gamble or use banned drugs, it has no policies for the discipline of athletes involved in domestic violence.[16] Violence prevention training should be included to deliver a message of mutual respect and conflict resolution.[17] Many trained professionals believe that the child's social milieu[18] is an important determinant of his future conduct. Back-end, punishment-only approaches cannot expunge the torment that domestic violence leaves behind.

Over the last three decades, our juvenile justice system has seen its policies and procedures mirror those of the Federal Juvenile Justice Delinquency Prevention Act of 1974. Most states, including Massachusetts, model their programs on this act in order to acquire federal funds. Caught between legal certainty of the deterrence theory and governmental complexities created by "status" offenders, the juvenile justice system has become a complex and fragmented system that provides little structure and less discipline for young people than ever before. Over the last two decades, juvenile violence has become one of our most compelling problems.[19]

At the nexus of the federal system is the belief that all but the most serious of juvenile crimes should be "status" offenses for which the offender *should not* be disciplined.[20]The Federal government has tended to discipline all juvenile offenders--violent and nonviolent alike--with lenient sanctions for their behavior. This policy is just as wrong as punishing all young offenders alike with harsh sentences. The goal of the juvenile justice system should be to teach young people that they will be held accountable for their behavior. Placing a 16-year-old who is guilty of a drive-by shooting, in the local YMCA for a few months until he reaches adulthood sends the wrong message to other young men in the community.

Even worse than the YMCA detention is a recent Massachusetts case. A 5-year-old boy was raped and abused by a 12-year-old boy. In court, the defendant admitted that he was guilty. The judge then declared that he was "not delinquent" and sent him back to the neighborhood where his victim is still in therapy suffering from the lingering trauma of the rape. Middlesex District Attorney Thomas F. Reilly asserts that cases like this are very common and he wonders just what kind of message we are sending to the defendants. Where is the justice for the victim?[21] In this case, the defendant did not even have to go to the YMCA. The judge did order that the defendant receive therapy. Maybe both victim and defendant can go to the same therapist.

Most of us, as parents, attempt to demonstrate to our children what the consequences of their actions will be. It seems extraordinary that as a nation of laws we cannot send the very same message to juvenile offenders in the criminal justice system. It stands to reason that if the juvenile justice system does not communicate individual accountability or personal responsibility to youthful offenders through the use of proper sanctions, then the criminal justice system will have its hands full when these youths become adult offenders. Chronic violent youthful offenders need to understand that sanctions will be sure and swift for their violent behavior and that they will be incarcerated regardless of age. If I am a victim of a 16- year-old youth or a victim of a 26-year-old adult, I am a victim never-the-less.

With young people, mostly male, committing more and more violent crimes and without any proper criminal sanctions combined with intensive probation and rehabilitation programs for this behavior, it stands to reason that their crimes may increase in severity as the offenders get older. Without question, almost everyone in the criminal justice system will agree that swift and sure punishment of criminal behavior is an important component of an effective crime policy. Without question almost everyone in the criminal justice system will agree that there is *no swift, sure and equitable punishment* for criminal behavior in the criminal justice system. These problems often start at home and in school where some young people show no respect for parents or peers. Without proper swift and sure sanctions by parents or the criminal justice system, that type of antisocial /criminal behavior continues into adulthood.

DETERRENCE AS PREVENTION

The 1991 *Funk & Wagnalls* dictionary defines a misdemeanor as "an offense of minor degree," and a felony as a "serious crime." Upon closer inspection, it becomes obvious to all concerned that domestic violence, in and of itself, is still not treated as a *serious crime* by the criminal justice system because *it is not by legal definition a serious crime*. In most states a misdemeanor is by legal definition a *minor crime*. If it walks like a duck, looks like a duck, and quacks like a duck, it is most likely a duck. A rose is a rose. This should not be a difficult concept to follow.

The following are some recommended solutions. Cut the ones you like out or copy them down and mail them to your legislators. Insist that you receive an answer of just what they intend to do. Follow up to ensure that the legislators do what they promised you they were going to do. You can become part of the process of change. If you are a woman and cannot run for political office, you must communicate your concern about domestic violence to your local politician. You can and will make a difference in the political process. Remember that *in the political process silence is acceptance.*

RECOMMENDATION ONE: *We must begin at the beginning.*
There must be another United States Attorney General's Task Force on Family Violence similar to the one in 1984. It was the 1984 recommendation that the confrontation of domestic violence in our society must *begin* with the criminal justice system that created many of our problems. We must begin at the beginning and it should be the business of the attorney general to understand that simple concept. It is the responsibility of the attorney general to initiate the proper course of action the second time around.

RECOMMENDATION TWO: *Let's get serious and make domestic violence a serious crime.*
Spousal or intimate partner assault and battery should be a *felony*. Spousal assault and battery could include married couples or others who live in a spousal relationship. Not until the police have responded and a report of spousal assault and battery is made and after criminal complaints have been issued or an arrest made should a court issue a *criminal* protective order. A violation of this criminal protective order would be a felony.

A conviction of the criminal violation order would cause the abuser to be affixed with an electronic monitoring device that would alert the victim and the police when the abuser comes within 1,000 feet of the victim. The abuser would be placed in an intensive probation program that would monitor the abuser much more closely than traditional probation. A second conviction of a violation of the criminal protective order would be a three-year felony. The abuser, after conviction, could then be given an option, at sentencing, to attend a "domestic violence boot camp." The boot camp would be a twenty-six week counseling and education program, followed by a three-week program addressing the impact of violence on children. Refusal to attend or complete the program would be cause for the three-year mandatory incarceration of the defendant. This process would provide that the only people who would be jailed for the three year sentence are those who leave us no other alternative. They have in effect sentenced themselves.

RECOMMENDATION THREE: *If we are serious, we must protect our children first.*
The Legislature should pass a "child endangerment law." This law would provide for the intervention of the Department of Social Services on behalf of the children in the homes of chronic domestic violence abusers and defendants upon the issuance of a criminal restraining order. This information should be passed to the Department of Social Services by the probation department of the District Court. Most offenders start their behavior as children. Two important risk factors for children are poor classroom performance or the early onset of aggressive behavior in school and experience as a victim of violence or witness of chronic violence in the family.

RECOMMENDATION FOUR: *Do we want to pay now or pay later?*
Intensive probation costs an average of $2,912 per offender a year. The average cost of a new prison cell is well over $100,000. The average cost to house a prisoner is over $22,000 and that does not include food and medical services.[22] Intensive probation would require the abuser to contact his probation officer two or three times a week. The probation officer would be required to ensure that the abuser successfully complete domestic violence programs and not violate any terms of probation. The probation officer must also include visits to the home of the victim.

RECOMMENDATION FIVE: *It is often "different strokes for different folks."*
Cultural class differences have become very apparent to the criminal justice system, and many immigrants have little understanding of the laws regarding domestic violence. A South Korean businessman was arrested in Boston for punching his wife. He said that the police were wrong to arrest him because his action is acceptable behavior in his native South Korea. His court-appointed lawyer told the court that cultural differences contributed to the arrest. "They were just visiting tourists, unfamiliar with the customs."[23]

An informational pamphlet should be developed for those immigrants involved in domestic violence. This pamphlet should describe what is prohibited behavior under local law and explain the consequences of their actions as well as the services that are available and ensure that the information will be provided in confidence.

RECOMMENDATION SIX: *"Once, shame on me, twice shame on you."*
Immediate revocation of probation/parole should be taken by a judge who determines that someone who is on probation or parole has a *criminal* protective order taken out against him or her. This is usually a message to the system that this person is a chronic offender.

RECOMMENDATION SEVEN: *If it is not sure, swift, and equitable, it will not work.*
We should establish a "Domestic Violence Court." Arraignment would occur within a week and trial within a month. This is a time when the victims are most vulnerable, and so sanctions must be sure and swift to have any effect on the behavior of the perpetrator.

RECOMMENDATION EIGHT: *Abuse of alcohol does not cause domestic violence but does add fuel to the fire.*
All alcohol containers should include a message that alcohol is often a contributing factor in domestic violence. Domestic violence education should be part of all alcohol-related programs.

RECOMMENDATION NINE: *Police should try to be as proactive as possible.*
Police departments should track repeat nonviolent family disturbance calls. These are the kinds of events that often precede domestic violence. Repeat nonviolent calls should be cause for both the police department and the women's advocacy agencies to follow up. Together they must determine the best process to prevent further calls and alleviate an escalation of violence.

RECOMMENDATION TEN: *Limit the process faced by many police officers of, "when in doubt, lock him/them up."*
The federal government should ensure that, when police respond to a domestic violence call and do not make an arrest, they will not be held civilly liable in federal court for failure to prevent future domestic homicide or serious injury. The police should, however, be made to log why an arrest was not made. In many states there are laws that provide for civil liability for police officers but the fact is that the public can and most often does bring suit in federal court.

RECOMMENDATION ELEVEN: *This will help ensure that there is a criminal justice system for the victim.*
Police departments should have a unit or an individual officer who monitors chronically violent couples. This unit/officer would be part of a team that

includes the prosecutor's office, court probation office, and women's advocacy groups. The team should meet with the couples and attempt to find a solution before the violence escalates.

RECOMMENDATION TWELVE: *The most difficult step many of us take is matrimony.*

We should impose a surcharge when issuing a marriage license. This surcharge would be for proactive domestic violence education and would be informational. Everyone would be required to attend a number of informational courses before the issuance of a marriage license. The program would not be pass or fail, attendance is all that would be necessary. Local advocacy groups could administer this type of proactive preventative program for battered women. For those who question the government's right to issue such a license, where were you when state and local governments began to hand out motor vehicle driving licenses?

EFFORTS BEYOND THE CRIMINAL JUSTICE SYSTEM

Ultimately, while in many states expanded powers are conferred on those in the criminal justice system, it is imperative that other men in the community hold abusers, who for the most part are men, accountable for their behavior. If there is no public shame or loss of public reputation in the eyes of one's peers in the local community, then there is little reason to expect that person to change his behavior. Many public policymakers and those within the criminal justice system continue to believe that local communities are unconcerned about private violence. It is important for the public to become aware of the insidious nature of domestic violence. The entire community, both men and women, must meet their obligations in condemning it.

In many states community concern can begin with the many neighborhood watch programs throughout the nation. These programs can use their special relationship with police departments to receive training in how to prevent family violence in the homes of their own neighborhoods. Community police workshops and training seminars can help send the message that their neighbors do care about their problems with domestic violence and that the victims are not alone.

Victims often refuse to report their problems to the criminal justice system and often do not even tell their family or relatives about the abusive relationship that they find themselves in. These same victims often share their experiences with close friends and neighbors. Neighborhood watch members can be asked to urge these victims to seek professional counseling and assistance and to provide literature with the many options open to the victim. Together with the police, they can bring this process directly into their neighborhoods and homes. This may be the only source that can convince the victim that they are not alone. The victim can observe that others often share their problem. All family members must learn that this violent behavior will not be accepted or tolerated in their community.

Public policymakers should look at what they intended to accomplish twenty years ago and recognize that domestic violence is not being *prevented* by these *reactive* approaches to the problem. They should revisit what outcomes, both positive and negative, their legislative performance has created. *Most important they should ask both victims and abusers why the system does not prevent domestic violence.* Victims of domestic violence deserve better treatment. These crime victims are often being revictimized by the criminal justice system.[24]

The problems are indeed complex but laws alone cannot save us from ourselves. "We should not expect the criminal justice system to correct all antisocial behavior . . . or to solve our social problems . . . "[25] There are no studies demonstrating that our current policies have slowed the steady rise of domestic violence calls. These policies provide only a slow and painfully ineffectual punishment for the abuser and little relief for the abused after the abuse has occurred.

The solutions do not lie in the interventionist policies of the criminal justice system but rather in the patterns of our social and cultural behavior. We raise boys in a culture where they take pride in tormenting, punching, wrestling, competing to be the best, bullying, and taking pride in being independent and disrespectful. Why do we seem surprised that many boys continue this behavior as men?

Precipitating variables such as class and gender must be addressed in order for appropriate solutions to be devised. The history of women has not always been a history of progress because in the past women have been denied involvement in the institutional and political process controlled by men. This is no longer true. The only people preventing the full empowerment of women are women themselves. The empowerment of police, however, is not a substitute for empowerment of women. Any legal or policy changes that increase the power of police without simultaneously striving for the empowerment of women will have the potential to decrease rather than improve the level of women's safety."[26]

After twenty years of failure to provide a remedy, it is time to reject the current legal concepts and the current array of independent and uncoordinated programs that provide little relief.[27] "The safety of millions of victims . . . depends ultimately on a cultural shift much larger than any law can guarantee."[28] Richard Gelles, a psychologist and sociologist at the University of Rhode Island, observed, "The more power women have, the less they're likely to be beaten."[29] We should begin to ask new questions of old sources to discover where we have failed as a society and where women have failed to become more involved in the political arena. It is time to use analytical tools taken from sociology and anthropology. These methodologies can yield fresh insight and help us probe for better answers to this old conundrum.

The understanding that socioeconomic status and cultural background are important determinants of behavior would be a good place to undertake the examination because those at the lower end of the socioeconomic ladder need the most help.[30] The best way to develop sound remedies for domestic violence is to diagnose it where it is most common. I believe that there are many women at the lower end of the socioeconomic strata who are willing to dispute the Justice Department's 1994 National Crime Victimization Survey which reported that there is only a 10 percent difference in the rate of family violence between those families that make less than $10,000 and those that make more than $50,000.[31] The National Center on Child Abuse and Neglect calculates that the mistreatment of children is ten times more likely among families with incomes below $7,000. According to the Massachusetts Department of Social Services, the cities and towns with the worst child abuse and neglect in 1993 were those with the most welfare cases. In the eight municipalities with the largest number of reports of child abuse or neglect, the average number of families on welfare was 40 percent. In the eight with the fewest reports, the average was 9.7 percent.[32]

A recent six-year study of 436 low-income families in Worcester, Massachusetts, by Dr. Ellen Bassuk, a Harvard Medical School psychiatrist, reveals the following: 84 percent of mothers had been victims of sexual or physical abuse at some time during their lives; 61 percent of mothers were victims of domestic abuse as adults; 27 percent of mothers had required medical care because of abuse by a male partner; 91 percent of women had been victims of sexual or physical abuse at some time during their lives; 33 percent of mothers were in ongoing domestic abuse situations; and 35 percent of mothers suffered from post-traumatic stress disorder.[33]

I will not dispute the fact that professional women with good jobs and financial security cannot be victims of domestic violence, just as I do not dispute the idea that men cannot become victims of domestic violence. But to imagine as Hillary Johnson, a contributing writer for *Working Woman* magazine "[a]ny advantages women of means may have over poor and blue-collar women are minimal . . . "[34] displays an improbable lack of understanding of the true character and nature of domestic violence. Johnson does not seem to understand that the problems of working-class, poor, and minority women concerning domestic violence are much more complex than hers.

Does Hillary Johnson believe that a young 18-year-old who was raped at age 11 by her mother's boyfriend, is a high school dropout, became pregnant by the same man who fathered her sister's two-year-old son, shares a one bedroom apartment with her father, and sits home all day endlessly smoking cigarettes in front of a TV set will receive the same advantages from the criminal justice system as Hillary Johnson or any woman of wealth or position can? Many working-class and minority women continue to view the feminist movement as a white, middle-class phenomenon.[35] I believe that many working class and minority women who have a problem with domestic violence are beginning to understand that without the money for a good lawyer, the criminal justice system will provide no long-term relief to their dilemma. The rich and the poor are not truly equal before the law.[36]

I believe that the difference in numbers of domestic violence victims is proportional to the wealth and education of the victim. In general, the violent crime rate decreases as income increases. Families with family incomes of less than $7,500 have higher rates of aggravated assault than families with incomes of more than $50,000 Individuals who have attained a college education have the lowest rates of violent crime victimization.[37] If wealth and education affect the general violent crime rate, how can we not expect the same effect on domestic violence? Murders and shootings that have become so common in our inner cities are rare in the suburbs. In the small, economically disadvantaged cities and towns, however, the rates of assault, rape, and child abuse remain high.[38]

Criminologist Elliott Currie studied two neighborhoods with roughly the same population for a year. One was a wealthy suburb of Chicago and the second an impoverished neighborhood in Detroit. In the wealthy neighborhood, there were no murders, no robberies, and one rape. In the low-income neighborhood, for the same period of time, there were *27 murders, 55 rapes, and 796 robberies.*[39] Since we have recently concluded that domestic violence is not just a family problem but a crime, is it not logical to conclude that there would be much higher rates of domestic violence in impoverished neighborhoods?

While domestic violence can and does occur in all strata of society, some studies demonstrate that "arrests in domestic disputes are disproportionately of lower class, minority residents of large cities . . . . "[40] The Department of Justice studies demonstrate that the rise in violent crime began suddenly in the mid-1980s. This sudden rise is concentrated greatly in poor neighborhoods ravaged by drugs, flooded with guns, and afflicted with a host of problems ranging from unemployment to broken homes to child abuse.[41] The 1994 Bureau of Justice Statistics Sourcebook details that the vast majority of the violent crimes: murder, rape, robbery, aggravated assaults, and other violent crimes are committed by young single males.[42] "Regardless of who or what is to blame for family decline, it is clear enough that the endemic violence of inner cities is closely related to their numbers of illegitimate children and single-parent households."[43]

Why should society expect that, considering the rampant violence in the streets of our inner cities, domestic violence will not similarly occur in the homes of those same neighborhoods? Studies demonstrate that although child abuse occurs in all racial, ethnic, cultural, and socioeconomic groups it is more common among people in poverty.[44] This does not mean that domestic violence is *confined* to inner cities, for it does indeed permeate through all racial and socioeconomic tiers. But it frankly means that it is more prevalent in the inner cities because of the population size and the socioeconomic status of those living there. Does educational and economic deprivation end at the stoops of those homes?

The vast majority of men and women who are college graduates and make over $50,000 a year do not have criminal records, nor are abuse prevention orders issued against them at the same rate as those with little education or money. "Studies conclusively demonstrate that economic inequality affects not only the extent of crime, but its seriousness as well."[45] "Although spousal assault can occur in all economic groups, the rate of spousal battering was five times higher in lower-income families than in the higher income brackets."[46] "In fact, domestic violence may well prove to be the most troubling issue facing poor, urban minority communities for a long time to come."[47]

Many feminists and victim advocates continue to insist that there is no common profile for a domestic violence abuser. A common profile for any type of offender does not propose that everyone who meets that profile will be an offender. A common profile for any offender does not propose that if you do not match the common profile you cannot be an offender. A common profile simply proposes that the *majority of offenders* do meet that profile. In Massachusetts, the computerized Registry of Restraining Orders reveals that the majority of batterers are young males who are not married to the victim. Over half of these abusers demonstrate either drug or alcohol abuse problems. Almost 77 percent of abusers are criminal offenders, many of whom have lengthy prior criminal records and histories of violence.[48]To many who fit this profile it can be a badge of honor, not to comply, but to defy authority. Most abusers who fit this profile will not be deterred by a piece of paper.

Many studies have demonstrated that poor children who have only one parent from birth nearly always stay poor. Approximately two-third of rapists and three-quarters of teenage murderers and long-term prisoners are young men who grew up without fathers in the house.[49] It is these chronic offenders that the criminal justice system should confront first.

Modern family settings, work responsibilities, our cultural milieu, and home lives must be scrutinized. Research of socioeconomic characteristics reveals that about 61 percent of the abusers have been unemployed during the past year. Almost 59 percent of the violators have trouble handling finances. The majority of restraining order violators have problems with stability in family and social relationships and have serious substance abuse problems, particularly with alcohol.[50]

Long-term progress will come only when *we begin to treat the cause of domestic violence rather than its symptoms.*[51] The educational system should serve as the foundation for this new approach and explore ways to include entire families. Abuse of others is often learned behavior and is not simply discovered during adulthood. Use of prevention/educational programs as a central element in curbing criminal domestic violence reflects the realization that enforcement alone is not enough to reduce domestic violence.

In this book I have provided a clear example of why the criminal justice system and public policymakers must shift from a primarily reactive approach to a holistic communitywide proactive approach. I believe that this change of direction will not take place until women become more involved with the political process. Equal access to politics is not the panacea for all the ills of domestic violence. It doesn't solve everything. But in a democracy social equity can and very well may proceed from institutional equity.

Integral to the intervention process is the involvement of the family, community, and social services and other agencies. With this innovative role, society and the criminal justice system will be taking on a much greater challenge than in the past, but doing so holds the promise of discovering a way of reducing domestic violence. Society must recognize that the burden of policing a democratic society does not lie with the criminal justice system, but with communities and citizens themselves. It remains the responsibility of women who want change to use the political process to ensure that change will take place. "The voice of family-instilled conscience is always more cost-effective than that of a police officer, especially if the officer is part of a criminal justice system that has become irrelevant to all but serious offenses and then not guaranteed to produce results."[52]

Public policymakers must establish a broad, interagency policy framework that specifies, in a clearly defined manner, the distinct and concordant goals for each agency. They must identify specific program strategies to coordinate the efforts of individual agencies and ensure cohesion and linkage of the criminal justice system with other social service agencies in the community. *This can only be accomplished by appointing a single oversight domestic violence agency that will provide guidance for the myriad of often disordered, independent, and uncoordinated agencies.* This principal agency must be given the power and authority to hold each of the other individual agencies responsible for completion of their assigned role. The oversight agency itself must be held responsible for the overall success or failure of the program.

With the assistance of current police department computer assisted dispatch systems, the chronically violent abusers can be identified. Just as the majority of crime is committed by a small number of chronic criminals, the majority of violent domestic violence incidents are perpetrated by those with records of prior arrests. Many criminologists believe that the most imperative issue facing the criminal justice system is the relatively small group of chronic offenders who consistently appear over and over again in the system and are committing a disproportionate amount of crime.[53]

A policy of "two strikes and you are out" should be instituted for these chronic abusers. Mandatory sentences should be in place for second time offenders that will provide equity of sanctions for these chronic offenders. First, a program must be established that provides for intensive probation, including weekly visits for both the defendant and his victim by the probation officer. If probation does not work, then incarceration is in order. The sentence does not need to be lengthy. If sanctions are intended as a deterrent, it is not the length of the sentence but the fact that the incarceration will be sure and swift that counts most. When abusers are released from prison, they should be placed in an intensive parole program for at least a year and again with weekly visits for both the defendant and his victim should be instituted. If abusers commit another act of domestic violence, they must be immediately jailed, held without bail, tried, and if convicted, must finish the term of their original sentence in prison.

This book is my contribution to the nation's discourse on domestic violence. We, both men and women, must learn that we have to understand the consequences of our behavior towards each other. Do we want our present behavior to be replicated by our children? Do we want them to live in our world or a better one? This book is intended to be a competent, yet compact, treatment of this complex subject. It speaks of the origins and nature of domestic violence, provides a history of criminal justice intervention, furnishes a configuration of current policy, charts new direction, and offers recommendations for change. The number of men who want to move on beyond the uncomfortable present and fashion a harmonious society built on mutual respect remains modest, but by working together with women socially significant change can occur.

My final appeal to women who want to end domestic violence is threefold. First, women must increase their intellectual curiosity as to why change in the fundamental assumptions about gender differences has been so slow in coming by looking inward and not outward for fundamental social change. Second, women must come to understand that the transformation of "how ought we order our lives together" will not occur until the majority of women pursue that ordering with a positive reformist zeal. Third, women must begin to display a professional political aggressiveness and themselves become the public policymakers who are after all, our agents of change. This is the most important task women face as they prepare for the twenty-first century.

NOTES

1. Peter K. Manning, "The Preventive Conceit," *American Behavioral Scientist* 36, no. 5 (1993): 648.

2. Peter T. Elikann, *The Tough-on-Crime Myth: Real Solutions to Cut Crime* (New York: Insight, 1996), p. 135.

3. David S. Broder, "Confronting Juvenile Crime," *Boston Globe,* February 26, 1997, p. A15.

4. Lawrence W. Sherman, *Policing Domestic Violence: Experiments and Dilemmas* (New York: Free Press, 1992), pp. 218-219.

5. Liane Evans, "Author Lectures on Codependency," *Portsmouth Herald,* April 18, 1995, p. B2-3.

6. Donald Cochran, *The Tragedies of Domestic Violence: A Qualitative Analysis of Civil Restraining Orders in Massachusetts* (Boston: Office of the Commissioner of Probation Massachusetts Trail Court, October 12, 1995), Executive Summary.

7. *Domestic Violence: Strategies for Prevention and Enforcement Supplement.* Prepared for Scott Harsbarger, Attorney General, Commonwealth of Massachusetts (1993), p. 3.

8. Larry Tye, "Addictive Personalities Formed Early, a Study Finds," *Boston Globe,* February 2, 1997, p. A3.

9. Cochran, *The Tragedies of Domestic Violence,* Executive Summary.

10. Karen Wright and Devin Wright, *Family Life, Delinquency, and Crime: A Policy Maker's Guide* (Washington, D.C.: U.S. Department of Justice, August 1995), p. 32.

11. Barrie Thorne and Zella Luria, "Sexuality and Gender in Children's Daily Worlds," in James M. Henslin, ed., *Down To Earth Sociology,* 8th ed. (New York: Free Press, 1995), pp. 137-148.

12. Joseph P. Kahn, "He Does Want to Talk About It," *Boston Globe,* April 7, 1997, p. C5.

13. Mark A. Stevens, "Stopping Domestic Violence: More Answers and More Questions Needed," *Counseling Psychologist* 22, no. 4 (October 1994): 587-592.

14. James M. Henslin, "On Becoming Male: Reflections of a Sociologist on Childhood and Early Socialization," *Down To Earth Sociology,* 8th ed. (New York: Free Press, 1995), pp. 126-138.

15. Stevens, "Stopping Domestic Violence," p. 590.

16. David Diamond, "Victory, Violence and Values," *USA Weekend* August 22-23, 1996, p. 4.

17. William D. Baker, "A New Approach to Domestic Violence," *FBI Law Enforcement Bulletin* 64, no. 9 (September 1995): 18-20.

18. Hamilton Cravens, *Before Head Start: The Iowa Station and America's Children* (Chapel Hill: University of North Carolina Press, 1993), p. 228.

19. Steven R. Dozinger, ed. *The Real War on Crime: The Report of the National Criminal Justice Commission* (New York: Harper Perennial, 1996), p. xii.

20. Judy A. Bradshaw, "The Juvenile Justice System: Is It Working?" *FBI Law Enforcement Bulletin* (May 1995): 14-16.

21. Eileen McNamara, "Parental Cry: This Is Justice?" *Boston Globe,* April 9, 1997, p. B1.

22. *The Real War on Crime,* pp. 49, 190.

23. John Ellement, "S. Korean Held in Assault on Wife," *Boston Globe,* December 31, 1996, p. B1.

24. *The Real War on Crime,* p. 217.

25. Ibid., p. 61.

26. Kathleen J. Ferraro and Lucille Pope, "Irreconcilable Differences: Battered Women, Police, and the Law," in N. Zoe Hilton, ed. *Legal Responses To Wife Assault* (Newbury Park, Calif: Sage Publications, 1993), p. 120.

27. John Ellement, "Study Details Domestic Violence," *Boston Globe,* October 12, 1995, p. 25.

28. Erica Goode et al. "Domestic Violence Is a Serious Problem for Women," in Karin L. Swisher, ed. *Domestic Violence* (San Diego: Greenhaven Press, 1996), p. 24.

29. Betty Grillo and Marleen Lee, "Domestic Violence Rate Still Reported to be Alarmingly High," *Boston Globe,* October 29, 1995, p. 25.

30. Lawrence W. Sherman, "The Influence of Criminology on Criminal Law: Evaluating Arrest for Misdemeanor Domestic Violence," *Journal of Criminal Law and Criminology* 83, no. 1 (1992): 35.

31. Hillary Johnson, "Domestic Violence Is a Serious Problem for Professional Women," in Karin L. Swisher, ed. *Domestic Violence* (San Diego: Greenhaven Press, 1996) , p. 29.

32. Jeff Jacoby, "A Blunt, Ugly Truth," *Boston Globe,* March 8, 1994, p. 15.

33. Michael Grunwald, "Welfare Revamp Softening," *Boston Globe,* February 15, 1997, p. 1.

34. Johnson, "Domestic Violence Is a Serious Problem for Professional Women," p. 36.

35. Kenneth C. Davis, *Don't Know Much About History* (New York: Avon, 1990), p. 361.

36. Robert Wright, "Politics Made Me Do It," *Time,* February 2, 1998, p. 34.

37. Steven Dilligham, ed., *Criminal Victimization in the United States, 1991* (Washington, D.C.: Bureau of Justice Statistics, 1991), p. 118.

38. Ellen O'Brien and David Armstrong, "Rape, Child Abuse, Neglect," *Boston Globe,* March 10, 1997, p. A1.

39. Dozinger, ed. *The Real War on Crime,* p. 196.

40. Manning, "The Preventive Conceit," p. 646.

41. Wright and Wright, *Family Life, Delinquency and Crime,* pp. 45-46.

42. *Bureau of Justice Statistics Sourcebook of Criminal Justice Statistics-1994,* eds. Kathleen Maguire and Ann L. Pastore (Washington, D.C.: U.S. Department of Justice, 1994), pp. 231-233.

43. David T. Courtwright, "Violence in America," *American Heritage*. 47, no. 5 (1996): 50.

44. Otto Johnson, ed. *1996 Information Please Almanac* (Boston: Houghton Miffin Co., 1996), p. 436.

45. Dozinger, ed., *The Real War on Crime*, p. 106.

46. Harvey Wallace, *Family Violence: Legal, Medical, and Social Perspectives* (Boston: Allyn & Bacon, 1996), p. 194.

47. Shawn Sullivan, "Domestic Violence Is a Serious Problem for Black Women," in Karin L. Swisher, ed., *Domestic Violence* (San Diago: Greenhaven Press, 1996), p. 37.

48. Donald Cochran, "The Invisible Problem," *Executive Exchange*, National Association of Probation Executives (Fall 1994), p. 3.

49. William D. Eggers and John O'Leary, *Revolution at the Roots: Making Our Government Smaller, Better, and Closer to Home* (New York: Free Press, 1995), p. 224.

50. Anne Powell, "Comparison of Restraining Order Violators and Other Risk/Need Offenders," *Executive Exchange* National Association of Probation Executives (Fall 1994), pp. 4-5.

51. N. Zoe Hilton, *Legal Responses to Wife Assault* (Newbury Park, Calif.: Sage Publications, 1993), p. 27.

52. Courtwright, "Violence in America," p. 51.

53. Matt Bai, "Chronic Offenders Grab System's Attention," *Boston Globe*, May 2, 1995, p. 17.

10

Afterword

A human being is not, in any proper sense, a human being until he is educated.

Horace Mann

On June 11, 1997, the day after the third anniversary of the murders of O.J. Simpson's wife, Nicole Brown Simpson, and Ronald Goldman, Boston Red Sox leftfielder Wilfredo Cordero was arrested by the Cambridge, Massachusetts police for allegedly hitting his wife with a telephone, choking her, and then threatening to kill her. This act of domestic violence apparently took place in the Cordero apartment with both of their children present.[1]

The O.J. Simpson double murder case was cited by many women's and victims' rights groups and public policymakers as a dramatic example of how domestic violence incidents can escalate to murder. It was postulated that the Simpson case, regardless of its outcome, would confirm that domestic violence can and often does escalate into more serious incidents if not confronted promptly and properly.

For almost two decades now, women's and victims' rights advocates as well as some public policymakers have attempted to convince contemporary American society that domestic violence is not a personal problem or a private matter. These advocates believe that society should recognize that domestic violence is a criminal act. Domestic violence, they maintain, will often repeat itself if effective intervention and proper sanctions by the criminal justice system are not applied. The Wilfredo Cordero incident provides an exemplar of the current status of domestic violence intervention and public awareness of the issue. This incident occurred two decades after the struggle to curb the dilemma of domestic violence that began in 1977 with the enactment of the landmark Abuse Act in Pennsylvanian. This act began an escalation to moderate or change this form of inappropriate social behavior by means of criminal sanctions.[2]

Ana Cordero testified to the Cambridge, Massachusetts, police as follows. Her husband Wilfredo Cordero came home drunk early on the morning of June

12, 1997. He began arguing with her, and he poked her in the face and chest with his fingertips. When she tried to call the police, he grabbed the phone from her and struck her in the head with it. Then she alleged that he tried to choke her. She broke free and ran outside clothed only in a shirt and underwear. Her fifteen-year-old son found some shorts for her. She then located a security guard and asked him to call 911 for her. Her husband followed her outside and told the security guard not to call the police. The Cambridge police dispatchers routinely call back to a 911 hangup. The police dispatcher told the responding officers that a man had answered and that she could hear a woman screaming in the background. The man on the phone refused to let the dispatcher speak to the woman screaming in the background and hung up.

The responding officers found Ana in the hallway of the apartment building. The officer's report indicates that she was bleeding from the nose and gasping for breath. The police spoke to Cordero, and he admitted to them that he had struck his wife. The officer's report also attests that they could see red marks on Ana where her husband had poked her with his fingers. He was placed under arrest. Before the officers left for the police station, however, Cordero asked the officers if he could give his baby daughter a kiss. They agreed and after Cordero kissed her, he then said something in Spanish to Ana. She told the officers that he was threatening to kill her. The police brought Cordero to the station where he was booked. The police helped Ana obtain an emergency restraining order and served it on Cordero, telling him that he was prohibited from returning home until after court the next morning.[3] Clearly, the actions of the Cambridge Police Department demonstrate that they take domestic violence seriously and that they did what was expected of them.

The Cambridge Police illustrate the two underlying themes of my book: The police should do what they have been trained to do, and the police, for the most part, should perform consistently concerning domestic violence. Much of the rest of the criminal justice system generally seems to be most concerned with political and professional posturing.

The police came, they saw, and they arrested. After an arrest by the police others in the criminal justice should step to the forefront. After spending less than an hour in the Cambridge Police Department's lockup, Wilfredo Cordero was a free man.[4] Regardless of what the *Boston Globe* editorial wrote in a June 14, 1997 article, Cordero was not released by the Cambridge police, instead, he was released on $200 cash bail by assistant court clerk James J. Lynch. The very same public policymakers who decry domestic violence are the very same policymakers who provide statute law for the procedure that Lynch was required to follow. Lynch did little different in this instance than he had done many times before under similar circumstances. Cordero had spent no more than an hour at the Cambridge Police Department.

Massachusetts top bail administrator, Michael J. McEneaney, under an avalanche of questioning by the media, launched an inquiry into the question of whether Cordero had received preferential treatment because he was released on bail less than an hour after being arrested. McEneaney reportedly said that he "had not been given any information to suggest Lynch acted inappropriately or improperly when he allowed Cordero to be released on $200 bail. Regardless of the public and professional outcry the only legal question of Lynch by McEneaney is, did Lynch attempt to contact Ana Cordero, as required by statue law in Massachusetts, before releasing him?"[5]

McEneaney should more appropriately question how many times the hundreds of Massachusetts assistant clerks of court failed to make a reasonable attempt to reach the thousands of less well-known and less affluent victims of domestic violence since that effort has been mandated by statute law. Assuredly if the abuser had been an unemployed carpenter or electrician, the top Massachusetts bail administrator would not have launched an inquiry into the expeditious issuance of bail.

Roxbury District Court Judge Milton L. Wright, Jr., issued the emergency restraining order against Cordero, after he received a telephone call from the Cambridge police department the night of Cordero's arrest. The Massachusetts Judicial Response System provides a means of resolving emergency legal situations when court is closed and is routinely used to issue emergency restraining orders that remain in effect only until the next court day.

A June 14, 1997 *Boston Globe* article headlined, "Judge Wright wanted Cordero held until court session, source says."[6] But there is no Massachusetts statute that could have prevented Cordero from being released on bail. Judge Wright may have wanted Cordero held until a court session but it appears that he was not aware that there was no legal procedure in place to do so.

In a June 12, 1997 article, a source told the *Boston Globe* that the Cambridge police had assured Judge Wright that Cordero would not be released. The source stated that the judge also thought that Cordero should have been held overnight for a cooling-off period. Judge Wright and the *Boston Globe* source were either being less than truthful or were demonstrating a lack of knowledge of Massachusetts statute law if either believed that *the police* had the authority to keep Cordero in custody for a cooling-off period. In Massachusetts, it is the judges and assistant court clerks who make the decisions concerning bail and not the police departments. Perhaps Judge Wright was not aware that the police cannot legally deny anyone the opportunity for bail or hold someone for a cooling-off period against their will. Massachusetts law stipulates that anyone arrested by the police must be allowed, within an hour, the use of a phone to call friends or an attorney, or to arrange for bail.[7] McEneaney understands that by Massachusetts law Cordero was legally entitled to bail as expeditiously as possible. No statute law could legally have prevented Cordero from being released. Judge Wright apparently needs to review Massachusetts statute law and court decisions concerning the rights of defendants.

In a June 12, 1997 article in the *Boston Globe*, Middlesex District Attorney Thomas F. Reilly contends that Cordero must have received preferential treatment in being bailed because of his celebrity status as a professional ballplayer. The district attorney insisted that, "it is very rare for a person accused of domestic violence to be immediately released." Apparently Riely also told the reporter that "The system failed Mrs. Cordero that night. She should have had the comfort of getting through one night in safety."[8]

On June 29, 1997, the *Boston Globe* reviewed the records of the Cambridge police that document the fact that the majority of those arrested for "beating up their wives or girlfriends during the night were bailed out of jail soon after their arrests instead of being held overnight."[9] Perhaps someone should ask District Attorney Reilly, who proclaims himself to be a domestic violence advocate, why he did not understand that the customary process was followed and that process is the system. *This type of incident is not rare and can and does occur regularly in the district attorneys' county and every other county in Massachusetts,* and most every other state in the United States for that matter. District Attorney Reilly does not seem to understand that the criminal justice system continues to fail the victims of domestic violence every night of the year in Massachusetts as well as nationwide. Instead of the usual political posturing and the pointing of blame elsewhere, the district attorney might have used this incident to demonstrate the flaws in the current system. *The flawed system did fail someone that night, just as it fails victims every night of the year.* The system worked in the same manner for Cordero as it does for others. The old saying in Massachusetts is, "If you have the bail, you are out of jail."

District Attorney Reilly, proclaims his office has a "no drop" policy and it intends to prosecute the case even though Ana Cordero has declined to testify against her husband. The lawyers for Cordero researched 109 domestic violence cases handled by the district attorneys office from January through August 1997. They claims that 76 percent of those cases the defendants were found not guilty, dismissed, continued without a finding, or pretrial probation.[10] Further, Cordero's lawyer claims that, "research conducted over the last couple of weeks found no defendants charged with assault and battery as a first offense who have gone to trial.[11] This information seems to bolster the district attorneys claim that this incident is being handled differently because of Cordero's celebrity status. However, this apparent political posturing seems to point the blame at his own office. His policy for most other abusers appears to be quite similar to neighboring Norfolk County's domestic violence policy.

In neighboring Norfolk County the District Attorney's Office does not agree with a mandatory "no drop" policy for every case. In the late 1970s former Norfolk District Attorney William D. Delahunt, a proponent of proactive domestic violence programs, formed a domestic violence unit that is arguably the best in the state. Delahunt states, "But [no drop policies] like anything else, these ironclad policies, like mandatory sentencing, in the real world they just simply do not work."[12]

In the June 12, 1997 article in the *Boston Globe,* the reporter quotes Wendy Murphy, a Boston attorney who specializes in women's and victims' rights, as saying, "Were Cordero an average citizen, they would absolutely hold him overnight." She is also quoted in the same article as stating that, "accused batterers are customarily jailed overnight."[13] Murphy, as the reader has already discovered, does not have her facts straight. The only perpetrators of domestic violence who are legally held overnight or on weekends when the courts are closed are those who cannot make bail. If she had stated, however, that those in society who are at the bottom of the socioeconomic ladder are customarily jailed overnight she would be right. To be evenhanded with Attorney Murphy, the reporter did write that she specialized in women's and victim's rights. In this era of specialization she may not necessarily know the rights of the defendants.

The reactions to this incident by the Boston Red Sox, their general manager Dan Duquette, the American League, Major League baseball, the baseball players union, Boston sports writers and many players from Cordero's past and present teams Cordero played on are illuminating. Many of their statements demonstrate that twenty years after domestic violence became a public issue, they are among many Americans who still don't have a clue about the subject.

At first, the Boston Red Sox, not knowing all of the facts, placed Cordero on administrative leave and kept him off the playing field while continuing to pay him. Soon a number of documents and facts came to light. The police report stated Ana had a bloody nose and Cordero threatened to kill her in front of the police officers;[14] the two 2-inch bruise on Ana's neck was noted when she made a court appearance the next morning;[15] reports that Cordero's first wife said he beat her on more than one occasion during his first marriage;[16] reports that Cordero's first wife made these allegations not out of spite but because she still cared for him only wanted him to get help to control his temper;[17] and reports that Cordero's ex-girlfriend, the mother of one of his children, alleged that Cordero beat her on various occasions.[18] In an ESPN television interview, a smiling Cordero denied anything had taken place, "What actions?" he asked and insisted he was not the kind of person who would hurt his wife and he emphatically stated that he and Ana did not need counseling. This is a classic example of the domestic abuser in denial. The day after Cordero's denial of abuse the Boston Red Sox canceled his administrative leave and inexplicably put him back on the playing field.[19]

After Cordero's arrest on criminal felony charges the Red Sox general manager, Dan Duquette, stated that he believed that this incident was a private family issue.[20] Duquette stated that he "had a soft spot for Wil and his family" and declared that "Our first concern is for Ana and Wil Cordero. We have concern for their well-being and will give them our support."[21] Soon afterwards the Red Sox placed Cordero on waivers and attempted to trade him. There were no takers.[22]

The American League, Major League baseball, and the players union all expressed concern over the issue but ultimately indicated that there was really nothing they could do. "Baseball's investigation does not supersede the club's own investigation of the matter."[23] The Player Relations Committee representative, Louis Melendez, stated that these events were, "only allegations" and that we should not forget due process.[24] I believe that the correct term for their collective reaction is stonewalling. Together they crossed their collective fingers and hoped that this incident would just go away. As for the players, most reactions would be similar to that of Baltimore Orioles second baseman Roberto Alomar: "I don't think he's that kind of person."[25] If nothing else, this event should demonstrate to the players that they do not know what kind of private persons their fellow players are.

The *Boston Globe* is not your average newspaper. It can be purchased or delivered throughout all of New England. In fact, it is mailed both nationwide and worldwide. It can be picked up at newsstands in most of our nation's major airports and can be found in most of this nation's major cities. It is among a handful of major daily newspapers that can influence public opinion.

The *Boston Globe* is committed to bringing the dilemma of domestic violence to its reader's attention. This incident demonstrates that even newspapers as conscientious as the *Boston Globe* can provide inaccurate information to the public concerning domestic violence. Clearly some members of the paper's editorial staff and some of its reporters have little real understanding of this complicated issue.

A *Boston Globe* editorial in the 14 June 1997 issue related, "Instead of being handled like anyone else facing allegations of domestic violence, Red Sox outfielder Wilfredo Cordero appears to have gotten celebrity treatment." They further wrote that, "Had Cordero been unknown, he might have been detained by police early Wednesday, the first time they arrested him."[26] The fact of the matter is that when anyone, average citizen or celebrity, is arrested for domestic violence related charges, he or she has the right to a bail hearing without delay.[27] After booking, the Cambridge police were mandated by law to provide that opportunity. The police have only the authority to arrest the perpetrator, and in fact they did just that. The police never release anyone who has been arrested; only a judge or a magistrate has that authority. Regardless of what the editors of the *Boston Globe* believe it was the job of the police to arrest and they did just that. Wilfredo Cordero was treated just like any other perpetrator that the police arrest. The only establishment that has provided celebrity treatment to Cordero is the *Boston Globe*. It is *only because of his celebrity status* that the paper put Cordero in its headlines and reported on the case almost daily.

The editorial further reports that after Cordero was released he went back to his apartment, in apparent violation of an emergency restraining order. The editorial states, "This action bullhorns the message: The courts can't stop me." What his action really bullhorns is that restraining orders are simply pieces of paper that are often ineffective in stopping domestic violence perpetrators. The *Globe*, as others in the nation have done, continues to ignore many studies that demonstrate the ineffectiveness of restraining orders. A stone's throw from the *Globe*, Andy Klein of the Quincy District Court published a study showing that that the restraining orders as currently promulgated in Massachusetts often prove to be ineffective. His study has been almost universally ignored *because many women's rights and victim's advocates want to believe that these orders work* and that they will deter future violence, despite the empirical evidence and common sense to the contrary. Public policymakers continue to believe in the effectiveness of these orders because the restraining order provides an easy, albeit ineffective, answer.

The last paragraph of the editorial offers some advice that the *Globe* itself should follow. "But when it comes to domestic violence, consistently equal treatment is the only way to protect everyone." If the *Boston Globe* provided for consistently equal coverage of all incidents of domestic violence in the same manner as it covered the Cordero incident, public awareness of the issue would not continue to be a problem.

A *Boston Globe* article of June 29, 1997 states, "For those charged with violating an existing restraining order, the decision is an easy one, no release" (p. B1.) It further relates that, "the Massachusetts Legislature enacted a law in 1992 that prohibits the release on bail of individuals charged with domestic abuse on nights or weekends while a restraining order is in place." In fact Massachusetts General Law 276.57 says no such thing. A change in Massachusetts General Law 276.57 prohibits bail by a clerk of court, a bail commissioner, or a master in chancery only. It *does not prohibit bail by a judge.* In fact, *Aime v. Commonwealth* (1993) 611 N.E.2d 204, 414 Mass. 667 struck down the section of 276.57 that allowed a judge to refuse bail if such a release would endanger the safety of anyone in the community.

On August 13, 1994, Massachusetts General Law 276.58A allowed for the attorney for the *Commonwealth* [district or assistant district attorney] to move for a hearing to determine whether a defendant can be held without bail. This statute clearly states that it is the *Commonwealth* that must request a dangerousness hearing at which the defendant has the right to have his attorney present to cross-examine witnesses produced by the *Commonwealth.* If there is *no request by the Commonwealth and a defendant requests bail from a judge,* [an appearance before the court] under MGL 276.58 *a judge shall/must determine bail or release the accused on personal recognizance.* A failure to do so would be in violation of the Massachusetts Constitution Article XXVI and Massachusetts's statute as well as court law. *Mendonza v. Commonwealth* (1996) 673 N.E. 2d 22, 423 Mass. 771 clearly states, "Only if the judge determines after a hearing that no condition of release will reasonably assure the safety of any persons may he order the pretrial detention." The defendant must be, baring a request for a hearing *by the Commonwealth,* be provided with the opportunity for bail by a judge. If a judge in Massachusetts refuses to issue bail to those detained by the police after their arrest that judge is not complying with the law and that defendant is being held overnight or for the weekend without full compliance of Massachusetts statute law. *Mendonza v. Commonwealth* was a review only of arraignment procedure and defendants request for bail prior to arraignment must be upheld. A judge, like everyone else in the criminal justice system, must follow the law and afford the defendant his Constitutional rights.

Also in the June 24, 1997 *Globe* article, Massachusetts Governor William F. Weld has proposed that, "only judges should set bail in domestic violence cases"(p. B1).[28] Samuel Zoll, chief administrative justice of the district courts of Massachusetts, is quoted in the same article as saying that, "the bill could have considerable administrative consequences for judges, who traditionally have refrained from setting bail at police stations." In the same article he also states that, "judges" are not supposed to do any bails."

Since the October 7, 1992 Massachusetts General Law 276.57 change, only judges have been authorized to set bail for defendants who violate restraining orders. Is it possible that Judge Zoll did not know of this almost five-year-old statute, or has he been misquoted? Traditionally, judges have refrained from setting bail, but by Massachusetts General Law 276.58 they are mandated to do so. It is also difficult to believe that Judge Zoll, as the chief administrative justice is not aware that under certain conditions, such as a violation of a restraining order, a judge not a clerk of court must determine release of the defendant or set bail. Does Governor Weld believe that judges are not mandated to follow the same bail guidelines set by the Massachusetts Constitution and Massachusetts statute law that the court clerks must adhere to?

In Massachusetts a man charged with trying to kill his wife was being held on $1 million dollars cash bail. Massachusetts Supreme Judicial Court Justice John M Greaney reduced it to $100,000 cash or surety. "The circumstances of the crime are horrible. . . . But the fact that a defendant is charged with having committed a heinous crime is not enough by itself to deny bail."[29] Furthermore, *Commonwealth v. Finelli* (1996) 666 N.E.2d 144 422 Mass.860, states that this statute, "providing that authorized persons shall hold hearing and admit person to bail when person is arrested, was not intended to give courts discretion to deny bail, but rather to establish right of accused, in most circumstances, to be admitted to bail." It further affords that the bail magistrate system is designed to provide rapid out-of-court bail hearings and inject quasijudicial officers into the criminal process at a very early stage."

The article also relates that "Unlike bail magistrates, judges can consider the dangerousness of defendants as one of the factors in setting bail." Again, the statute states that "The hearing shall be held at the *request of the Commonwealth* immediately upon the prisoner's first appearance before the court unless that prisoner, or the attorney for the Commonwealth, seeks a continuance." This law does not appear to supersede the defendants right to request bail at night or during a weekend at a police station. Throughout Massachusetts these hearings are not being held, but the defendants are being detained nevertheless.

Few people in Massachusetts or anywhere else will acknowledge that much of the information provided to the *Boston Globe* concerning domestic violence is inaccurate and in some instances misleading. Little to no effort has been made to correct the inaccuracies and misinformation provided to the newspaper reporters from the Attorney General's Office, domestic violence advocates, judges, magistrates, or attorneys concerning this potentially dangerous misinformation. The ill-omened sad political dance of producing simple answers to complex problems continues.

I believe that the Wilfredo Cordero incident demonstrates that after twenty years of effort, many who are truly concerned with domestic violence have yet to understand precisely what their role is and many still continue to disagree what it should be. Worse still is that many still know little to nothing concerning the roles of others. More importantly, those who care about creating positive change must come to a better understanding of the policies, procedures, and legislative limitations presented by our civil and criminal justice systems. There is no reason for me not to believe that most individuals involved with the Cordero incident are concerned with the issue of domestic violence. Yet after all these years there is little to no continuity or cohesion of effort.

We have not yet reached a national unity of purpose concerning domestic violence in the criminal justice system because there is no national unity of purpose outside the criminal justice system. This single incident in Massachusetts is not a solitary unique anecdotal tale without substance. Massachusetts has one of the most scholarly judiciaries in America and according to many advocates is one of the more enlightened states in the battle against domestic violence. Police logs across this nation will demonstrate that incidents similar to this one, without similar extensive media coverage, occur each and every day across this nation. This and all similar incidents should consummately demonstrate that good intent alone is not enough if the right hand still does not know what the left hand is doing.

Mere individual awareness of solitary domestic violence incidents in contemporary American society should provide little satisfaction to advocates who for twenty years have endeavored to convince the general public that domestic violence is a criminal act and that its perpetrators are criminals. We must acknowledge that our current criminal justice efforts to resolve many domestic violence incidents have often been ineffectual.

We need to identify why the policies based in the criminal justice system have not adequately reduced the number of spousal assault. We must begin this examination by understanding that the present policy of emphasizing the police officers power of arrest has achieved little success for many thousands of victims such as Ana Cordero. Ana Cordero has said that "We are working through our problems and I support Wilfredo."[30] On July 24, 1997, Wilfredo was in Cambridge District Court with Ana by his side. Leroy Vaughn, a family friend, said of Cordero, "I saw tears in his eyes. You look at his armor, but deep down inside he has a heart. These are kids, and they need our help." [31] Two days after the court date, before beginning batting practice for a game, Cordero was signing autographs for adoring fans. Later in the game, he received ovations and applause from thousands of fans at Fenway Park when he delivered a game-winning hit.[32] Hours after the end of the season Cordero was released by the Red Sox, making him a free agent.

On November 4, 1997 Cordero pleaded guilty and was given a suspended sentence of ninety days in the Middlesex House of Correction and was sentenced to complete a forty-week state approved domestic violence course for batterers. Not a single day in jail, no fine, and sentenced to a batterers program where there is very little evidence that any current program is effective.[33] This is the punishment meted out to a man who made $3.5 million last year? An editorial writer for the *Globe* states that this case serves to demonstrate that "No one can get away with domestic violence."[34] Middlesex Assistant District Attorney Anne Edwards, who prosecuted this case, states that she is pleased with these results.[35] After no jail and no fine, Cordero left Massachusetts and did not attend a Massachusetts approved program. This is punishment?

In a December 6, 1997 *Globe* article that he subtitles "Clip and Save" Will McDonough, a well respected *Globe* sports reporter, remains so deep in denial about the subject of domestic violence that he continues to write about the incident as when Cordero, "*allegedly beat his wife*." Perhaps McDonough does not read his own or any other newspaper. McDonough's article was written *after* Cordero admitted in open court that he was guilty. Cordero has admitted in open court that he hit his wife and McDonugh still refers to the incident as the "alleged incident." McDonough provides an affidavit in his article that asserts that Cordero was calm and polite and that there were no marks or bruises on Ana Cordero. The affidavit further proclaims that Wilfredo Codero was the "calming influence in trying to defuse the situation." After providing an affidavit that states what McDonough presumably believes is the truth, McDonough then implies that "the media and the Middlesex County District Attorney's Office" made this simple little misunderstanding a contrived event. Even though I "clipped it and saved it" I find it hard to believe that McDonough would display his bias and ignorance concerning domestic violence for everyone to read. Just as surprising to me is the fact that there was no reaction to McDonough's obvious belief, implied in his *Globe* article, that *Wilfredo Codero is the victim*. It should be the responsibility of newspapers not to allow their reporters to refer to any incident, domestic violence or otherwise, as an "*alleged incident*" after the guilty party admits his or her guilt in court. I remain convinced the Will McDonough is not the only person on the staff of the *Globe* or elsewhere that continues to believe domestic violence is just a lot of media hype.[36]

Just six days after McDonough's column Ana Codero called the police, this time back in Mayaguez, Puerto Rico, and complained that Wilfredo had threatened her. "He told her he was going to rip off her head and then shut the door," stated Mayaguez Police Captain David Ortiz. She requested and received another restraining order.[37] On December 19, 1997 Ana Codero requested that the restraining order be removed. Cordero's lawyer, Jose Quinones Cruz stated that it is all just a misunderstanding "The mentality of Americans is a little different from ours in cases like this."[38] I bet Will McDonough believes many Americans do have that same mentality.

On March 23, 1998 Cordero signed a one year contract with the Chicago White Sox for a guaranteed one million dollars. The agreement could be worth as much as much as five million if Cordero gets enough plate appearances. Not until the signing of this contract did Cordero admit any remorse for his past behavior. Some people will say anything for money. Concerning fan acceptance of Cordero, White Sox manager Jerry Manuel stated, "I think as long as we come back into Chicago playing good, hard-nosed, aggressive baseball, I feel our fans will accept us."[39] I believe that Cordero has demonstrated that he can be hard-nosed and aggressive.

This sorrowful incident demonstrates that little genuine progress has been accomplished.[40] Public policymakers, women and victim rights advocates, and the criminal justice system have yet to agree on coherent, logical, systematic and unified positive goals, policies, procedures, sanctions, and programs that must proceed and follow the arrest process. A review of this nation's newspapers would reveal that the Cordero case is not an isolated incident. After twenty years there remains not even a universal definition of domestic violence nor is there a collective national method of implementation all agencies are willing to accept. While laws have changed dramatically attitudes have not.[41] While laws have changed dramatically little to no thought has been given to the logistical problems these legislative changes have created. The educational process must become the constructive course that will allow us to rethink current assumptions and provide the aggregate link between public awareness and a unified and clear sense of resolve that is understandable and acceptable to all concerned.

A proper and amicable commitment ought to start with a commonsense agreement among all three of the above groups. The lack of collaboration between these groups has delayed the proper development of appropriate and proper policies. Agreement must be reached that a proactive resolution for all domestic violence incidents can not and ought not to begin with the reactive policies of the criminal justice system.

NOTES

1. Gordon Edes, "Cordero: Day in Court," *Boston Globe*, June 12, 1997, p. D1.

2. Eve S. Buzawa and Carl G. Buzawa, *Domestic Violence: The Criminal Justice Response* (Newbury Park, Calif.: Sage Publishing, 1990) p. 82.

3. Gordon Edes, "Cordero Charged in Wife's Beating," *Boston Globe*, October 12, 1997, p. A30

4. John Ellement and William F. Doherty, "Judge Wanted Cordero Held Until Court Session, Source Says," *Boston Globe*, June 14, 1997, p. B2.

5. Matthew Brelis and Judy Rakowsky, "Cordero Case Spotlights Bail Flaws," *Boston Globe*, June 29, 1997, p. B1.

6. Ellement and Doherty, "Judge Wanted Cordero Held," p. B2.

7. *Massachusetts General Law* 276.33A

8. Edes, "Cordero," p. A30.

9. Brelis and Rakowsky, "Cordero Case Spotlights Bail Flaws," p. B1.

10. Will McDonough, "Cordero's Lawyers Cry Foul," *Boston Globe*, August 30, 1997, p. F1.

11. Gordon Edes, "Stressed-out Cordero Asks for a Night Off," *Boston Globe*, September 1, 1997, p. B1.

12. Patricia Nealon, "Prosecutors Altering Approach to Help Press Cases," *Boston Globe*, September 25, 1994, p. 28.

13. Edes, "Cordero," p. A30.

14. Eileen McNamara, "Fans' Trust Takes a Beating," *Boston Globe*, June 28, 1997, p. B1.

15. Edes, "Cordero," p. D1.

16. Stephen Kurkjian and Matthew Brelis, "Cordero's Ex-Wife Said He Beat Her During Marriage," *Boston Globe*, June 27, 1997, p. A1.

17. Judy Rakowesky, "Cordero Needs Help, Ex-Wife Says," *Boston Globe*, June 28, 1997, p. A1.

18. Tito Stevens and Judy Rakowesky, "More Abuse Alleged," *Boston Globe*, July 1, 1997, p. C1.

19. *Boston Globe*, 12 July 1997: A10.

20. Eileen McNamara, "Red Sox Have Short Memory," *Boston Globe*, June 14, 1997, p. B1.

21. Kurkjian and Brelis, "Cordero's Ex-Wife Said He Beat Her," p. A8.

22. Stevens and Rokowesky, "More Abuse Alleged," p. C1.

23. Gordon Edes, "League Office to Investigate Allegations," *Boston Globe*, June 28, 1997, p. G2.

24. Ibid. p. G2.

25. Lee Jenkins, "Incident Baffles, Bothers Orioles," *Boston Globe,* June 12, 1997, p. D6.

26. *Boston Globe,* "For the Sake of Ana Cordero," June 14, 1997, p. A14.

27. *Massachusetts General Law* 276.42.

28. Doris Sue Wong, "Weld Advocates Broad Changes in Bail System," *Boston Globe,* July 24, 1997, p. B2.

29 John Ellement, "Bail Reset for Spouse Held in Plot to Kill Wife," *Boston Globe,* December 2, 1997, p. B3.

30. Marvin Pave, "The Cordero Fallout," *Boston Globe,* June 20, 1997, p. C1

31. Gordon Edes, "Vaughn's Parents Show up for Corderos," *Boston Globe,* July 25,1997, p. E6.

32. Dan Shaughnessy, "It's Time to Speak his Piece on Sports World," *Boston Globe,* July 28, 1997, p. D1.

33.Niel Jacobson and John Gottman, *When Men Batter Women* (New York: Simon & Schuster, 1998), p. 44.

34. *Boston Globe,* "The Next Step For a Batterer," November 5, 1997, p. A22.

35. Stephen Kurkjian and Gordon Edes, "Cordero Pleads Guilty to Assault," *Boston Globe,* November 5, 1997, p. B1.

36. Will McDonough, "Jacksonville Foes go on a Talking Jag," *Boston Globe,* December 6, 1997, p. D1,

37. Stephanie Ebbert and Jenifer B. McKim, "Restraining Order Issued to Keep Cordero From Wife," *Boston Globe,* December 13 1997, p. B3.

38. Associated Press, "Order Against Cordero Lifted," *Boston Globe,* December 18, 1997, p. B2.

39. Gordon Edes, "Cordero Gets Pact," *Boston Globe,* March 24, 1998, p. E1.

40. Nancy A. Crowell and Ann W. Burgess, eds. *Understanding Violence Against Women* (Washington, D.C. National Academy Press, 1996) p. v.

41. Eileen McNamara, "Batterers Win Another Round," *Boston Globe,* May 13, 1998, p. B1.

Appendix I

The National Institute of Justice Studies

In the 1970s, feminist activists and domestic violence advocacy groups lobbied our public policymakers to improve the criminal justice system's response to domestic violence. The Law Enforcement Assistance Administration of the Federal Justice Department funded twenty-three different programs and studies between 1976 and 1981.

With the support of a grant from the National Institute of Justice, the Minneapolis Police Department and the Police Foundation conducted the Minneapolis Domestic Violence Experiment. The Minneapolis study is in fact the first scientifically controlled test of the effect of arrest for any crime. The Minneapolis experiment remains, to many public policymakers and women's advocates, the most influential research of police response to domestic violence to date. It does not make that claim, however. The study was in fact followed by other studies of police response to domestic violence studies funded by grants from the National Institute of Justice. Many of the results of these follow-up studies did not produce the findings anticipated (that the intervention of arrest by police will deter domestic violence) by many public policymakers and women's advocates. Inexplicably, most results of these followup studies have essentially been ignored.

The Minneapolis Domestic Violence Experiment was performed from early 1981 to mid-1982. The purpose of the experiment was to attempt to provide an answer to the much-debated question of how police should respond to *misdemeanor cases of domestic violence*. Early on, I believe, criminologists and women's advocacy groups should have noted that misdemeanor crimes are in fact and in point of law considered by law enforcement to be minor crimes. It is my earnest opinion that little thought was given to the reality that, as long as domestic violence calls remain misdemeanors, they will remain just what the law states they are, minor crimes. Misdemeanors will continue to be considered as minor crimes by most police departments, prosecutors, and the courts. Since these studies little effort has been made to make domestic violence assault or domestic violence assault and battery a crime in and of itself. And, yes, I do understand that I seem to be repeating myself many times concerning this same simple detail. Frankly, I cannot understand how something so significant continues to be ignored or misunderstood by those outside law enforcement. If domestic violence is to be considered a serious issue by the criminal justice system, why is it so difficult to make domestic violence a felony?

Social progress is often dependent on opinions fostered by public policy-makers. It should be important to these public policymakers to ensure that when these ideas become public policy, they are supported by evidence that confirms that these concepts make sense. There must be some demonstrative evidence that their opinions are substantiated by the fact that their ideas are the right ideas.

In May 1984, the U.S. National Institute of Justice announced the findings of the Minneapolis study. Four months later, the attorney general of the United States issued a report recommending that arrest be made the standard treatment in cases of misdemeanor domestic assault.[1] Inside of two years, either mandatory or preferred arrest policy became the most common practice of urban police departments. By 1991, fifteen states and the District of Columbia had passed mandatory arrest statutes for many cases of misdemeanor domestic violence.[2] This dramatic shift in police response created intense controversy nationwide. The most common criticism was that the Minneapolis experiment was simply too limited. In response, the National Institute of Justice sponsored studies to reevaluate the findings of the Minneapolis experiment in six other cities--Atlanta, Charlotte, Colorado Springs, Metro-Dade, Omaha, and Milwaukee. These studies were replicated to determine whether arrest alone would have the deterrent effect it had in Minneapolis. To date, no researcher has discovered any information about the Atlanta study. The major conclusions of the completed studies are summarized as follows:

- Arrest increases domestic violence among people who have nothing to lose, especially the unemployed.
- Arrest deters domestic violence in cities with higher proportions of white and Hispanic suspects.
- Arrest deters domestic violence in the short run but escalates violence later on in cities with higher proportions of unemployed black suspects.
- A small but chronic portion of all violent couples produces the majority of domestic violence incidents.
- Offenders who flee before police arrive are substantially deterred by warrants for their arrests, at least in the Omaha study.[3]

A conference hosted in the spring of 1995 by the National Institute of Justice (NIJ) and the Department of Health and Human Services concluded that the final answer to domestic violence lies beyond the criminal justice system because the answer involves societal behavior and values that cannot altered by the criminal justice system. While the Minneapolis study was a major media story, it was difficult, if not impossible to find the results of this conference. The solution for domestic violence is in the hands of all of us and not the criminal justice system.[4]

For over 20 years, research on the effects of increased criminal justice involvement on domestic violence has emphasized systemic reforms and efforts to increase the rate at which legal sanctions are applied. Yet there remains inconsistent and inconclusive knowledge about the effectiveness of criminalizing domestic violence on controlling repeat victimization . . . We simply do not know what the effects of legal sanctions for domestic violence are, whether there are differences in these effects for specific population groups, what the theoretical bases are for their effects or noneffects, and what the risks and limitations of a policy of "criminalization" are.[5]

The following are very condensed summaries of the results of all six studies. I believe that it is difficult to avoid bias in this summarization process. Simply because I believe one section is more important than the other does not make any particular section more important than the other. It should be a requirement that any and all professionals concerned with domestic violence read these studies in their entirety. Since the completion of these studies, I have attended numerous conferences, meetings, symposiums, and debates concerning the subject of domestic violence. I have yet to meet anyone, including those in law enforcement, who has read all of these studies. In fact, a great many of the participants of these meetings, other than the Minneapolis Experiment, do not even know of the existence of these other NIJ studies.

Copies or information on how to get copies can be obtained by writing to the National Institute of Justice, P.O. Box 6000, Rockville, Md. 20850 or by calling 800-851-3420. The reader may also consult *Journal of Criminal Law and Criminology*, Northwestern University School of Law, Volume 83, Number 1, Spring 1992. Any and all professionals who have a passionate concern about the issue of domestic violence and the criminal justice system must read Lawrence W. Sherman's *Policing Domestic Violence.* For the criminal justice practitioners, our public policymakers, and particularly for feminist activists and advocacy groups for battered women, it is critical that they read the National Institute of Justice Research Report, *The Criminalization of Domestic Violence: Promises and Limits* authored by Jeffrey Fagan. A copy can be obtained using the same information above from the National Criminal Justice Reference Service. It is requisite reading.

THE MINNEAPOLIS DOMESTIC VIOLENCE EXPERIMENT

In order to find which police approach was most effective in deterring future domestic violence, the design of the experiment used three different police responses. The suspect would be either arrested, sent away from the scene of the assault for eight hours, or given some form of advice, which would include mediation by the responding officers. Officers who responded to the scene provided a total of 314 cases. The police officers agreed to meet monthly with Lawrence W. Sherman, the project director, and Nancy Wester, the project manager. A predominantly female research staff was to contact the victims for a detailed in-person interview. This interview would then be followed by telephone interviews every two weeks for twenty-four weeks. Only 205 of the cases could be located and interviews obtained.

Two kinds of measures of repeat violence were used. One was a police record of an offender repeating domestic violence during the six-month followup period. The second came from interviews in which the victims were asked if there had been a repeat incident with the same subject. The repeat incident was defined to be an actual assault, threatened assault, or property damage.

The findings demonstrate that arrest was the most effective of the three methods used by the officers. The other two, attempting to counsel both parties or sending assailants away from home for several hours, were found to be less effective in deterring future violence.

The preponderance of evidence did suggest that the police should use arrest in most domestic violence cases. It also reported that these results do not imply that all suspected assailants in all domestic violence incidents should be arrested. It concluded that other experiments in other settings were needed before any major policy changes should take place. These other experiments are needed because the cultural context of other cities would produce different effects of police actions. This study is the most widely cited and often misunderstood by domestic violence victim advocates and remains the most influential of all the National Institute of Justice criminal justice experiments.

THE MILWAUKEE DOMESTIC VIOLENCE EXPERIMENT

This replication experiment in Milwaukee, Wisconsin, again had Lawrence Sherman as director and again it used three different police responses. Police officers were randomly assigned to arrest under a mandatory arrest policy, and the suspect was eligible for release on $250. This process would vary but averaged about eleven hours. The suspect was to be arrested but to be released on personal recognizance, with no money involved, about three hours after booking at the police station. The third process provided for no arrest at all but a warning of arrest if the police had to return within twenty-four hours. In this experiment both the arrested suspect and victim were immediately interviewed. The officers assigned provided a total of 1,200 cases.

The outcomes of the three different responses were measured by known repeat offenses within six months of the initial police response. The second again was by interview with the victim, this time six months later.

This analysis of the data discovered no evidence of an overall long-term deterrent effect with the use of standard arrest. Initial deterrent effects observed for up to thirty days after the incident quickly disappeared. In fact, one year later the arrest response had produced an escalation effect. The first reported act of repeat violence occurred about 20 percent sooner than it did following the warning process. Arrest was also found to have different effects on different kinds of people; employed, married, white high school graduates, for example, were more likely to be deterred by arrest than were unemployed, unmarried, black high school dropouts. Violence with the latter group tended to escalate with arrest. The experiment concluded that the deterrence effectiveness of arrest of the alleged abuser varied according to many characteristics and in many cases correlated with an escalation of domestic violence.

THE OMAHA DOMESTIC VIOLENCE EXPERIMENT

This replication experiment took place in Omaha, Nebraska and used three different police responses. The suspect would be either arrested, given some form of mediation by the responding officers, or separated for a minimum of eight hours. In all, the officers who responded provided a total of 330 cases.

The outcomes of the three different responses were measured by new arrests and complaints for any crimes committed by the suspect against the victim. The second was by an interview of the victim within the first week following the offense and then a second six months later.

This analysis of the data discovered that arrest by itself did not appear to deter subsequent domestic violence any more than separating or mediation. It did appear that what the police did in Omaha after responding to cases of misdemeanor domestic assault neither helped nor hurt victims in terms of subsequent conflict. The failure to replicate the Minneapolis study should cast some doubt on the wisdom of a mandatory or even a preferred arrest policy for cases of misdemeanor domestic assault.

The study suggests as an alternative policy one that encourages arrest when probable cause for arrest exists. It suggests that the police prefer to arrest when there is probable cause for an arrest and the failure to do so in many cases of domestic assault is often due to the belief that the justice system does not follow through with prosecution and sanctions in cases where arrests for misdemeanor domestic assault have been made.

It did find that abusers who had fled the scene before the arrival of the police were less likely to engage in subsequent conflict if they were subjected to a warrant for their arrest. This result suggests that an outstanding warrant a greater deterrent than an actual arrest. According to the report, before consideration of change in police policy decisions concerning warrants, we should wait for more results from other studies.

THE CHARLOTTE DOMESTIC VIOLENCE EXPERIMENT

This replication experiment took place in Charlotte, North Carolina, and used three different police responses. The police officers advised and sometimes separated the couple, issued a citation for the offender to appear in court, or arrested the offender at the scene of the incident. In all, the officers assigned provided a total of 650 cases.

The outcomes of the three different responses were measured by known repeat offenses within six months of the initial police response. The second measure was by initial interview with the victim, followed by another interview six months later.

The report delineates the relative failure rates of each of the three police responses in deterring subsequent abuse. Arrest was not found to be a greater deterrent than advising/separating or issuing a citation. The six-month followup period showed higher proportions of at least one repeat arrest among the suspects randomly assigned to arrest and citation than among those assigned to advice/separation. The followup interviews also revealed substantially more subsequent abuse than did the official arrest data. The experiment also revealed that spouse abusers are rarely found guilty and rarely spend any significant time in jail. An analysis of how soon the first repeat arrest occurred also shows that the formal sanctioning treatments increased violence significantly over the informal treatment. The report concludes that even though arrest was not shown to have a particular deterrent or punitive value, the decision to arrest may be the correct conscientious choice. It must be beyond my meager intellectual capacities to understand how the report findings, which in part demonstrate that formal sanctioning treatments such as arrest *may increase violence significantly* over informal treatments, can possibly be the correct conscientious choice for those who will suffer increased abuse. I warned you earlier against my bias, and I suppose here it is on display.

COLORADO DOMESTIC VIOLENCE EXPERIMENT

This replication experiment took place in Colorado Springs, Colorado, and used four different police responses. Police officers were randomly assigned to arrest the suspect and include with the arrest an emergency protection order to stay away from the victim. This order was issued at the time of the arrest. The police would provide immediate crisis counseling for the suspect at police headquarters and issue an emergency protection order but would not arrest the suspect. Police officers could issue an emergency protection order with no arrest and no counseling. The officers could restore order and provide advice at the scene. The officers who responded provided a total of 1,658 cases.

The outcomes of the three different responses were measured by new arrests and complaints for any future crimes against the victim. There would be an initial interview followed by another interview six months later.

Analysis of the data showed that arrest does not deter repeat domestic crime, while according to the opinions of victim interview data it did. This paradox may have been caused because the majority of crimes in the sample did not entail violence: 54 percent of the calls were for harassment, 3 percent for menacing complaint, and in 2 percent the suspect would not allow the victim to leave the home. This result could have been produced by the low victim response rate (58%) for the six-month followup interview.

THE METRO-DADE DOMESTIC VIOLENCE EXPERIMENT

This replication experiment was performed in the Miami Metro-Dade area and used four different police responses. Arrest and no arrest response were each divided into two groups: those with and without followup counseling by a Safe Streets Unit of the police department. In all, the officers who responded provided a total of 907 cases.

The outcomes of the different responses were measured by the suspect against the victim. A followup visit/interview was provided by a specially trained police unit within two weeks of the original call. The experiment provided for an initial interview and a followup interview six months later. A completed comprehensive questionnaire covered the history of the victim's relationship with the suspect.

This analysis of the data demonstrated the significant deterrent effects of the arrest policy. The interviews showed significant effects attributable to the arrest treatment with respect to both prevalence and incidence of physical assaults against the victim. No effect attributable to followup by the special domestic violence police unit was found.

NOTES

1. U.S. Attorney General's Task Force on Family Violence, *U.S. Department of Justice Final Report*, 1984, pp. 10-26.

2. Lawrence W. Sherman, and Ellen G. Cohen, "The Impact of Research on Legal Policy: The Minneapolis Domestic Violence Experiment," *Law and Society Review* 23, no. 1 (1989): 117-126, 333.

3. Stephen Goldsmith, ed., *Prosecutor's Perspective*, Winter 1993, Editor's Note.

4. Jeremy Travis, "Violence Against Women: Reflections on NIJ's Research Agenda," *National Institute of Justice Journal* (February 1996): 25.

5. Jeffrey Fagan, *The Criminalization of Domestic Violence Promises and Limits* (Washington, D.C.: U.S. Department of Justice, National Institute of Justice, January, 1996), p. 40.

Appendix II

Family Disputes

When I joined the Brockton Police Department in 1975, the following was the family dispute policy of the department. It would have been the domestic violence policy of its day. This policy presumably used the national policy guidelines of the International Chiefs of Police as its boilerplate. For that reason, the Brockton policies should not have been dramatically different from those of most other police departments during this time period.

At many of the domestic violence forums I have attended over the years, I quite often would hear complaints from various other agencies about police policy and procedures concerning domestic violence from many people, who when I inquired, admitted that they had never read any police policy and procedures. In fact, many who complained specifically about the Brockton Police Departments response to domestic violence had never read nor did they know what the specific policy and procedures of the Brockton Police Department were. There seemed never to be a lack of people who willingly displayed little understanding of the problems our department faced. Displaying only a limited knowledge is often a dangerous practice. When I asked these agencies if I could see their policy and procedures concerning domestic violence most of them admitted that they did not have any. As of this writing most agencies in the criminal justice system, other than police departments, and those agencies concerned with domestic violence were not able to produce any written domestic violence policies.

This appendix provides an opportunity for people who did understand police policy at that time to revisit some of those issues, and it will permit a fair comparison with some of the current policies and can demonstrate how much police policies have changed. It also provides an opportunity for critics, both past and present, to see whether or not they were correct in their criticism.

These guidelines demonstrate that some senior police officers long removed from street duty do not understand what is important to the street/patrol officers and the difficulties they face in these types of calls. I am not sure how many officers after responding as quickly as possible, often with lights and siren on, believe that it is important that they "inspect their uniform and equipment before making entry."

BROCKTON POLICE DEPARTMENT FAMILY DISPUTES

A. GENERAL CONSIDERATIONS AND GUIDELINES

Numerous activities unrelated to crime control or law enforcement make demands on police time and manpower. This is reflected in many calls for assistance involving complaints of a personal or interpersonal nature. Those involving family disputes are sufficient in number and seriousness to warrant particular treatment.

When responding to a situation involving a family dispute, an officer must be vigilant and anticipate the unexpected. What appears to be an argument of a minor nature may soon escalate to a conflict of dangerous proportions. Family disputes are often characterized by anger, frustration, and pitched emotions. These feelings can easily be redirected towards a police officer, with the result that it is the officer who becomes the focus and target of the violence. It is not unusual for uncontrolled aggressive outbursts within families to lead to serious bodily injury or death, with the officers themselves becoming the victims.

Despite such conditions, the police role is often not that of law enforcer, but rather counselor and peacemaker. However, officers should not become personally involved or spend an undue period of time on any one dispute. The goal of the police should be to calm the emotional conflicts and reconcile the disputing parties. To achieve the proper result, the police officer must remain objective and neutral. Proper guidelines are intended to aid in successful police response to family disputes. Without them, unskilled and unguarded police performance may endanger members of the force as well as innocent parties and may fail to prevent the eventual commission of crime.

B. FIRST STAGE-THE INITIAL CONTACT

The entrance of police officers onto the scene of a family dispute can have great impact and usually causes an impasse in the fighting or other dispute at least temporarily. If properly exploited, this impact can be used to extend and suppress the dispute altogether.

The object of the intervention at this stage is to take the disputants' attention away from each other and to direct it toward the police officer in such a way as to allow a breathing spell during which tempers may subside, making resolution of the dispute possible.

To accomplish this, the police officer shall be governed by the following guidelines:

1. Officers should await the arrival of a backup unit if assigned to a oneman car and otherwise refrain from taking action pending the arrival or presence of a second officer. Where circumstances require a single officer to act independently, he shall exercise caution to ensure his own safety and rely on common sense and field experience in deciding when and how to proceed.

2. Upon establishing initial contact with the disputants, the officer should convey a professional image, which is reflected by his calm and helpful attitude.

   a. Beforehand, inspect his uniform and equipment. Neatness and cleanliness can have an important impact upon entry.

   b. Introduce himself by giving his name and title.

   c. Explain that a call has been received and that he would like to be of assistance.

   d. Avoid profanity or the excessive use or impression of authority. (Even where no crime has been committed, the decision to call the police indicates that someone is deeply upset. The goal of the police is to calm such emotions and reconcile the parties.)

   e. Do not degrade or show disrespect to the disputants or any member of the family. Anger can very easily be redirected toward the officer where family unity is threatened.

   f. Indicate neutrality; show that as a police officer he will not take sides. (Since it is frequently the woman of the house who summons the police, the man of the house commonly sees him as an agent of his wife and transfers to the officer the anger he previously directed against his wife. It is therefore crucial to immediately assure the man of complete neutrality.)

3. Since the officer is responding to a request for police assistance, he should remain until entry is granted and not leave until he has accomplished his purpose.

   a. At a minimum, this requires an officer to ensure that peace is restored. This usually consists of an opportunity to observe and ask a few questions.

   b. However, these specific guidelines shall govern any situation:

      i. An officer may enter any private premises where one or both of the parties grant permission or where there is probable cause to believe a felony is being committed or there is virtual certainty of violence resulting in death or physical injury or where a breach of the peace has taken place in his presence.

ii. An officer must leave if both parties request that he do so unless there is probable cause to believe that a felony has been committed or a crime is occurring in the officer's presence.

iii. An officer having probable cause to believe that a felony or an arrestable misdemeanor has occurred may force entry for the purpose of making an arrest or to make an appropriate disposition short of arrest.

4. Upon entry, immediately evaluate the emotional state of the people present at the scene and beware of evidence of weapons or injuries.

C. SECOND STAGE-RESTORATION OF CALM

Upon entry to the premises, the officer should make every effort to extend the impasse in the dispute generally precipitated by his arrival and to restore calm. To achieve this goal, the police officer should be governed by the following guidelines:

1. If violence is occurring, physically intervene and arrest, if necessary.

2. Assume a firm and neutral attitude. Don't shout. By speaking firmly, yet softly, the disputants will usually moderate their voices too.

3. Whenever possible, avoid having children present at the scene.

4. Third parties should not be permitted to intervene unless they can make a contribution to the resolution of the dispute.

5. If summary arrest is required, it should be made. Avoid arrest if possible, unless other measures have failed or would be obviously futile.

6. In separating the persons involved, make a quick visual survey of the area for objects that could be used as weapons, and control the movements of those present as much as possible.

7. Disputants should be separated with sufficient distance between them so that each may relate his or her story individually without interruption. Take them to separate rooms if possible. At the same time, try to always maintain visual contact with the other police officer. Where any kind of anger has been displayed, do not take a person into the kitchen because of the increased availability of weapons.

8. Carefully listen to the person's story. This is important for two reasons. First, facts may be needed upon which to base a later course of action. Second, the person's opportunity to vent his or her anger and tell his or her story to an interested third party can, by itself, contribute in a major way to the defusing of

the person's rage. Avoid any display of disinterest. If the officer is not attentive, the person will be frustrated even more and so the chance of a violent outbreak will increase.

9. For disputes involving children or teenagers, avoid the adult tendency to use an overbearing attitude in calming or distracting the youth. Treat them as adults. By so doing, the youth will feel that he is being approached and treated with respect.

10. Consider a parent's bitter indictment of his or her children with a little skepticism. Keep in mind when attempting to assess the situation that parents frequently use their children as scapegoats for their own problems, inadequacies, and frustrations.

11. Never take verbal or emotional reactions as personal affronts or as insults to the integrity of the department. Remember that the appearance of police on the scene allows the disputants to ventilate their anger and that the officer is seen as a symbol of authority; the people react emotionally to the presence of authority in their own home where they have traditionally been in charge. In such situations, the officer should indicate that it is not his intention or purpose to challenge the person's authority, but to assist in resolving the dispute.

12. When necessary, inform the parties of the limits of police authority. Normally, civil matters are not a police concern. Family disputes are an exception, however, because of their tendency toward violence and the ease with which they can be renewed.

D. THIRD STAGE-FACT FINDING

The purpose of this stage of the intervention is to gather information that will assist in the effective evaluation and handling of the problems involved.

1. To deal intelligently with the situation, an officer must ask questions. Certain fundamentals must be followed while keeping the interruptions to a minimum.

   a. Obtain information regarding identities and family relationships.

   b. Unless necessary, never demand answers or ask a question in such a manner that it is a command.

   c. Avoid questions that belittle or reflect poorly on the individual.

   d. Do not emphasize or question in depth on personal matters if there is an indication that the person would rather not discuss them more fully.

e. Attempt to discover if there is a prior history of such disputes and the nature and extent of them.

f. Express appreciation for the person's cooperation.

2. Consumption of alcohol or mental illness always aggravates a situation. Officers should recognize such conditions and the resulting necessity for greater patience in handling the dispute. Procedures for handling alcoholics and mentally ill should also be followed.

3. Keep in mind that he may be in a household where the ethnic, economic, and social atmosphere may be completely different from his own. Because of this, the officer may find himself shocked or confused about what he hears; but if he is to be effective, he must remain neutral and polite. Here are some suggestions for the approach:

a. Avoid the use of phrases or expressions which challenge the person's dignity, family pride, or general background.

b. Refer to those present as 'Mr.' and 'Mrs.'

c. Use normal asking and receiving terms; for example; 'Please', 'Thank you', 'Yes Sir', and 'No Sir'.

d. Arrange for an interpreter, if possible, if the disputants do not speak English. Ensure that the interpreter is neutral in the dispute, and where appropriate, get both parties to approve of the selection. Using other members of the family for interpreting is usually not advisable due to emotional ties or the tendency to interpret to the advantage of the party they favor.

D. FOURTH STAGE-FINAL DISPOSITION

After establishing an atmosphere of relative calm, gather the accounts from the disputants, and observing other significant facts, the next step is to attempt a solution.

1. Mediation within a reasonable time is the primary goal of intervention, and except where serious crimes have occurred necessitating arrest, all efforts should be directed toward achieving a real mediation.

a. Keep in mind the important role of the participants in deciding on any solution. A settlement cannot be imposed. Unless the parties themselves agree that a given solution is proper, any agreement between them will quickly disappear after the officers leave the premises. Ask each person to discuss his or her views in the presence of the other and to offer solutions. Remind them that any real settlement must be reached based on their own initiative and willingness to help themselves.

b. Offer positive aspects of the home that can be brought to the attention of the disputants. There is always something complimentary that can be said, whether it be that the children appear well cared for or that they act politely, or that the home is neat, and so on. The point in doing this is that when you as an outsider recognize some attribute of the home and compliment the people on it, this eases the embarrassment of having the police in their home and allows them to share a common pride. Bringing people together ultimately contributes to resolution.

c. As to the content of the mediations, this cannot be specified beforehand. Essentially what is to be sought is the recognition by each party as to how he contributed to the problem, and a commitment to solve the problem by alternative methods other than fighting, screaming, or disruption. Frequently, a referral is made for future consultation.

2. Referrals. Where outside counseling appears advisable, but before suggesting a referral, carefully consider what the most appropriate referral would be. It is essential that the disputants be referred only to an agency that is equipped to help with their particular problem. A full list of social service agencies is available through the Multi-Health Center, and police officers as a part of their general responsibilities should make a continuing effort to become familiar with the agencies' services and personnel.

a. When making a referral, write down the name of the agency, the address, and the telephone number. If someone at the agency is known personally, write down his or her name. Parties are much more likely to take advantage of services offered when they have a specific person to ask for upon arrival at the facility.

b. If there is a choice between agencies, make the referral to the agency or organization closest to the home of the disputants.

c. Never use referrals as a means of avoiding the problem. A useless referral will only lead to more calls and an increased potential for violence.

3. Temporary separation. Sometimes as a part of mediation, and in addition to referral, it may be advisable to separate the participants temporarily while emotions subside. This solution must be arrived at by mutual agreement and may be facilitated by a friend or relative living nearby on a short-term basis.

4. Arrest. Some situations offer no reasonable alternative but to arrest, for instance, where there has been a serious assault committed in the officer's presence. As a general guideline, however, arrest should be avoided where

possible since it does not constitute a lasting solution to a family dispute. Too often the situation between the disputants worsens or creates a serious danger for the arresting officer due to possible efforts to resist arrest. This is especially true when a husband or father is arrested in his home or in the presence of his family.

    a. If it appears that no crime or a minor crime has been committed and one of the disputants insists on an arrest, the officer should explain the extent and consequences of such action.

        i. Court proceedings.

        ii. Loss of income.

        iii. Perpetual hostility.

    b. It is not unusual in such disputes for the person who insists upon an arrest in the heat of a quarrel to refuse to cooperate later in court and even to criticize police for taking such action after the fact.

F. POLICE REPORTS

Officers shall file all necessary or appropriate reports prior to the conclusion of his tour of duty in accordance with the current department procedures.

Appendix III

Police Policy and Procedure

Most police departments in Massachusetts have implemented policies involving domestic violence that have replaced the old policy and procedure of family disputes. In the past two decades proper law enforcement intervention concerning domestic violence has emerged as a major concern. The primary purpose of these policies is to provide a clear written policy regarding the dramatic change in how police departments handle domestic violence calls for service. The adoption and implementation as part of a department's written directive system will help reduce the exposure of the chief, the officers who respond, and the community they serve, in civil liability demands. These policies and procedures are intended to be used in conjunction with a department's in-service training programs.

In addition, Massachusetts law Chapter 403 of the Acts of 1990 requires that the secretary of public safety issue a model domestic violence law enforcement policy for local police. The police departments may adopt the model guideline in whole or in part. The Executive Office of Public Safety then reviews and approves the policy. The majority of departments have used these guidelines provided by the Municipal Police Institute and the Massachusetts Chiefs of Police Association to ensure uniformity. These guidelines included and expanded those issued by the Executive Office of Public Safety.

DOMESTIC VIOLENCE

I. GENERAL CONSIDERATIONS AND GUIDELINES

Among the most difficult and sensitive calls for police assistance are those involving domestic violence. When responding to a domestic disturbance, officers must be both alert and impartial, and must be concerned with the needs of victims where domestic violence is apparent or alleged. At the same time, officers must always anticipate the unexpected. What appears to be a dispute of a minor nature may quickly escalate into a conflict of dangerous proportions because of the potentially violent nature of such incidents. Domestic violence situations are often characterized by anger, frustration, intense emotions and a batterer's attempt to control household members. These feelings can easily be directed against the responding officers, who can suddenly become the focus and target of ensuing violence. It is not unusual for aggressive outbursts within families to lead to serious bodily injury or even death. For this reason, whenever possible, at least two police officers should be assigned to a domestic violence situation unless immediate intervention is necessary to prevent serious physical harm.

II. G.L.C209A ABUSE PREVENTION LAW

Whenever any law officer has reason to believe that a family or household member has been abused or is in danger of being abused, such officer shall use all reasonable means to prevent further abuse. The officer shall take, but not be limited to the following action:

A. Remain on the scene where the abuse occurred or was (or is) in danger of occurring as long as the officer has reason to believe that at least one of the parties involved would be in immediate physical danger without the presence of a law officer for a reasonable period to prevent abuse.

B. Assist the abused person in obtaining medical treatment necessitated by an assault, which may include driving the victim to the emergency room of the nearest health care facility, notwithstanding any law to the contrary.

C. Assist the abused person and dependent children in locating and getting to a safe place, including but not limited to a designated meeting place for a shelter or a family member's or friend's residence (or a similar place of safety). The officer shall consider the victim's preference in this regard and what is reasonable under all the circumstances.

D. Give abuse victims immediate and adequate notice of their rights by handing them and reading a form detailing their rights; where said person's native language is not English, the statement shall be then provided in said person's native language whenever possible.

E. Assist the abused person by activating the Emergency Judicial System (generally by contacting the state police, unless some other procedure has been established) when the court is closed for business.

F. Inform the victim that the abuser will be eligible for bail and may be promptly released.

G. Arrest any person the officer witnesses or has probable cause to believe has violated a temporary or permanent vacate, restraining, or no-contact order or judgment.

H. Where there are no vacate, restraining or no-contact orders or judgments in effect, arrest shall be the preferred response, that is, whenever an officer witnesses or has probable cause to believe that a person

1. has committed a felony; or

2. has committed an assault and battery in violation of G.L.c.265,s.13A; or

3. has committed a misdemeanor involving abuse.

NOTE: Arrest for a misdemeanor not committed in the officer's presence is a statutory exception to the long-standing rule that limited misdemeanor arrests to those committed in the officer's presence. Officers are now authorized to arrest for past misdemeanors not committed in their presence as long as the officers have probable cause to believe that a misdemeanor involving "abuse" occurred. Such misdemeanors include but are not limited to threats to commit crimes against the person or property of another (G.L.c.275,s.2).

For the purposes of this law, "abuse" is defined as "the occurrence of one or more of the following acts between family or household members: (a) attempting to cause or causing physical harm; (b) placing another in fear of imminent physical harm; (c) causing another to engage involuntarily in sexual relations by force, threat of force or duress."

The safety of the victim and any involved children shall be paramount in any decision to arrest. Any officer arresting both parties is required by law to submit a detailed, written report in addition to an incident report, setting forth the grounds for dual arrest. (Dual arrests, like the issuance of mutual restraining orders, trivialize the seriousness of domestic abuse and increase the danger to its victims.)

Officers investigating an incident of domestic violence shall not threaten, suggest, or otherwise indicate the arrest of all parties for the purpose of discouraging requests for law enforcement intervention by any party.
Regardless of arrest, whenever an officer investigates an incidence of domestic violence, the officer shall immediately file a written incident report on the prescribed departmental form. The victim shall be provided a copy of the full incident report at no cost, upon request to the police department.

Family or household members are persons who:

1. are or were married to one another;

2. are or were residing together in the same household;

3. are related by blood or are or were related by marriage;

4. have a child in common regardless of whether they have ever married or lived together; or

5. are or have been in a substantial dating relationship as determined by a court. (This includes same-sex relationships.)

Chapter 209A specifically provides that police shall make a warrantless arrest of a person whom the officer has probable cause to believe has committed a misdemeanor by violating a temporary or permanent vacate, restraining or no-contact order or judgment (G.L.c.276,s.20). Even if the victim is unwilling to bring a complaint against the alleged abuser, officers are expected to arrest where probable cause exists. (*NOTE*: While G.L.c.276,s.28 concerning arrest without a warrant for a violation of certain statutes, among which is listed c.209A, uses the word "may," this is superseded by the provisions of c.209A which specifies that officers "shall" make such a warrantless arrest.)

In additionally, the trespass law-G.L.c.266,s.120 has been amended by including within its scope a violation of a "get-out" order issued pursuant to G.L.c.208,s.234B, or G.L.c.209A.

An officer may arrest and detain a person charged with a misdemeanor, without having a warrant for such arrest in his possession, if the officer has actual knowledge that a warrant then in full force and effect for the arrest of such person has in fact been issued. (G.L.c.276,s.28.)

According to Chapter 403 of the Acts of 1990: "No law officer shall be held liable in any civil action regarding personal injury or injury to property brought by any party to a domestic violence incident for an arrest based on probable cause when such officer acted reasonably and in good faith and in compliance with this chapter and the statewide policy as established by the secretary of public safety."

It is strongly recommended that all reasonable measures be taken to ensure cooperation among law enforcement personnel and those social service agencies involved with domestic violence incidents.

III. RESPONSE

The unique nature of domestic violence situations requires that an officer immediately proceed to the place of the dispute. Check with the dispatcher about previous incidents and existing orders. If possible, a backup up officer should also be dispatched to the scene.

   A. The initial contact by the responding officers must convey a professionally calm and helpful attitude.

      1. The officers shall state their reason for being present.

      2. They must be considerate and attentive toward all parties.

      3. Upon entering, they shall prevent the physical movement of the parties as much as possible and control their access to any potential weapons.

   B. Officers are authorized by c.209A to transport victims of domestic violence to the emergency room of the nearest hospital. However, the preferred method of transportation is via ambulance, or if the victim is not seriously injured, in their own vehicle or that of a friend. Officers should receive approval from their supervisor prior to transporting victims of domestic violence abuse in a cruiser, except in an emergency.

   C. The responding officer(s) must take immediate control of the situation and should separate the parties to prevent any violent action. However, if there are two officers present at the scene, they should remain within view of each other to avoid any subsequent allegations of mistreatment.

   D. The use of alcohol and drugs, or a condition of mental illness, can aggravate a domestic violence situation, requiring far greater patience on the part of the responding officer(s).

   E. The provisions of G.L.c.209A impose specific responsibilities upon the police as regards to a domestic abuse situation. All officers are expected to be thoroughly familiar with the contents of this statute (as amended from time to time) and to act with discretion and competence in carrying out its provisions.

IV. INVESTIGATION

Officers responding to domestic violence calls should conduct thorough investigations, including interviewing children, neighbors and other potential witnesses. Keep in mind that the same standards for probable cause apply to domestic violence offenses as for any other crimes.

A. When investigating a report of domestic violence, officers should be thorough and observe the following guidelines:

1. These specific guidelines shall govern any situation:

a. Officer(s) may enter private premises at the request of someone in lawful control of the premises, or to enforce the provisions of a protective court order or to take reasonable measures to prevent any further abuse under the authority of G.L.c.209A.

b. Officer(s) may enter private premises where there is probable cause to believe that a felony has been or is being committed or that there is imminent danger of violence which could result in death or serious physical injury or where a breach of the peace has been committed in the officer(s) presence.

c. Officer(s) must leave if both parties request that they do so unless there is probable cause to believe that a felony has been committed or that their continued presence is necessary to prevent physical harm or to carry out the provisions of G.L.c.209A.

d. "Private premises" includes a house, an apartment, a condominium, a hotel room, a mobile home, or a house trailer.

2. In attempting to ascertain the facts in the dispute, the officer(s) should allow each party to present his or her story individually, avoiding any unnecessary interruptions or undue interference by either party. While keeping all parties and officers in view, separate the parties sufficiently to allow each to relate matters to an officer without being overheard by the other party.

3. To deal with the situation, the officer(s) must ask pertinent questions, and certain fundamentals must be followed:

a. Obtain information regarding identities and relationships, including children. Obtain the phone number of the residence and include it in the incident report for use by the bailbonds-person in informing the victim of the abuser's release on bail. Inform the victim that if the victim intends to leave the residence, and wishes to be informed of such release, the victim must inform the police department of a number where the victim can be reached, or where a message of such release can be safely relayed to the victim.

b. Obtain information about firearms.

c. Unless necessary, avoid emphasis or in-depth questioning on personal matters if there is an indication that the person would rather not discuss them more fully.

d. Ascertain if there is a prior history of such disputes and whether there are any vacate, restraining, no-contact, or other protective orders currently in effect.

e. Determine, when appropriate, who has lawful custody of any minors involved and whether court approved visitation rights are being transgressed.

f. As a standard precaution, police should check for outstanding arrest warrants on persons encountered during a domestic dispute. Since official court orders and other court papers are the best source for much of this information, police should ask the parties to produce copies of court orders or other court papers to verify their claims. In addition, the police records bureau may be checked, or appropriate courts, social service agencies or attorneys contacted.

g. Gather information, where applicable, which will assist the District, Probate or Boston municipal courts in determining whether a "substantial dating relationship" exists. This is especially helpful if the officer anticipates activating the Emergency Judicial Response System. Chapter 209A specifies that such courts will take into consideration the following factors:

    i. the length of time of the relationship;

    ii. the type of relationship;

    iii. the frequency of interaction between the parties; and

    iv. if the relationship has been terminated by either person, the length of time elapsed since the termination of the relationship.

h. Provide the addresses and telephone numbers of available crisis centers or emergency shelters and, where appropriate, advise any victims or witnesses of the Victim-witness Assistance Program administered by the local District Attorney's office.

V. CHILDREN

A. When children are present at a domestic dispute, their welfare and safety must be a major consideration. Any evidence of neglect or emotional, physical, or sexual abuse of children under 18 shall be carefully noted. Whenever a police officer, in his professional capacity, has reasonable cause to believe that a child under 18 is suffering serious physical or emotional injury resulting from abuse, including sexual abuse, or by witnessing domestic abuse, or from neglect, including malnutrition, or if a child is determined to be physically dependent upon an addictive drug at birth, the officer shall make a full report to his superior such that an oral and written report can be made to the Department of Social Services as required by G.L.c.119.s.51A. If an officer believes that a child under 18 has died because of neglect, abuse, or drug addiction, or is present in a household in which the officer observes the presence of drugs or evidence of drug use, he shall make a full report to his superior in addition to the report to the Department of Social Service in accordance with that same statute.

B. Officers should be aware that in serious cases of child neglect or abuse "any person" may apply to an appropriate juvenile court to have custody of a child under eighteen taken away from the parents or other neglectful or abusing custodian and have custody transferred, on an emergency basis, to the Department of Social Services or a licensed child care agency or individual.

VI. PROPERTY

The relationship of the parties and their property interests complicate domestic violence situations. When a party to a domestic dispute is accused of removing or attempting to remove property from the dwelling or is accused of damaging or destroying property, he or she should be warned of the potential civil or criminal consequences of his or her conduct, and both parties should be advised to seek legal counsel. A vacate order issued pursuant to c.209A includes the following requirements:

The defendant shall not damage any of the plaintiff's belongings or those of another occupant and shall not shut off any utilities or mail delivery to the plaintiff.

VII. FIREARMS

When a firearm or other weapon is present at the scene of a domestic violence situation or the responding officer(s) are informed that a firearm or weapon has been or may be involved in the dispute, the officer(s) shall:

A. Request that the firearm or weapon be placed in their custody temporarily.

B. Search for and take custody of the firearm or weapon if one of the parties requests they do so.

C. Seize and take temporary custody of the firearm or weapon to alleviate the threat of serious violence that it poses.

D. Determine whether a firearm is lawfully possessed before returning the same.

E. If the officer determines that the weapon cannot be seized:

> 1. the judge can order defendant to surrender guns, License to Carry, and FID card; and

> 2. the chief can revoke a License to Carry for cause and an FID card for: felony convictions, drug use, possession or sale; and mental illness.

VIII. INCIDENT REPORTS

The reporting procedures of any other crime scene should be applied to domestic violence incidents. Prosecution and subsequent legal action can be greatly helped by documentation and description of physical injuries, photographs of the injuries, and/or noting the presence of children in the household, and other information specified under Section IV.

IX. SERVICE OF ORDER

Service of orders shall be in hand unless otherwise ordered by the court. Chapter 209A, section 7, requires that "law enforcement agency shall promptly make its return of service to the court."

Without Judicial authorization, officers should not accompany defendants to the property for any reason.

NOTE: The victim's safety should be considered in the timing of the service of orders.

Appendix IV

Domestic Violence Policy Involving Law Enforcement Personnel

GOVERNOR'S COMMISSION ON DOMESTIC VIOLENCE
POLICY FOR INCIDENTS OF DOMESTIC VIOLENCE
INVOLVING LAW ENFORCEMENT PERSONNEL

The majority of police departments in the Commonwealth of Massachusetts have adopted this type of policy or policies very much like it. This is a specific policy designed to assist and guide investigating officers when members of a police department are suspected of being a domestic violence abuser. It is not the intent of this policy to increase a police officer's exposure, its adoption and implementation should reduce the exposure of liability for the officers of the department, and the chief of police and the municipality they serve.

Most police agencies in Massachusetts and nationwide have a written policy that provides appropriate rules and regulations concerning the conduct of the departments officers. This writer knows of no department that believes its officers are above the law or are exempt from any crimes other than those that provide immunity for reasons of public safety by statute law such as exceeding the speed limit during an emergency call. Many policy officers have lost their jobs because of a deviation form their department rules and regulations that delineate the high standard of comportment expected from police officers. There has been little to no implementation of written rules and regulations concerning domestic violence from other personnel in the criminal justice system. Although there are isolated courts, judges, and prosecutors who urge change there remains little to no systematic change other than police departments.

Most police departments in Massachusetts have established guidelines based on the Governor's Commission on Domestic Violence. Most police departments in Massachusetts continue to wait for the adoption of similar guidelines by others in the criminal justice system. No where in the criminal justice system has the process of change been as comprehensive as the police. It would seem the most appropriate role models would be the Executive Office of Public Safety and those in the office of the attorney general.

1.0 PURPOSE

The Commonwealth of Massachusetts recognizes Domestic Violence as a universal problem that affects people from all walks of life in every community. It is the Law Enforcement Community that this policy addresses. The purpose of the policy is to establish guidelines and to give direction when dealing with domestic violence incidents in which sworn officers are defendants. Domestic Violence is a criminal activity in which arrest is the appropriate and preferred response. No person is exempt, whatever his or her occupation, from the consequences of their actions that result in a violation of M.G.L.c.208, 209,209A, 209C and/or Superior Court injunctions. Therefore, this policy is issued to:

- Ensure the safety of the victims;
- Ensure compliance with all provisions of a court order;
- Ensure compliance with Mass. General Laws, policy, and procedures, rules and regulations; to include: M.G.L.c.208, 209A, 209C; M.G.L.c.140, &129B (An Act Relative To Firearms, Effective July 1, 1994); Executive Office of Public Safety's Policy for Law Enforcement Response to Domestic Violence;
- provide procedures for the uniformity of the investigation, notification and reporting of said incidents and;
- preserve the integrity of the investigation;
- provide for the securing of department issued weapons and personal weapons.

1.   2.0 DEFINITIONS:

Domestic Violence Situations - Those situations involving domestic violence as described in accordance with M.G.L.c.209As1, and c.209ASec6.

Abuse - The occurrence of one or more of the following acts between family or household members:

1. Attempting to cause or causing physical harm;

2. Placing another in fear of physical harm;

3. Causing another to engage involuntarily in sexual relations by force, threats, or duress.

Family or Household Members-Persons who:

1. Are or were married to one another,

2. Are or were residing together in the same household.

3. Are or were related by blood or marriage;

4. Have a child in common regardless of whether they have ever married or lived together; or

5. Are or have been in a substantive dating relationship.

3.0 PROCEDURES

The following procedures shall be adhered to when responding to a domestic violence situation involving a sworn law enforcement officer:

3.1 Responsibilities of Officer(s) Responding to Incident

A. Immediate action shall be taken to ensure the safety of the victim;

B. The responding officer shall proceed with the investigation in accordance with MGLc.208, 209, 209A, 209C, c.140, &129B court orders, policy and procedures, rules, and regulations.

C. A supervisor, who is of higher rank than the involved officer, is to be called to the scene;

D. The responding officer will remain on the scene until relieved by the responding supervisor.

E. Reports are to be completed prior to the end of the officer's tour of duty.

3.2 Responsibilities of the Responding Supervisor

A. Proceed to the scene of the incident;

B. Assess the actual and potential harm to the victim.

C. Ensure enforcement of MGLc.208, 209, 209A, 209C, c.140, &129B, court orders, Policy and Procedures Rules and Regulations.

D. The supervisor will check of LEAPS data-base to determine if there are outstanding restraining orders and/or warrants in effect against the officer.

E. The supervisor shall submit, through the Department's appropriate chain of command a report detailing his/her assessment of the incident and action taken before the end of the supervisor's tour of duty.

3.3 The On-duty Commanding Officer's Responsibilities

The Commanding Officer in charge of the officer(s)/supervisor assigned the initial investigation upon being notified of a domestic violence incident involving a sworn officer, shall:

A.   Ensure that the supervisor has responded to the scene and commenced an investigation.

B.   Ensure enforcement of all provisions of MGLc.208.209, c.140 & 129B, Court orders, policy and procedures, rules, and regulations.

C.   Ensure reports and proper documentation of the facts and circumstances of the incident and the action taken are submitted through proper channels in accordance with department procedures.

C.   Ensure that appropriate notifications are made in accordance with department procedure and chain of command. Notifications should include the commanding officer of the officer involved.

3.4 The Responsibilities of the Involved Officer

A sworn officer who has:

- been served with a Restraining Order, or
- learns that s/he is a defendant named in any such order/complaint
- involving abuse; or
- is arrested for any crime involving abuse shall:

A.   Immediately provide oral notification officer of his or her permanent assignment assignment, naming the investigation Police department (example: police officer lives in town other than where he or she is employed.)

B.   Within 24 hours provide written notification to the commanding Officer of his or her permanent assignment. A copy of the restraining Order (if applicable) shall be attached.

C.   Upon being served with a restraining order, the officer shall immediately surrender his or her license to carry/FID card, department-issued firearms in compliance with MGLc.140, & 129B. The officer may file an affidavit that a firearm is necessary for employment and request an expedited hearing on the suspension and surrender order.

3.5 The Responsibilities of the Commanding Officer of the Involved Officer

A Commanding Officer, upon being notified that an employee under his/her command has been served a restraining order and/or has been involved in a domestic violence, shall take the following actions:

A. Ensure the safety of the victim;

B. Order that all appropriate notifications be made and that required documentation be completed and review all documents and reports;

C.   Determine, in accordance with departmental procedure, the employee's work status and if applicable, the appropriate disciplinary action.

Appendix V

A Clear and Concise Policy

As the Brockton Police Department continually constructed and amended its domestic violence policies and procedures, it became apparent that these policies were adding up to thousands of words, were increasingly more detailed, and were enlarging and expanding every year. The rules and regulations, policies and procedures were in danger of comprising an instruction manual that few could clearly and precisely understand. Worse still, the department, like so many public policymakers, was in danger of deluding itself that with an abundance of procedural protection, the employees would read them all, and of course abide by them. Bureaucrats everywhere would have been proud. The department achieved the ability to shroud individual responsibility and accountability in a sheath of procedural process that would take the blame for failure rather than assign individual failure. Thus when confronted with failure, members of the department can simply state, "I know it does not make any sense, but that is what the rules are and we followed the rules as we understood them." The bureaucratic Nirvana had been consummated.

What the department needed was a policy that would protect *everyone's* rights and be simple enough to be understood by everyone. What the chief of police needed was the ability to incontestably hold each and every *individual* accountable. The idea of holding an individual and not a procedure responsible for the completion of a task or their own actions or inactions is becoming a lost art in contemporary society.

The captain of operations and the domestic violence coordinator must understand that the purpose of this policy is not complex (to protect everybody's rights) and must be given both the authority and the discretion necessary to complete the assignment. *People, not process must ultimately decide what is equitable.*

It is important to note that the Brockton Police Department alone did not develop this policy. It was developed through the coordinated efforts of the

Brockton Police Department, the Domestic Violence Action Program at Brockton Family and Community Resources, Inc. and the Domestic Violence Unit of the Plymouth County district attorney. Inasmuch as these efforts must be collaborative in nature the three agencies felt it was important to include a system of checks and balances so as not to infringe any one of the agency employees' constitutional rights.

PROCEDURE FOR DEPARTMENTAL PERSONNEL INVOLVED IN DOMESTIC VIOLENCE

A. PROCEDURE

When employees of this department are involved in a domestic violence situation and sworn personnel are dispatched or called to the scene, the following procedures shall be followed:

1. The responding officer(s) shall include a supervisor. This includes the service of abuse prevention orders.

2. The responding supervisor shall notify his/her commanding officer/officer-in-charge from the scene on or before the end of the shift.

3. The commanding officer/officer-in-charge shall notify the captain of operations and the domestic violence coordinator from the scene or before the end of the shift.

4.Copies of the investigative report and all other investigative files shall be provided to the captain of operations and the domestic violence coordinator within 48 hours.

5. If the investigating supervisor determines that either criminal complaints will be issued.or an arrest will be made, that information shall be turned over to the district attorney's office as soon as possible for prosecution and/or further investigation.

B. MANDATORY REPORTING

1. If any employee of this department has knowledge of an on-going domestic violence situation involving another employee or an employee's family member, the incident shall be reported to the employee's immediate supervisor, who will begin an investigation into the allegations. The captain of operations and domestic violence coordinator shall be informed within 48 hours.

2. The provisions of this roll call are intended to further the credibility of this department and are to be in no way construed as creating a standard of response or investigation that automatically assumes guilt, penalizes, punishes, or exonerates departmental employees.

Appendix VI

Massachusetts General Law C.290A

The small number of my colleagues that have read any of the National Institute of Justice sponsored studies concerning domestic violence continues to surprise me. In the same way, I am often more astonished by the small number of my colleagues and domestic violence victim advocates in this state who have read and more importantly understand the Massachusetts Abuse Prevention Act. The Act in this book pertains only to Massachusetts, however, all states have some type of legislation similar to it. Anyone working in any sector, public or private that is concerned about domestic violence is urged to become familiar with their local laws and legislation.

The Massachusetts Abuse Prevention Act G.L.c.209A was passed in 1978. It was amended in 1983 to further regulate police procedures and to require police to adhere to specific guidelines. It was amended yet again in 1987 to further increase the powers and duties of police officers. In 1990, an amendment was added requiring the secretary of public safety to establish and implement specific operational guidelines and to require that local police departments submit their procedures to the secretary. The Act mandated that a law enforcement officer arrest anyone when he or she witnesses or has "probable cause to believe a person has violated certain criminal provision of a court ordered restraining order." There are some sections, such as those relating to support and custody that are noncriminal and no arrest should me made for violations of those sections. The fact that on the first page of the Massachusetts order in large red letters it states, "VIOLATION OF THIS ORDER IS A CRIMINAL OFFENSE," leads many, including many attorneys not familiar with the Act, to believe that all violations of the order mandate mandatory arrest. The officer must be able to determine if there is probable cause that the defendant has violated a *criminal provision* and there must be more than "*he said, she said*" accusations. The fact is that only the criminal sections include mandated mandatory arrest.

Arrest is to be the "preferred response" for those instances where there is not a court order, but where an officer witnessed or has probable cause to believe that a person has committed an act of abuse as defined under the guidelines of the Act. It also provides that the Department of Public Health certify batterers' treatment program standards and guidelines appropriate for court referrals. In 1993, an amendment at the end of the final sentence of the chapter substituted "General Fund" for "Domestic Violence Victims' Assistance Fund."

Chapter 209A contains ten sections. Section one defines, "abuse," "court," "family or household member," "law officer," and "vacate order." Section two defines which courts may be used and explains venue. Section three describes the types of court orders that a victim may request. Section three A describes the nature of the proceedings and provides the plaintiff with further information from the district attorney's office in regard to criminal complaints. Section three B describes actions the court can take in regard to firearms concerning an emergency or temporary order. Section three C describes action upon continuation or modification of the order. Section four describes the procedure for obtaining a temporary order. Section five provides for 24-hour service by allowing orders to be issued from police departments with telephone authority from an on-call judge. Section six describes the powers and duties of the police and the rights of the plaintiff. Section seven describes the procedure for search for a past domestic violence history or outstanding warrants. This section also regulates the service of court orders and other actions the court may take. Section eight describes the proceedings to ensure the confidentiality of all records of the court procedures. Section nine requires the courts to have a standard complaint form. Section ten describes the assessments for persons referred to batterers' programs.

C.209A Section 1. Domestic Definitions.

As used in this chapter the following words shall have the following meanings:

"Abuse," the occurrence of one or more of the following acts between family or household members:

(a) attempting to cause or causing physical harm;

(b) placing another in fear of imminent serious physical harm;

(c) causing another to engage involuntarily in sexual relations by force, threat or duress.

"Court," the superior, probate and family, district or Boston municipal court departments of the trial court, except when the petitioner is in a dating relationship when "Court" shall mean district, probate, or Boston municipal courts.

"Family or household members," persons who:

(a) are or were married to one another;

(b) are or were residing together in the same household;

(c) are or were related by blood or marriage;

(d) having a child in common regardless of whether they have ever married or lived together; or

(e) are or have been in a substantive dating or engagement relationship, which shall be adjudged by district, probate or Boston municipal courts consideration of the following factors:

(1) the length of time of the relationship;

(2) the type of relationship;

(3) the frequency of interaction between the parties; and

(4) if the relationship has been terminated by either person, the length of time elapsed since the termination of the relationship.

"Law officer," any officer authorized to serve criminal process.

"Vacate order," court order to leave and remain away from a premises and surrendering forthwith any keys to said premises to the plaintiff. The defendant shall not damage any of the plaintiff's belongings or those of any other occupant and shall not shut off or cause to be shut off any utilities or mail delivery to the plaintiff. In the case where the premises designated in the vacate order is a residence, so long as the plaintiff is living at said residence, the defendant shall not interfere in any way with the plaintiff's right to possess such residence, except by order or judgment of a court of competent jurisdiction pursuant to appropriate civil eviction proceedings, a petition to partition real estate, or a proceeding to divide marital property. A vacate order may include in its scope a household, a multiple family dwelling and the plaintiff's workplace. When issuing an order to vacate the plaintiff's workplace, the presiding justice must consider whether the plaintiff and defendant work in the same location or for the same employer.

C.209A Section 2. Domestic Venue

Proceedings under this chapter shall be filed, heard, and determined in the superior court department or the Boston municipal court department or respective divisions of the probate and family or district court departments having venue over the plaintiff's residence. If the plaintiff has left a residence or household to avoid abuse, such plaintiff shall have the option of commencing an action in the court having venue over such prior residence or household, or in the court having venue over the present residence or household.

C.209A Section 3. Complaint Requesting Protection from Abuse

A person suffering from abuse from an adult or minor family or household member may file a complaint in the court requesting protection from such abuse, including, but not limited to, the following orders:

(a) ordering the defendant to refrain from abusing the plaintiff, whether the defendant is an adult or minor;

(b) ordering the defendant to refrain from contacting the plaintiff, unless authorized by the court, whether the defendant is an adult or minor;

(c) ordering the defendant to vacate forthwith and remain away from the household, multiple family dwelling, and workplace. Notwithstanding the provisions of section thirty-four B of Chapter two hundred and eight, an order to vacate shall be for a fixed period of time, not to exceed one year, at the expiration of which time the court may extend any such order upon motion of the plaintiff, with notice to the defendant, for such additional time as it deems necessary to protect the plaintiff from abuse;

(d) awarding the plaintiff temporary custody of a minor child;

(e) ordering the defendant to pay temporary support for the plaintiff or any child in the plaintiff's custody or both, when the defendant has a legal obligation to support such a person. In determining the amount to be paid, the court shall apply the standards established in the child support guidelines;

(f) ordering the defendant to pay the person abused monetary compensation for the losses suffered as a direct result of such abuse. Compensatory losses shall include, but not be limited to, loss of earnings or support, costs for restoring utilities, out-of-pocket losses for injuries sustained, replacement costs for locks or personal property removed or destroyed, medical and moving expenses, and reasonable attorney's fees;

(g) ordering the plaintiff's address to be impounded as provided in section nine;

(h) ordering the defendant to refrain from abusing or contacting the plaintiff's child, or child in plaintiff's care or custody, unless authorized by the court;

(i) the judge may recommend to the defendant that the defendant attend a recognized batterers' treatment program.

No filing fee shall be charged for the filing of the complaint. Neither the plaintiff nor the plaintiff's attorney shall be charged for certified copies of any orders entered by the court, or any copies of the file reasonably required for future court action or as a result of the loss or destruction of plaintiff's copies.

Any relief granted by the court shall be for a fixed period of time not to exceed one year. Every order shall on its face state the time and date the order is to expire and shall include the date and time that the matter will again be heard. If the plaintiff appears at the court at the date and time the order is to expire, the court shall determine whether or not to extend the order for any additional time reasonably necessary to protect the plaintiff or to enter a permanent order. When the expiration date stated on the order is on a weekend day or holiday, or a date when the court is closed to business, the order shall not expire until the next date that the court is open to business. The plaintiff may appear on such next court business day at the time designated by the order to request that the order be extended. The court may also extend the order upon motion of the plaintiff, for such additional time as it deems necessary to protect from abuse the plaintiff or any child in the plaintiff's care or custody. The fact that abuse has not occurred during the pendency of an order shall not, in itself, constitute sufficient ground for denying or failing to extend the order, of allowing an order to expire or be vacated, or for refusing to issue a new order.

The court may modify its order at any subsequent time upon motion by either party. When the plaintiff's address is impounded and the defendant has filed a motion to modify the court's order, the court shall be responsible for notifying the plaintiff. In no event shall the court disclose any impounded address.

No order under this chapter shall in any manner affect title to real property.

No court shall compel parties to mediate any aspect of their case. Although the court may refer the case to the family service office of the probation department or victim/witness advocates for information gathering purposes.

A court shall not deny any complaint filed under this chapter solely because it was not filed within a particular time period after the last alleged incident of abuse.

A court may issue a mutual restraining order or mutual no-contact order pursuant to any abuse prevention action only if the court has made specific written findings of fact. The court shall then provide a detailed order, sufficiently specific to apprise any law officer as to which party has violated the order, if the parties are or appear to be in violation of the order.

Any action commenced under the provisions of this chapter shall not preclude any other civil or criminal remedies. A party filing a complaint under this chapter shall be required to disclose any prior or pending actions involving the parties for divorce, annulment, paternity, custody or support, guardianship, separate support or legal separation, or abuse prevention.

If there is a prior or pending custody support order from the probate and family court department of the trial court, an order issued in the superior, district, or Boston municipal court departments of the trial court pursuant to this chapter may include any relief available pursuant to this chapter except orders for custody or support.

If the parties to a proceeding under this chapter are parties in a subsequent proceeding in the probate and family court department for divorce, annulment, paternity, custody or support, guardianship or separate support, any custody or support order or judgment issued in the subsequent proceeding shall supersede any prior custody or support order under this chapter.

C.209A Sec.3A. Information Required to Be Given to Complainant

Upon the filing of a complaint under this chapter, a complainant shall be informed that the proceedings hereunder are civil in nature and that violations of orders issued hereunder are criminal in nature. Further, a complainant shall be given information prepared by the appropriate district attorney's office that other criminal proceedings may be available and such complainant shall be instructed by such district attorney's office relative to the procedures required to initiate criminal proceedings including, but not limited to, a complaint for a violation of section forty-three of chapter two hundred and sixty-five. Whenever possible a complainant shall be provided with such information in the complainants' native language.

C.209A Sec.3B. Suspension and Surrender of Firearms

Upon issuance of a temporary or emergency order under section four or five of this chapter, the court shall, if the plaintiff demonstrates a substantial likelihood of immediate danger of abuse, order the immediate suspension and surrender of any license to carry firearms and or firearms identification card which the defendant may hold and order the defendant to surrender all firearms, rifles, shotguns, machine guns and ammunition which he then possesses in accordance with the provisions of this chapter and any license to carry firearms or firearms identification cards which the defendant may hold shall be surrendered to the appropriate law enforcement officials in accordance with the provisions of this chapter. Notice of such suspension and ordered surrender shall be appended to the copy of abuse prevention order served on the defendant pursuant to section seven. Law enforcement officials, upon the service of said orders, shall immediately take possession of all firearms, rifles, shotguns, machine guns, ammunition, any license to carry firearms and any firearms identification cards in control, ownership, or possession of said defendant. Any violation of such orders shall be punishable by a fine of not more than five thousand dollars, or by imprisonment for not more than two and one half years in a house of correction, or by both such fine and imprisonment.

Any defendant aggrieved by an order of surrender or suspension as described in the first sentence of this section may petition the court which issued such suspension or surrender order for a review of such action and such petition shall be heard no later than ten court business days after the receipt of the notice of the petition by the court. If said license to carry firearms or firearms identification card has been suspended upon the issuance of an order issued pursuant to section four or five, said petition may be heard contemporaneously with the hearing specified in the second sentence of the second paragraph of section four. Upon the filing of an affidavit by the defendant that a firearm, rifle, shotgun, machine gun or ammunition is required in the performance of the defendant's employment, and upon a request for an expedited hearing, the court shall order said hearing within two business days of receipt of such affidavit and request but only on the issue of surrender and suspension pursuant to this section.

C.209A Sec.3C. Continuation of Suspension and Surrender Order of Firearms

Upon the continuation and/or modification of an order issued pursuant to section four of this chapter or upon a petition for review described in section 3B of this chapter, the court shall also order or continue to order the immediate suspension and surrender of the defendant's license to carry firearms and firearms identification card and the surrender of all firearms, rifles, shotguns, machine guns and ammunition which he then possesses if the court makes a determination that the return of said license to carry firearms identification card or firearms, rifles, shotguns, machine guns, and ammunition presents a likelihood of abuse to the plaintiff. A suspension and surrender order issued pursuant to this section shall continue so long as the restraining order to which it relates is in effect.

C.209A Sec.4. Protection Pendente Lite

Upon the filing of a complaint under this chapter, the court may enter such temporary orders as it deems necessary to protect a plaintiff from abuse, including relief as provided in section three. Such relief shall not be contingent upon the filing of a complaint for divorce, separate support, or paternity actions.

If the plaintiff demonstrates a substantial likelihood of immediate danger of abuse, the court may enter such temporary relief orders without notice as it deems necessary to protect the plaintiff from abuse and shall immediately thereafter notify the defendant that the temporary orders have been issued. The court shall give the defendant an opportunity to be heard on the question of continuing the temporary order and of granting other relief as requested by the plaintiff no later than ten court business days after such orders are entered.

Notice shall be made by the appropriate law enforcement agency as provided in section seven. If the defendant does not appear at such subsequent hearing, the temporary orders shall continue in effect without further order of the court.

C.209A Sec.5. Emergency Orders

When the court is closed for business, any justice of the superior, probate and family, district, or Boston municipal court departments may grant relief to the plaintiff as provided under section four if the plaintiff demonstrates a substantial likelihood of immediate danger of abuse. In the discretion of the justice, such relief may be granted and communicated by telephone to an officer or employee of an appropriate law enforcement agency, who shall record such order on a form of order promulgated for such use by the chief administrative justice and shall deliver a copy of such order on the next court day to the clerk-magistrate of the court having venue and jurisdiction over the matter. If relief has been granted without the filing of a complaint pursuant to this section of this chapter, then the plaintiff shall appear in court on the next available business day to file said complaint. Notice to the plaintiff and defendant and an opportunity for the defendant to be heard shall be given as provided in said section four.

Any order issued under this section and any documentation in support thereof shall be certified on the next court day by the clerk-magistrate or registrar of the court issuing such order to the court having venue and jurisdiction over the matter. Such certification to the court shall have the effect of commencing proceedings under this chapter and invoking the other provisions of this chapter but shall not be deemed necessary for an emergency order issued under this section to take effect.

C.209A Sec. 6. Duties of Law Officer; Notice of Rights

Whenever any law officer has reason to believe that a family or household member has been abused or is in danger of being abused, such officer shall use all reasonable means to prevent further abuse. *The officer shall take, but not be limited to the following action:*

(1) remain on the scene of where said abuse occurred or was in danger of occurring as long as the officer has reason to believe that at least one of the parties involved would be in immediate physical danger without the presence of a law officer. This shall include, but not be limited to remaining in the dwelling for a reasonable period of time;

(2) assist the abused person in obtaining medical treatment necessitated by an assault, which may include driving the victim to the emergency room of the nearest hospital, or arranging for appropriate transportation to a health care facility, notwithstanding any law to the contrary;

(3) assist the abused person in locating and getting to a safe place; including but not limited to a designated meeting place for a shelter or a family member's or friend's residence. The officer shall consider the victim's preference in this regard and what is reasonable under all the circumstances;

(4) give such person immediate and adequate notice of his or her rights. Such notice shall consist of handing said person a copy of the statement which follows below and reading the same to said person. Where said person's native language is not English, the statement shall be then provided in said person's

language whenever possible. "You have the right to appear at the Superior, Probate and Family, District or Boston Municipal Court, if you reside within the appropriate jurisdiction, and file a complaint requesting any of the following applicable orders:

(a) an order restraining your attacker from abusing you;

(b) an order directing your attacker to leave your household, building or workplace;

(c) an order awarding you custody of a minor child;

(d) an order directing your attacker to pay support for you or any minor child in your custody, if the attacker has a legal obligation of support; and

(e) an order directing your attacker to pay you for losses suffered as a result of abuse, including medical and moving expenses, loss of earnings or support, costs for restoring utilities and replacing locks, reasonable attorney's fees, and other out-of-pocket losses for injuries and property damage sustained.

For an emergency on weekends, holidays, or weeknights, the police will refer you to a justice of the superior, probate and family, district, or Boston municipal court departments.

You have the right to go to the appropriate district court or the Boston municipal court and seek a criminal complaint for threats, assault and battery, assault with a deadly weapon, assault with intent to kill, or other related offenses.

If you are in need of medical treatment, you have the right to request that an officer present drive you to the nearest hospital or otherwise assist you in obtaining medical treatment.

If you believe that police protection is needed for your physical safety, you have the right to request that the officer present remain at the scene until you and your children can leave or until your safety is otherwise ensured. You may also request that the officer assist you in locating and taking you to a safe place, including but not limited to a designated meeting place for a shelter or a family member's or a friend's residence, or a similar place of safety.

You may request a copy of the police incident report at no cost from the police department."

The officer shall leave a copy of the foregoing statement with such person before leaving the scene or premises.

(5) assist such person by activating the emergency judicial system when the court is closed for business;

(6) inform the victim that the abuser will be eligible for bail and may be promptly released; and

(7) arrest any person a law officer witnesses or has probable cause to believe has violated a temporary or permanent vacate, restraining, or no-contact order or judgment issued pursuant to section eighteen, thirty-four B or thirty-four C of chapter two hundred and eight, section thirty-two of chapter two hundred and nine, section three, four or five of this chapter, or sections fifteen or twenty of chapter two hundred and nine C. *When there are no vacate, restraining, or no-contact orders or judgments in effect, arrest shall be the preferred response whenever an officer witness or has probable cause to believe that a person:*

(a) has committed a felony;

(b) has committed a misdemeanor involving abuse as defined in section one of this chapter;

(c) has committed an assault and battery in violation of section thirteen A of chapter two hundred and sixty-five.

The safety of the victim and any involved children shall be paramount in any decision to arrest. Any officer arresting both parties must submit a detailed, written report in addition to an incident report, setting forth the grounds for dual arrest.

No law officer shall be held liable in any civil action regarding personal injury or injury to property brought by any party to a domestic violence incident for an arrest based on probable cause when such officer acted reasonably and in good faith and in compliance with this chapter and the statewide policy as established by the secretary of public safety.

Whenever any law officer investigates an incident of domestic violence, the officer shall immediately file a written incident report in accordance with the standards of the officer's law enforcement agency and, wherever possible, in the form of the National Incident-Based Reporting System, as defined by the Federal Bureau of Investigation. The latter information may be submitted voluntarily by the local police on a monthly basis to the crime reporting unit of the criminal history systems board.

The victim shall be provided a copy of the full incident report at no cost upon request to the appropriate law enforcement department.

When a judge or other person authorized to take bail bails any person arrested under the provisions of this chapter, he shall make reasonable efforts to inform the victim of such release prior to or at the time of said release.

When any person charged with or arrested for a crime involving abuse under this chapter is released from custody, the court or the emergency response judge shall issue, upon the request of the victim, a written no-contact order prohibiting the person charged or arrested from having any contact with the victim and shall use all reasonable means to notify the victim immediately of release from custody. The victim shall be given at no cost a certified copy of the no-contact order.

C.209A Sec. 7. Search of Domestic Violence Records; Outstanding Warrants

When considering a complaint filed under this chapter, a judge shall cause a search to be made of the records contained within the statewide domestic violence record-keeping system maintained by the office of the commissioner of probation and shall review the resulting data to determine whether the named defendant has a civil or criminal record involving domestic or other violence. Upon receipt of information that an outstanding warrant exists against the named defendant, a judge shall order that the appropriate law enforcement officials be notified and shall order that any information regarding the defendant's most recent whereabouts shall be forwarded to such officials. In all instances where an outstanding warrant exists, a judge shall make a finding, based upon all of the circumstances, as to whether an imminent threat of bodily injury exists to the petitioner. In all instances where such an imminent threat of bodily injury is found to exist, the judge shall notify the appropriate law enforcement officials of such finding and officials shall take all necessary actions to execute any such outstanding warrant as soon as is practicable.

Whenever the court orders under sections eighteen, thirty-four B, and thirty-four C of chapter two hundred and eight, section thirty-two of chapter two hundred and nine, sections three, four and five of this chapter, or section fifteen and twenty of chapter two hundred and nine C, the defendant to vacate, refrain from abusing the plaintiff or to have no contact with the plaintiff or the plaintiff's minor child, the registrar or clerk-magistrate shall transmit two certified copies of each such order and one copy of the complaint and summons, forthwith to the appropriate law enforcement agency which, unless otherwise ordered by the court, shall serve one copy of each order upon the defendant, together with a copy of the complaint, order and summons and notice of any suspension or surrender ordered pursuant to section three of this chapter. The law enforcement agency shall promptly make its return of service to the court.

Law enforcement officers shall use every reasonable means to enforce such abuse prevention orders. Law enforcement agencies shall establish procedures adequate to insure that an officer on the scene of an alleged violation of such order may be informed of the existence and terms of such order. The court shall notify the appropriate law enforcement agency in writing whenever any such order is vacated and shall direct the agency to destroy all record of such vacated order and such agency shall comply with that directive.

Each abuse prevention order issued shall contain the following statement: VIOLATION OF THIS ORDER IS A CRIMINAL OFFENSE.

Any violation of such order shall be punishable by a fine of not more than five thousand dollars, or by imprisonment for not more than two and one-half years in a house of correction, or by both such fine and imprisonment. Where the defendant has no prior record of any crime of violence and where the court believes, after evaluation by a certified or provisionally certified batter's treatment program, that the defendant is amenable to treatment, the court may, in addition to any other penalty, order appropriate treatment as specified in this section.

If a defendant ordered to undergo treatment has received a suspended sentence, the original sentence shall be reimposed if the defendant fails to participate in said program as required by the terms of his probation.

When a defendant has been ordered to participate in a treatment program pursuant to this section, the defendant shall be required to regularly attend a certified or provisionally certified batterers' treatment program. To the extent permitted by professional requirements of confidentiality, said program shall communicate with local battered women's programs for the purpose of protecting the victims' safety. Additionally, it shall specify the defendant's attendance requirements and keep the probation department informed of whether the defendant is in compliance.

In addition to, but not in lieu of, such orders for treatment, if the defendant has a substance abuse problem, the court may order appropriate treatment for such problem. All ordered treatment shall last until the end of the probationary period or until the treatment program decides to discharge the defendant, whichever comes first. When the defendant is not in compliance with the terms of probation, the court shall hold a revocation of probation hearing. To the extent possible, the defendant shall be responsible for paying all costs for court-ordered treatment.

In each instance where there is a violation of an abuse prevention order, the court may order the defendant to pay the plaintiff for all damages including, but not limited to, cost for shelter or emergency housing, loss of earnings or support, out-of-pocket losses for injuries sustained or property damaged, medical expenses, moving expenses, cost for obtaining an unlisted telephone number, and reasonable attorney's fees.

Any such violation may be enforced in the superior, the district or Boston municipal court departments. Criminal remedies provided herein are not exclusive and do not preclude any other available civil or criminal remedies. The superior, probate and family, district and Boston municipal court departments may each enforce by civil contempt procedure a violation of its own court order.

The provisions of section eight of chapter one hundred and thirty-six shall not apply to any order, complaint, or summons issued pursuant to this section.

C.209A Sec.8. Confidentiality of Plaintiff's Address; Records Involving Minors

Upon the request of the plaintiff, the court shall impound the plaintiff's address by excluding same from the complaint and from all other court documents which are available for public inspection, and shall ensure that the address is kept confidential from the defendant and defendant's attorney.

The records of cases arising out of an action brought under the provisions of this chapter where the plaintiff or defendant is a minor shall be withheld from public inspection except by order of the court; provided that such records shall be open, at all reasonable times, to the inspection of the minor, said minor's parent, guardian, attorney, and to the plaintiff and the plaintiff's attorney, or any of them.

C.209A Sec.9. Form of Complaint

The administrative justices of the superior court, probate and family court, district court, and the Boston municipal court departments shall jointly promulgate a form of complaint for use under this chapter which shall be in such form and language to permit a plaintiff to prepare and file such complaint pro se.

C.209A Sec.10. Assessments against persons referred to certified batterers' treatment programs as condition of probation

The court shall impose an assessment of three hundred dollars against any person who has been referred to a certified batterers' treatment program as a condition of probation. Said assessment shall be in addition to the cost of the treatment program. In the discretion of the court, said assessment may be reduced or waived when the court finds that the person is indigent or that payment of the assessment would cause the person, or the dependents of such person, severe financial hardship. Assessments made pursuant to this section shall be in addition to any other fines, assessments, or restitution imposed in any disposition. All funds collected by the court pursuant to this section shall be transmitted monthly to the state treasurer, who shall deposit said funds in the General Fund.

Appendix VII

Massachusetts General Law 265 S.43, Stalking

In May 1992 the Massachusetts legislature passed two new laws with the intent to deter the stalking of domestic violence victims and stalking in violation of a domestic violence court order. There are increased penalties for the second and subsequent convictions of stalking.

In section (a) you may note that another, more correct title for this law should be the Stalking and Threat Law. If the abuser continues to willfully, maliciously, and repeatedly follow or harass the domestic violence victim, but makes no threats, he or she *has not* violated this statute. There also seems to be little doubt that if a landlord repeatedly harassed and placed a tenant in fear of serious bodily injury, the landlord would have violated this statute. If you are looking for a law that does not make much sense, you quest is now over. I find it difficult to believe that this was the intent of the legislature. I find it more difficult to understand that, for almost five years now, the legislature has not been able to change this statute so that it says what it supposed to say. Its intent was to prevent stalking and it does not.

(a) Whoever willfully, maliciously, and repeatedly follows or harasses another person and who makes a threat with the intent to place that person in imminent fear of death or serious bodily injury shall be guilty of the crime of stalking and shall be punished by imprisonment in the state prison for not more than five years or by a fine of not more than one thousand dollars, or imprisonment in the house of correction for not more than two and one-half years or both.

(b) Whoever commits the crime of stalking in violation of a temporary or permanent vacate, restraining, or no-contact order or judgment issued pursuant to sections eighteen, thirty-four B, or thirty-four C of chapter two hundred and eight; or section thirty-two of chapter two hundred and nine; or sections three, four, or five of chapter two hundred and nine A; or sections fifteen or twenty of chapter two hundred and nine C; or a temporary restraining order or preliminary or permanent injunction issued by the superior court, shall be punished by imprisonment in a jail or the state prison for not less than one year and not more than five years. No sentence imposed under the provisions of this subsection shall be less than a mandatory minimum term of imprisonment of one year.

(c) Whoever, after having been convicted of the crime of stalking, commits a second or subsequent such crime shall be punished by imprisonment in a jail or the state prison for not less than two years and not more than ten years. No sentence imposed under the provisions of this subsection shall be less than a mandatory minimum term of imprisonment of two years.

(d) For the purposes of this section, "harasses," means a knowing and willful pattern of conduct or series of acts over a period of time directed at a specific person, which seriously alarms or annoys the person. Said conduct must be such as would cause a reasonable person to suffer substantial emotional distress.

Appendix VIII

Definition of Terms

Abuse: "the occurrence of one or more of the following acts between family or household members:

(a) attempting to cause or causing physical harm.

(b) placing another in fear of imminent physical harm.

(c) causing another to engage involuntarily in sexual relations by force, threat, or duress."

Assault: Any willful attempt or threat to inflict injury upon the person of another, when coupled with an apparent present ability to do so, and any intentional display of force such as would give the victim reason to fear or expect immediate bodily harm, constitutes an assault. An assault may be committed without actually touching, or striking, or doing bodily harm, to the person of another.

Assault and battery: Any unlawful touching of another which is without justification or excuse. The two crimes differ from each other in that battery requires physical contact of some sort (bodily injury or offensive touching), whereas assault is committed without physical contact.

Assault and battery with a dangerous weapon: Unlawful causing of bodily harm without justification or excuse by use of any instrument calculated to do harm or cause death.

Assault with dangerous weapon: An unlawful attempt or offer to do bodily harm without justification or excuse by use of any instrument calculated to do harm or cause death. An aggravated form of assault as distinguished from a simple assault; for example, pointing a loaded gun at one is an assault with a dangerous weapon.

Assault with intent to commit rape: Crime is constituted by the existence of the facts which bring the offense within the definition of an assault, coupled with the intention to commit the crime of rape.

De facto: In fact, in deed, actually. That phrase is used to characterize an officer, a government, a past action, or a state of affairs that must be accepted for all practical purposes.

Felony: A crime of a graver or more serious nature than those offenses designated as misdemeanors. Under Massachusetts law, a state statute that is punishable by death or imprisonment for a term exceeding 2 1/2 years in state prison.

Misdemeanor: Offenses lower than felonies and generally those punishable by fine or imprisonment otherwise than in state prison. Under Massachusetts law a state statute that is punishable by imprisonment for a term not exceeding 2 1/2 years in a county house of correction.

Probable Cause: A combination of facts and circumstances that would warrant a person of reasonable caution and prudence to believe that a crime has been or is being committed and that the person to be arrested is guilty of such crime.

Rape: Whoever has sexual intercourse or unnatural sexual intercourse with a person, and compels such person to submit by force and against his or her will, or compels such person to submit by threat of bodily injury . . . In *Commonwealth v Chretien*(1981), the fact that the victim was the spouse of the defendant will not prevent conviction of rape.

Status Offense: A status offense that is age related. That is, the act would not be an offense if the person committing it were an adult. Therefore the term "status offense" applies to all laws and city ordinances in which condition of age determines if there has been a violation.

Bibliography

Adams, David. "Identifying the Assaultive Husband in Court: You Be the Judge." *Boston Bar Journal* 33, no. 4 (1989) 23-25.

Adams, Sandra L. "Restraining Order Trend Analysis and Defendant Profile." *Executive Exchanges*, National Association of Probation Executives (Fall 1994).

Aime v. Commonwealth (1993) 611 N.E.2d 204, 414 Mass. 667

Asseo, Laurie. "Single-Sex Education: Implications of VMI Case." *Charleston, S.C. Post and Courier*, October 29, 1995, p. 1995, p. 21A.

Associated Press. "Custody Ruling May Help O.J." *Charleston, S.C. Post and Courier*, December 22, 1996, p. 6A.

Associated Press. "Father Blames System for Daughter's Death." *Brockton Enterprise*, September 5, 1994, p. 9.

Associated Press. "Home Violence Underreported." *Boston Globe*, August 25, 1997, p. A5.

Associated Press. "Order Against Cordero Lifted," *Boston Globe*, December 18, 1997, p. B2.

Associated Press. "Prosecutor Splits a Bullet." *Boston Globe*, May 27, 1997, p. A11.

Associated Press. "The Simpson Trials, by the Numbers." *Boston Globe*, February 11, 1997, p. A10.

Associated Press, "Violent Crime Dropped in 95 in Major U.S. Cities, FBI Says." *Boston Globe*, October 13, 1996, p. A18.

Bai, Matt. "Chronic Offenders Grab System's Attention." *Boston Globe*, May 2, 1995, p.17.

Baker, William D. "A New Approach to Domestic Violence." *FBI Law Enforcement Bulletin* 64, no. 9 (September 1995) 18-20.

Bard, Morton and Harriet Connolly. "The Police and Family Violence: Practice and Policy." *Battered Women: Issues of Public Policy*. Washington D.C.: U.S. Civil Rights Commission, 1978.

Barnicle, Mike. "Case Becomes Open-and-Shot." *Boston Globe*, February 6, 1997, p. B1.

Barta, Carolyn. "Women to Be Major Force Entering the Next Century." *Charleston, S.C. Post and Courier*, March 30, 1997, p. 5G.

Baskervile, Stephen. "The Family in Puritan Political Theology." *Journal of Family History* 18, no. 2 (1992) 157-177.

Bass, Alison. "The War on Domestic Abuse." *Boston Globe*, September 25, 1994, p. 1.

Bateson, Mary Catherine. "Holding Up the Sky Together." *Civilization* 2, no. 3(1995) 29-31

Battered. Narr. Lesley Stahl. Prod. Kathleen Sciere, CBS 60 Minutes, WBZ, Boston. April 30, 1995.

Beccaria, Cesare. *On Crimes and Punishments*. David Young. Trans. David Young. Indianapolis, Ind: Hacket, 1963.

Bennet, Richard R., and Sandra Baxter. "Police and Community Participation in Anti-Crime Programs." Ed. James J. Fyfe, *Police Management Todays Issues and Case Studies*. Washington, D.C.: International City Management Association. 1985, pp. 132-146.

Berger, Peter L. *Invitation to Sociology: A Humanistic Perspective*. New York: Doubleday, 1963

Berk, Richard A., et al. "A Bayesian Analysis of the Colorado Springs Spouse Experiment." *Journal of Criminal Law and Criminology* 83, no. 1 (Spring 1992): 170-200.

Berk, Richard A., and Phyllis J. Newton. "Does Arrest Really Deter Wife Battery?" *American Sociological Review* 50, no. 2 (April 1985): 253-262.

Blackman, Ann, et al. "When Violence Hits Home." *Time*, July 4, 1994, p. 21.

Bloomfield, Maxwell. "Law." Eds. Charles Regan Wilson and William Ferris, *Encyclopedia of Southern Culture*. Chapel Hill: University of North Carolina Press, 1993.

Bograd, Michele. "Battering, Competing Clinical Models, and Paucity of Research: Notes to Those in the Trenches." *Counseling Psychologist* 22, no. 4 (1994): 593-597.

Boston Globe. "Dangerous Denial." July 12, 1997, p. A10.

Boston Globe. "Defenders for the Undefended." October 11, 1996, p. A18.

Boston Globe. "Easing Battered Lives." October 12, 1996, p. A18.

Boston Globe. "In Memoriam." December 31, 1995, p.84.

Boston Globe. "The Next Step For a Batterer." November 5, 1997, p. A22.

Boston Globe. "For the Sake of Ana Cordero." June 14, 1997, p. A14.

Bowman, Cynthia Grant. "A Feminist Critique." *Journal of Criminal Law and Criminology* 83, no. 1 (1992): 201-208.

Bradshaw, Judy A. "The Juvenile Justice System: Is It Working?" *FBI Law Enforcement Bulletin*, May 1995: 14-16.

Brelis, Matthew and Judy Rakowsky. "Cordero Case Spotlights Bail Flaws." *Boston Globe*, June 29, 1997, p. B1.

Briggs, John B., and Kevin F. Collins. *Evaluating the Quality of Learning*. New York: Academic Press, 1982.

Bureau of Justice Assistance Program Brief. "Family Violence: Interventions for the Justice System." U.S. Department of Justice, Washington, D.C., October 1994

Bureau of Justice Statistics Sourcebook of Criminal Justice Statistics-1994. Eds. Kathleen Maguire and Ann L. Pastore. Washington, D.C.: U.S. Department of Justice, 1994.

Buzawa, Eve S., and Thomas L. Austin. "Determining Police Response to Domestic Violence Victims: The Role of Victim Preference." *American Behavioral Scientist* 36 (May/June 1993): 611-623.

Buzawa, Eve. S., Thomas L. Austin, and Carl G. Buzawa. "The Role of Arrest in Domestic Versus Stranger Assault." Eds. Eve S. and Carl G. Buzawa, *Do Arrests and Restraining Orders Work*? Thousand Oaks, Calif.: Sage Publishing, 1996, pp. 150-175.

Buzawa, Eve S., and Carl G. Buzawa. *Do Arrests and Restraining Orders Work*? Thousand Oaks, Calif: Sage Publishing, 1996.

___. *Domestic Violence: The Criminal Justice Response*. Newbury Park, Calif.: Sage Publishing, 1990.

____. "The Impact of Arrest on Domestic Violence." *American Behavioral Scientist* 36, no. 5 (1993): 558-573.

Caldwell, Robert G. *Red Hannah: Delaware's Whipping Post.* Philadelphia: University of Pennsylvania Press, 1947.

Canellos, Peter S. "Two Trials, Two Verdicts, Many Theories." *Boston Globe,* February 6, 1997, p. A1.

Cardarelli, Albert P., and Jack McDevitt. *Public Safety in Massachusetts: An Overview of Critical Issues Facing Law Enforcement.* April 1994.

Carden, Ann D. "Wife Abuse and the Wife Abuser: Review and Recommendations." *Counseling Psychologist* 22, no. 4 (October 1994): 539-573.

Challenges and Opportunities in Drug Prevention. National Crime Prevention Council, Washington, D.C., April 1990.

"Child Abuse Fatalities." *Virginia Child Protection Newsletter,* Fall 1990.

Chiu, Alexis. "Abuse in Gay Partners Detailed." *Boston Globe,* September 3, 1997, p. B1.

Cochran, Donald. "Domestic Violence: The Invisible Problem." *Executive Exchange,* National Association of Probation Executives (Fall 1994).

____. *Project History of the Massachusetts Statewide Automated Restraining Order Registry.* Boston: Office of the Commissioner of Probation Massachusetts Trail Court, 1994.

____. The Tragedies of Domestic Violence: A Qualitative Analysis of Civil Restraining Orders in Massachusetts. Office of the Commissioner of Probation Massachusetts Trial Court. October 12, 1995.

____. *Young Adolescent Batterers: A Profile of Restraining Order Defendants in Massachusetts.* Boston: Office of the Commissioner of Probation Massachusetts Trial Court. April 1994.

Commonwealth v. Andres W. Jacobsen. 419 Mass. 269. Barnstable, Mass., 1995.

Commonwealth v. Chretien. 383 Mass. 417 N.E. 2d 1203 1981.

Courtwright, David T. "Violence in America." *American Heritage* 47, no. 5 (1996): 36-51.

Cravens, Hamilton. *Before Head Start: The Iowa Station and America's Children.* Chapel Hill: University of North Carolina Press, 1993.

Crowell, Nancy A., and Ann W. Burgess, eds. *Understanding Violence Against Women.* Washington, D.C.: National Academy Press, 1996

Dallas Morning News, "75 Years After Suffrage," *Boston Globe,* June 4, 1995, p. 12.

Davis, Kenneth C. *Don't Know Much About History.* New York: Avon, 1990.

DeBecker, Gavin. *Gift of Fear.* Boston: Little, Brown and Company, 1997.

Diamond, David. "Victory, Violence and Values." *USA Weekend,* August 1996, pp. 23-25.

Dillingham, Steven, ed. *Criminal Victimization in the United States, 1991.* Washington, D.C.: Bureau of Justice Statistics, 1991.

Doggett, Maeve E. *Marriage, Wife-Beating, and the Law in Victorian England.* Columbia: University of South Carolina Press, 1994.

Donziger, Steven R., ed. *The Real War on Crime: The Report of the National Criminal Justice Commission.* New York: Harper Perennial, 1996.

Droz, Beverly. "Massachusetts Women Politicians." *Boston Globe,* December 18, 1996, p. A24.

Duffy, Barbara. "Using a Creative Teaching Process with Adult Patients." *Home Health Nurse* 15, no. 2 (1997): 102-108.

Dunford, Franklyn W. "The Measurement of Recidivism in Cases of Spouse Assault." *Journal of Criminal Law and Criminology* 83, no. 1 (1992): 120-136.

Durkin, Tish. "Domestic Violence Harms Both Men and Women." Ed. Karin L. Swisher, *Domestic Violence*. San Diego: Greenhaven Press, 1996, pp. 65-70.

Ebbert Stephanie, and Jenifer B. McKim, "Restraining Order Issued to Keep Codero From Wife." *Boston Globe*, December 13, 1997, p. B3.

Edes, Gordon. "Cordero Charged in Wife's Beating." *Boston Globe*, October 12, 1997, p. A30.

___. "Cordero: Day in Court." *Boston Globe,* June 12, 1997, p. D1.

___. "Cordero Gets Pact." *Boston Globe*, March 24, 1998, p. E1.

___. "League Office to Investigate Allegations." *Boston Globe*, June 14, 1997, p. B1.

___. "Stressed-out Cordero Asks For a Night Off." *Boston Globe*, September 1, 1997, p. C1.

___. "Vaughn's Parents Show up for Cordero." *Boston Globe*, July 25, 1997, p. E6.

Eggers, William D., and John O'Leary. *Revolution at the Roots: Making Our Government Smaller, Better, and Closer to Home.* New York: Free Press, 1995.

Elikann, Peter T. *The Tough on Crime Myth: Real Solutions to Cut Crime.* New York: Insight, 1996.

Ellement, John. "Bail Reset for Spouse Held in Plot to Kill Wife." *Boston Globe*, December 2, 1997, p. B3.

___. "Fight on DNA Test Case Gives Murder Suspect a Long Wait." *Boston Globe*, November 26, 1996, p. A1.

___. "Police Union: Judge's Ruling Morally Wrong." *Boston Globe*, October 20, 1995, p. 29.

___. "S. Korean Held in Assault on Wife." *Boston Globe*, December 31, 1996, B1.

___. "Study Details Domestic Violence." *Boston Globe*, October 12, 1995, p. 25.

Ellement, John, and William F. Doherty. "Judge Wanted Cordero Held Until Court Session, Source Says." *Boston Globe*, June 14, 1997, p. B1.

Elshtain, Jean Bethke. "What Feminists Could Learn from Ms. Anthony." *Civilization* 2, no. 6 (1995): 51-55.

Evans, Liane. "Author Lectures on Codependency." *Portsmouth N.H. Herald,* April 18, 1995, p. B2-3.

Evans, Paul F., and Alan Fox. "Our Anticrime 'Miracle.'" *Boston Globe*, February 18, 1997, p. A11.

Fagan, Jeffrey. *The Criminalization of Domestic Violence: Promises and Limits.* Washington, D.C.: U.S. Department of Justice, National Institute of Justice January 1996.

Ferdind, Pamela. "Scales Tip Against Dangerous Defendants." *Boston Globe*, December 2, 1996, p. B1.

Ferraro, Kathleen J., and Lucille Pope. "Irreconcilable Differences: Battered Women, Police, and the Law." Ed. N. Zoe Hilton, *Legal Responses to Wife Assault.* Newbury Park, Calif.: Sage Publications, 1993, pp. 96-121

Finn, Peter. "Civil Protection Orders: A Flawed Opportunity for Intervention." Ed. Michael Steinman, *Women Battering: Policy Responses.* Cincinnati: Anderson, 1991.

Finn, Peter, and Mary O'Brian Hylton. *Using Civil Remedies for Criminal Behavior: Rational, Case Studies, and Constitutional Issues.* Washington D.C.: National Institute of Justice, 1994.

Finn, Peter, and Sarah Colson. *Civil Protection Orders Legislation, Current Court Practice, and Enforcement.* Washington, D.C.: National Institute of Justice, 1990.

Fischer, David Hackett. *Historians' Fallacies.* New York: Harper & Row, 1970.

Fisher, Mary P., and Robert Luyster. *Living Religions.* Englewood Cliffs, N.J.: Prentice Hall, 1991.

Fitzgibbons, Robert E. *Making Educational Decisions*. New York: Harcourt Brace Jovanovich, 1981.

Fletcher, Connie. "What Cops Know." *On Patrol* (Summer 1996): 44-50.

Flowers, R. Barri. "The Problem of Domestic Violence Is Widespread." Ed. Karin L. Swisher, *Domestic Violence*. San Diego: Greenhaven Press, 1996, pp. 10-21.

Foldberg, Steven. "The Inevitability of Patriarchy." Ed. James P. Sterba, *Morality in Practice*. Belmont, Calif.: Wadsworth Publishing Co., 1984, pp. 217-221.

Frisch, Lisa A. "Research That Succeeds, Policies That Fail." *Journal of Criminal Law and Criminology* 83, no. 1 (1992) 209-216.

Fuhrman, Mark. *Murder in Brentwood*. Washington, D.C.: Regnery Publishing, 1997.

Gage, Matilda Josylin. *Women, Church, and State*. Watertown, Mass.: Persephone Press reprint, 1980; original edition, 1803.

Gallagher, Robert S. "The Fight for Women's Suffrage: An Interview with Alice Paul." Ed. John A Garraty. *Historical Viewpoints: Notable Articles from American Heritage*. New York: Harper & Row, 1981.

Garfield, Bob. "Do Lawyers Deserve Their Bad Name?" *Civilization* 4, no. 2 (1997): 50-53.

Garraty, John A. *1,001 Things Everyone Should Know About American History*. New York: Doubleday, 1989.

Gelles, Richard J. "Abused Wives: Why Do They Stay?" *Journal of Marriage and the Family* 38 (1976): 659-668.

___. "Constraints Against Family Violence" *American Behavioral Scientist* 36, no. 5 (1993): 575-586.

___. *The Violent Home: A Study of Physical Aggression Between Husbands and Wives*. Beverly Hills, Calif.: Sage Publications, 1970.

Gelles, Richard J., and Donileen R. Loseke, eds. *Current Controversies on Family Violence*. Newbury Park Calif.: Sage Publications, 1993.

Gelles, Richard J., and Murray A. Straus. *Intimate Violence: The Definitive Study of the Causes and Consequences of Abuse in the American Family*. New York :Simon & Schuster, 1988.

Goldsmith, Stephen, ed. *Prosecutors Perspective*. National District Attorneys Association, Winter 1993.

Goode, Erica. "Domestic Violence Is a Serious Problem for Women." Ed. Karin L. Swisher, *Domestic Violence*. San Diego: Greenhaven Press, 1996, pp. 22-27.

Goodman, Ellen. "I'd Have Let Him Walk." *Washington Post*, December 14, 1991, p. A27.

___. "Making This Man's World Fairer, Safer for Women." *Boston Globe*, September 3, 1995, p. 83.

Goolkasian, Gail A. *Confronting Domestic Violence: A Guide for Criminal Justice Agencies*. Washington, D.C.: U.S. Department of Justice, National Institute of Justice, May 1986.

Gordon, Linda. *Heroes of Their Own Lives: The Politics and History of Family Violence*. New York: Viking Press, 1988.

Grau, Janice, Jeffrey Fagan, and Sandra Wexler. "Restraining Orders for Battered Women: Issues of Access and Efficacy." *Women and Politics* 4 (1984): 13-18.

Grillo, Betty, and Marleen Lee. "Domestic Violence Rate Still Reported to Be Alarmingly High." *Boston Globe*, October 29, 1995, p. 25.

Grisham, John. *The Rainmaker*. New York: Doubleday, 1995.

Grunwald, Michael. "Welfare Revamp Softening." *Boston Globe*, February 15, 1997, p. 1.

Hamberger, L. Kevin, and James E. Hastings. "Recidivism Following Spouse Abuse Abatement Counseling: Treatment Program Implications." *Violence and Victims* 5 no. 33 (Fall 1990): 157-170.

Hancock, Marilyn. "Dangers From Without and Within." *Brockton Enterprise*, October 1, 1995, p. 1.

Harlow, Caroline W. *The Female Victims of Violent Crime*. Washington, D.C.: Bureau of Justice Statistics, January 1991.

Hart, Barbara. "Battered Women and the Criminal Justice System." *American Behavioral Scientist* 36 no. 5 (1993): 624-638.

_____. *Violent No More: Intervention Against Woman Abuse in Ohio*. Columbus: Ohio Department of Human Services in cooperation with the Ohio Domestic Violence Network, 1990.

Hartzler v. City of San Jose. 46 Cal. App. 3d 6, 120. Cal. Rptr.5 (1975).

Henslin, James M. "On Becoming Male: Reflections of a Sociologist on Childhood and Early Socialization." *Down to Earth Sociology*. 8th ed., New York: Free Press, 1995, pp. 126-138.

Hilton, N. Zoe. *Legal Response to Wife Assault*. Newbury Park, Calif.: Sage Publications, 1993.

Hirsch, E.D.Jr., Joseph F. Kett, and James Trefil, eds. *Dictionary of Cultural Literacy*. Boston: Houghton Mifflin Co., 1993.

Hirschel, David J., and Ira Hutchinson. "Police-Preferred Arrest Policies." *Woman Battering: Policy Responses*. Cincinnati: Anderson, 1991.

Hoffman, Jan. "When Men Hit Women." *New York Times Magazine*, February 16, 1994: 23-27.

Hofford, Meredith. "Family Violence: Challenging Cases for Probation Officers." *Federal Probation*, September 1991: 12-17.

Holmes, William M., et al. *Mandatory Arrest and Domestic Violence in Massachusetts*. Boston: Statistical Analysis Center Massachusetts Committee of Criminal Justice, 1993.

Howard, Philip K. *The Death of Common Sense*. New York: Random House, 1994.

Hunt, Marilee Kenney. "A Call for Court Advocates." *Governor's Commission on Domestic Violence* 1, no. 22 (1994): 1-2.

Jacobson, Niel, and John Gottman, *When Men Batter Women*. New York: Simon & Schuster, 1998.

Jafe, Peter G., et al. "The Impact of Police Laying Charges." Ed. N. Zoe Hilton. *Legal Responses to Wife Assault*. Newbury Park, Calif.: Sage Publications, 1993, pp. 62-95.

Jecoby, Jeff. "A Blunt, Ugly Truth." *Boston Globe*, March 8, 1994, p. 15.

Jenkins, Lee. "Incident Baffles, Bothers Orioles." *Boston Globe*, June 14, 1997, p. A14.

Johnson, Hillary. "Domestic Violence Is a Serious Problem for Professional Women." Ed. Karin L. Swisher. *Domestic Violence*. San Diego: Greenhaven Press, 1996, pp. 28-36.

Johnson, Otto, Ed. *1996 Information Please Almanac*. Boston: Houghton Miffin Co., 1996

Judicial Response System. *Commonwealth of Massachusetts Administrative Office of the Trial Court*, October 1994.

Kagan, Donald. "History's Largest Lessons." *American Heritage* 48, no. 1 (1997): 59-67.

Kahn, Joseph P. "He Does Not Want to Talk About It." *Boston Globe*, April 7, 1997, p. C5.

___. "The Professor of Carnal Knowledge." *Boston Globe*, March 26, 1997, p. D1.

Kaminer, Wendy. *It's All the Rage*. Reading, Mass.: Addison-Wesley, 1995.

Kanon, Joseph. *Los Alamos*. Broadway Books: New York, 1997.

Kaplan, Fred. "Two Found Guilty in Crown Heights Rights Case." *Boston Globe*, February 11, 1997, p. A13.

Kelling, George E., et al. *The Kansas City Preventive Patrol Experiment.* Washington, DC: Police Foundation, 1974.

Kenney, Charles. *Hammurabi's Code.* New York: Simon & Schuster, 1995.

Killacky, Keith F. *Towards a New Model in Police In-Service Training.* Quantico, Va.: FBI Academy.

Klein, Andrew R. "Re-Abuse in Population of Court-Restrained Male Batterers." Eds. Eve S. Buzawa and Carl G. Buzawa, *Do Arrest and Restraining Orders Work?* Thousand Oaks, Calif.: Sage Publications, 1996.

___. *Spousal/Partner Assault: A Protocol for the Sentencing and Supervision of Offenders.* Swampscott, Mass.: Production Specialties, 1993.

Krupa, Gregg. "Concern Voiced over Restraining Order Abuse." *Boston Globe*, March 3, 1994, p. 24.

Kurkjian, Stephen, and Matthew Brelis. "Cordero's Ex-Wife Said he Beat Her During Marriage." *Boston Globe,* June 27, 1997, p. A1.

Kurkjian, Stephen, and Gordon Edes, "Cordero Pleads Guilty to Assault." *Boston Globe*, November 5, 1997, p. B1.

Langan, Patrick A., and Christopher A. Innes. *Preventing Domestic Violence Against Women.* U.S. Department of Justice, Bureau of Justice Statistics, Special Report, August 1986.

Legal Update FY 95 Inservice. Massachusetts Criminal Justice Training Center at Plymouth, 1995.

Lehigh, Scott. "The Decadence of Privilege." *Boston Globe*, May 4, 1997,

Leo, John. "The Media Misreport Domestic Violence." Ed. Karin L. Swisher, *Domestic Violence.* San Diego: Greenhaven Press, 1996.

Lerman, Lisa G. "The Decontextualization of Domestic Violence." *Journal of Criminal Law and Criminology* 83, no. 1 (1992): 217-240.

Lerner, Gerda. *The Creation of Feminist Consciousness: From the Middle Ages to Eighteen-Seventy.* New York: Oxford University Press, 1993.

Lewis, Diane E. "On the Job." *Boston Globe*, March 18, 1997, p. C16.

Loewen, James W. *Lies My Teacher Told Me.* New York: Touchstone, 1995.

Mailer, Norman. *The Executioner's Song.* New York: Warner Books, 1979.

Manning, Peter K. "The Preventive Conceit." *American Behavioral Scientist* 36, no. 5 (1993): 639-650.

Martin, Del. "The Historical Roots of Domestic Violence." Ed. Daniel Jay Sonkin, *Domestic Violence on Trial: Psychological and Legal Dimensions of Family Violence.* New York: Springer, 1987, pp. 1-32.

Massachusetts Index Crimes-1960-1993. Massachusetts State Police Crime Reporting Unit, 1994.

McDonough, "Jacksonville Foes go on a Talking Jag." *Boston Globe*, December 6, 1997, p. D1.

McNamara, Eileen. "Batterers Win Another Round." *Boston Globe,"* May 13, 1998, p. B1.

___. "Parental Cry: This Is Justice." *Boston Globe*, April 9, 1997, p. B1.

___. "Fans' Trust Takes a Beating." *Boston Globe*, June 28, 1997, p. B1.

___. "Red Sox Have Short Memory." *Boston Globe*, June 14, 1997, p. B1.

McPherson, James M. *For Cause & Comrades.* New York: Oxford University Press, 1997.

Mendonza v. Commonwealth (1996) 673 N.E. 2d, 423, Mass. 771

Mitchell, David B. "Contemporary Police Practices in Domestic Violence Cases: Arresting the Abuser: Is it Enough?" *Journal of Criminal Law and Criminology* 83 no. 1 (1992): 241-249.

Nealon, Patricia. "Prosecutors Altering Approach to Help Press Cases." *Boston Globe*, September 25, 1994, p. 28.

O'Brien, Ellen, and David Armstrong. "Rape, Child Abuse, Neglect." *Boston Globe*, March 10, 1997, p. A1.

Pave, Marvin. "The Cordero Fallout." *Boston Globe*, June 27, 1997, p. C1.

Patterson, Jeffrey. "Community Policing." *FBI Law Enforcement Bulletin* (November 1995): 5-10.

Pearson, Patricia. *When She Was Bad: Violent Women and the Myth of Innocence.* New York: Viking, 1997.

Pertman, Adam. "Reverberations: A Year of Simpson." *Boston Globe,* June 11, 1995, p. 30.

Pleck, Elizabeth. "Criminal Approaches to Family Violence, 1640-1980." *Family Violence.* Vol. 2. *Crime and Justice: A Review of Research.* Eds. Lloyd Ohlin and Michael Tonry. Chicago: University of Chicago Press. 1989.

___. *Domestic Tyranny: The Making of Social Policy Against Family Violence from Colonial Times to the Present.* Chicago: University of Chicago Press, 1987.

Polsby, Daniel D. "Suppressing Domestic Violence with Law Reforms." *Journal of Criminal Law and Criminology* 83, no. 1 (1992): 250-253.

Powell, Anne. "Comparison of Restraining Order Violators and Other Risk/Need Offenders." *Executive Exchange National Association of Probation Executives* (Fall 1994).

Prothrow-Stith, Deborah. "A New Approach to Violence Prevention." *School Safety*, Spring 1992.

Rakowesky, Judy. "Cordero Needs Help, Ex-Wife Says." *Boston Globe,* June 28, 1997, p. A1.

Robarchek, Clayton, and Carole Robarchek, *Waorani: The Contexts of Violence and War.* New York: Harcourt Brace, 1998.

Roesch, Ronald, Stephen D. Hart, and Laurene J. Wilson. "Future Prospects for Intervention and Evaluation." Ed. N. Zoe Hilton, *Legal Responses to Wife Assault.* Newbury Park, Calif.: Sage Publications, 1993, pp. 289-303.

Rogers, Patrick M. *1995 Statutory Criminal Law of Massachusetts.* Fall River, Mass.: Commonwealth Police Services, 1995.

Rothwax, Harold J. Guilty: *The Collapse of Criminal Justice.* New York: Warner Books, 1996.

Sagan, Carl. *The Dragons of Eden.* New York: Ballatine Books, 1977.

Sagan, Carl, and Ann Druyan. *Shadows of Forgotten Ancestors: A Search for Who We Are.* New York: Random House, 1992.

Sanday, Peggy Reeves. *Female Power and Male Dominance: On the Origins of Sexual Inequality.* New York: Cambridge University Press, 1981.

_____. "The Socio-Cultural Context of Rape: A Cross-Cultural Study." *Journal of Social Issues* 37, no 4. (1976): 5-27.

Schmidt, Janell D., and Lawrence W. Sherman. "Does Arrest Deter Domestic Violence?" *American Behavioral Scientist* 36 (1993): 601-609.

Service Provider Perspectives on Family Violence Interventions. "Proceedings of a Workshop." Washington, D.C.: National Academy Press, 1995.

Shaughnessy, Dan. "It's Time to Speak His Piece on Sports World." *Boston Globe*, July 28, 1997, p. D1.

Sherman, Lawrence W. "The Influence of Criminology on Criminal Law: Evaluating Arrests for Misdemeanor Domestic Violence." *Journal of Criminal Law and Criminology* 83, no. 1 (1992): 1-45.

_____. *Policing Domestic Violence: Experiments and Dilemmas.* New York: Free Press, 1992.

_____. *The Minneapolis Domestic Violence Experiment.* Washington, D.C.: Police Foundation Report 1, 1984.

Sherman, Lawrence W., and Ellen G. Cohen. "The Impact of Research on Legal Policy: The Minneapolis Domestic Violence Experiment." *Law and Society Review* 23, no. 1 (1989): 117-144.

Sherman, Lawrence W., and Richard A. Berk. "The Specific Deterrent Effects of Arrest on Domestic Violence. "*American Sociological Review* 49, no. 2 (1989): 261-272.

Sigler, Robert T., and David Lamb. "Community-Based Alternatives to Prison: How the Public and Court Personnel View Them." *Federal Probation,* June 1995: 3-9

Sloan, Ron, Robert Trojanowicz, and Bonnie Bucqueroux. *Basic   Issues in Training: A Foundation for Community Policing.* National Center for Community Policing, Michigan State University, November 1992.

Slover, Pete. "Report Has McVeigh Describing Blast." *Boston Globe,* March 1, 1997, p. A3.

Smith, Douglas A., and Jody Klein. "Police Control of Interpersonal Disputes." *Social Problems* 31 (1984): 468-481.

Solomon, Robert C. *Introducing Philosophy.* 5th ed. New York: Harcourt Brace Jovanovich, 1993.

Somers, Ira, and Deborah Baskin. "Sex, Race, Age, and Violent Offending." *Violence and Victims* 7, no. 3 (Fall 1992): 191-201.

Stanko, Elizabeth. "Domestic Violence." Eds. Gary W. Cordner and Donna C. Hales, *What Works in Policing: Operations and Administration Examined.* Cincinnati: Anderson Publishing, 1992.

Stark, Evan. "Mandatory Arrest of Batterers: A Reply to Its Critics." *American Behavioral Scientist* 36, no, 5 (May/June 1993): 651-680.

Stein, Diane. *The Women's Spirituality Book.* St. Paul, Minn.: Liewellyn Publications, 1993.

Steinman, Michael. "Anticipating Rank and File Police Reactions to Arrest Policies Regarding Spouse Abuse." *Criminal Justice Research Bulletin* 4 (1988): 1-5.

___. "Coordinated Criminal Justice Interventions and Recidivism Among Batterers." *Woman Battering: Policy Responses.* Cincinnati: Anderson Publishing, 1991.

Stevens, Mark A. "Stopping Domestic Violence: More Answers and More Questions Needed." *Counseling Psychologist* 22, no, 4 (October 1994): 587-592.

Stevens, Tito, and Judy Rakowesky. "More Abuse Alleged." *Boston Globe,* July 1, 1997, p. C1.

Straus, Murray A. "Domestic Violence Is a Problem for Men." Ed. Karin Swisher, *Domestic Violence.* San Diego: Greenhaven Press, 1996, pp. 50-64.

_____. "Identifying Offenders in Criminal Justice Research on Domestic Assault." *American Behavioral Scientist* 36, no. 5 (1993): 587-600.

_____. *Manual for the Conflict Tactics Scales.* Durham, N.H.: University of New Hampshire, Family Research Laboratory, 1989.

Straus, Murray A., and Richard J. Gelles. *Physical Violence in American Families.* New Brunswick, N.J.: Transaction Books, 1990.

Sullivan, Shawn. "Domestic Violence is a Serious Problem for Black Women." Ed. Karin
    L. Swisher, *Domestic Violence*. San Diego: Greenhaven Press, 1996, pp. 37-
    40.
Swisher, Karin L., ed. *Domestic Violence*. San Diego: Greenhaven Press, 1996.
Tannen, Deborah. *Talking From 9 to 5: Women and Men in the Workplace*. New York:
    Avon Books, 1995.
Taylor, Matthew, and Shirley Leung. "Son Had Been Called Dangerous." *Boston Globe*,
    April 29, 1997, p. B1.
Third Annual Police Chiefs' Conference. Prepared for Scott Harsbarger, Attorney
    General, Commonwealth of Massachusetts. Bentley College, Waltham, Mass.
    November 1993.
Thurman v. City of Torrington. 595 F.Supp. 1521 D.Conn. 1984.
Thorne, Barrie, and Zella Luria. "Sexuality and Gender in Children's Daily Worlds."
    Down to Earth Sociology, 8th ed. Ed. James M. Henslin. New York: Free
    Press, 1995, pp. 137-149.
Toobin, Jeffrey. *The Run of His Life. The People v. O.J. Simpson*. New York: Random
    House, 1996.
Travis, Jeremy. "Violence Against Women: Reflections on NIJ's Research Agenda."
    National Institute of Justice Journal. (February 1996).
Trojanowicz, Robert, and Bonnie Bucqueroux. *Community Policing: A Contemporary
    Perspective*. Cincinnati: Anderson Publishing, 1990.
Trojanowicz, Robert, and Merry Murash. *Juvenile Delinquency: Concepts and Control*.
    Englewood Cliffs, N.J.: Prentice Hall, 1992.
Turow, Scott. *The Laws of Our Fathers*. New York: Farrar Straus Giroux, 1996.
Tye, Larry. "Addictive Personalities Formed Early, a Study Finds." *Boston Globe*
    February 2, 1997, p. A3.
U.S. Attorney General's Task Force on Family Violence. *U.S. Department of Justice
    Final Report*, 1984, pp. 10-26.
U.S. Commission of Civil Rights. *Battered Women: Issues of Public Policy*. Washington,
    D.C.: Government Printing Office, 1978.
Van Der Hagg, Ernst. "How to Cut Crime." *National Review,* May 30, 1994.
Violence Against Women, Thousand Oaks, Calif.: Sage Periodicals Press, 2, no. 4
    (December 1996).
Wallace, Harvey. *Family Violence: Legal, Medical, and Social Perspectives*. Boston:
    Allyn & Bacon, 1996.
Ware, Susan. *Partner and I: Molly Dawson, Feminism, and New Deal Politics*. New
    Haven, Conn.: Yale University Press, 1987.
Widom, Cathy Spatz. "The Cycle of Violence." *National Institute of Justice: Research in
    Brief*. October 1992.
Wilson, Charles, and William Regan Ferris, eds. *Encyclopedia of   Southern   Cultures*.
    Chapel Hill: University of North Carolina Press, 1993.
Wilson, William Julius. *The Truly Disadvantaged: The Inner City, the Underclass, and
    Public Policy*. Chicago: University of Chicago Press, 1987.
Winfeld, Liz. "Domestic Partner Benefits Getting to be Routine." *Boston Globe*, March
    23, 1997, p. E3.
Wolfgang, Marvin E. *Patterns in Criminal Homicide*. Philadelphia: University of
    Pennsylvania Press, 1958.
Wong, Doris Sue. "Unions Question Domestic-Violence Order." *Boston Globe*, August
    2, 1997, p. B2.
_____. "Weld Advocates Broad Changes in Bail System." *Boston Globe*, July 24, 1997,
    p. B2.

Wrangham, Richard, and Dale Peterson. *Demonic Males*. Boston: Houghton Mifflin Co., 1996.

Wright, Karen, and Devin Wright. *Family Life, Delinquency, and Crime: A Policymaker's Guide*. Washington, D.C.: U.S. Department of Justice August 1995.

Wright, Robert. "Politics Made Me Do It." *Time*. February 2, 1998: 34.

Wright, Robin. "Brutality Defines the Lives of Women Around the World." *Boston Globe*, September 2, 1995, p. A2.

Zobel, Hiller B. "The Jury on Trial." *American Heritage* 46, no. 4 (1995): 48-51.

Zorza, Joan. "The Criminal Law of Misdemeanor Domestic Violence, 1970-1990." *Journal of Criminal Law and Criminology* 83, no.1 (1992): 46-72.

Index

About the Author

RICHARD L. DAVIS is Adjunct Professor of Sociology at Quincy College at Plymouth. He is also a retired police lieutenant for the Brockton, Massachusetts Police Department.

ISBN 0-275-96126-5

90000>

EAN

9 780275 961268

HARDCOVER BAR CODE